THE POLITICS OF CONFORMITY IN
LATIN AMERICA

The
Politics of Conformity
in Latin America

Edited by
CLAUDIO VELIZ

Issued under the auspices of the
Royal Institute of International Affairs

OXFORD UNIVERSITY PRESS
LONDON   NEW YORK   TORONTO
1967

Oxford University Press, Ely House, London W.1

GLASGOW   NEW YORK   TORONTO   MELBOURNE   WELLINGTON
BOMBAY   CALCUTTA   MADRAS   KARACHI   LAHORE   DACCA
CAPE TOWN   SALISBURY   NAIROBI   IBADAN   ACCRA
KUALA LUMPUR   HONG KONG   TOKYO

PRINTED IN GREAT BRITAIN
BY
THE EASTERN PRESS LTD.
OF LONDON AND READING

Contents

Foreword

THIS volume has been a long time in the making and the better efforts and advice of many have been involved in its completion. The contributors certainly have a special debt of gratitude to Andrew Shonfield, Emanuel de Kadt, and Alan Angell who made the task of binding together these different themes so much more effective with their perceptive and valuable comments.

The revision of manuscripts from different authors, some originally prepared in languages other than English, has been accomplished with the skill which has by now become the trademark of Miss Hermia Oliver and Miss Katharine Duff, while the secretarial tasks were patiently and most efficiently performed by Miss Hilary Rawlings. The Editor wishes finally to express his gratitude to Don Eugenio González, Rector of the University of Chile, with whom he had the invaluable opportunity of discussing at length the more controversial historical aspects of his Introduction.

However, the responsibility for everything included in the Introduction evidently rests solely with the Editor.

January 1967   C. V.

Abbreviations

AD:	*Acción Democrática* (Venezuela).
AP:	*Ação Popular* (Brazil).
	Acción Popular (Peru).
APRA:	*Alianza Popular Revolucionaria Americana* (Peru).
CLAPESC:	*Centro Latino-Americano de Pesquisas em Ciências Sociais.*
CNBB:	*Conferência Nacional dos Bispos do Brasil.*
CNC:	*Confederación Nacional Campesina* (Mexico).
COPEI:	*Comité Organizador por Elecciones Independientes* (Venezuela).
DGE:	*Dirección General de Estadística.*
DNE:	*Directorio Nacional de Estudantes* (Brazil).
ECLA:	UN, Economic Commission for Latin America.
FALN:	*Fuerzas Armadas de Liberación Nacional* (Venezuela).
FERES:	*Federación Internacional de los Institutos Católicos de Investigaciones Sociales y Socioreligiosas.*
FEU:	*Federación de Estudiantes Universitarios* (Cuba).
FRAP:	*Frente de Acción Popular* (Chile).
JUC:	*Juventude Universitaria Católica* (Brazil).
MEB:	*Movimento de Educação de Base* (Brazil).

MIR: *Movimiento de Izquierda Revolucionaria* (Peru
                and Venezuela).

MNR: *Movimiento Nacionalista Revolucionario*
                (Bolivia).

ORMEU: *Oficina Relacionadora de Movimientos Estu-
                diantiles Universitarios* (Chile).

PRI: *Partido Revolucionario Institucional* (Mexico).

SPES: *Síntese Política Econômica Social* (Rio).

UCV: *Universidad Central de Venezuela.*

UNAM: *Universidad Nacional Autónoma de México.*

UNE: *União Nacional de Estudantes* (Brazil).

Introduction

CLAUDIO VELIZ

THE words reform and change have been overworked in Latin America during the last two decades. Perhaps nowhere else and at no other time have so many governments, political parties, international agencies, and pressure groups with otherwise obviously conflicting interests publicly agreed so wholeheartedly on the desirability of a profound alteration of the institutional structure of society. At the same time, seldom have so many influential would-be improvers had so little to show for their efforts. This has naturally led many students of the contemporary situation in Latin America to search for the cause of such a striking discrepancy between expressed intentions and actual performance. The resulting studies—often less critical than necessary—have generally tended to accept the assumptions on which the unsophisticated case for fundamental reform is apparently founded. Such an uncritical approach has been only marginally the result of bad scholarship: mostly it reflects the commitment to reform which is common to informed public opinion throughout the region.

Of the assumptions basic to the reformist case, probably the most important are, first, that the changes advocated are not only ethically desirable, but are also a technically necessary condition of accelerated economic growth, and, secondly, that there are in Latin America dynamic, forward-looking, self-conscious, and politically important social groups which, for economic or social reasons, are determined to achieve far-reaching reforms, of which the redistribution of land and the modernization of the fiscal system and of the central administrative structure are considered the most essential. An interesting corollary of these assumptions is that the frustration of these reformist expectations will almost certainly have explosive social consequences.

These assumptions appear less convincing today than they did some years ago and the worth of the large number of studies based on them is more open to question. No doubt important obstacles to desirable changes have been carefully identified and described and the consequences of their presence sometimes analysed in a scholarly manner, but, in spite of the fact that much impressive work has been completed, the feeling persists that the basic outline of the problem is still hazy, that intelligent answers are being given to the wrong questions: it would seem that the time has arrived when these assumptions ought to be re-examined.

The first is evidently an integral part of the general acceptance of the idea of progress characteristic of much contemporary political thinking: the word 'development' is used as scarcely more than a euphemism for the more straightforward but outmoded 'progress', the distance between them being roughly the same as that which separates 'underdevelopment' from 'backwardness'. In spite of its popularity and the many worthy ideals it represents, it would be encouraging to know that the validity of this current notion of development will be scrutinized rigorously in the future. It is difficult not to suspect that behind an indiscriminate usage, which often borders on the sentimental, there lies a hidden faith in an historical progression towards a technically feasible, inevitable improvement of everything in sight. Pleas for accelerated development and meticulous descriptions of the conditions and characteristics of the process have only drawn attention to the frequency with which the panacea fails. It is evident that humanitarian zeal has moved too many who ought to know better to place excessive trust in the application of technical solutions to problems which are essentially political ones.

Ultimately, the achievement of development may well prove as complex and sometimes as elusive for Latin Americans today as was that of progress for Europeans a century ago.

The second assumption—that there are groups so fundamentally committed to these reforms and occupying positions of such actual or potential power that the failure of their endeavours will almost certainly lead to social violence—is more obviously mistaken and has greater immediate importance, and it is to this that the title of this book refers.

Of the eight essays included, those by Professor François Chevalier and Dr Richard Adams were first presented before the 1964 Chatham House conference on Obstacles to Change in Latin America. Since then they have been revised and brought up to date for inclusion in this volume. Six additional essays were commissioned to be published under the collective title *The Politics of Change in Latin America*. The underlying idea behind the project was that the principal problems of development in Latin America were political in nature. It was hoped that the volume would shed light on the political ideas and activities of those social groups most obviously and efficiently determined to bring about profound changes in the institutional structure of Latin American society. Some of the essays were also intended to examine in detail the most important situations in which these political issues came to the fore, devoting special attention to the problems arising from the transition between rural and urban conditions.

Such a straightforward project became increasingly complicated as the finished contributions were submitted. Soon it was obvious that the title was no longer appropriate, and the whole framework of the book had to be reconsidered. There were three reasons for this. In the first place it was not at all clear that the structural reforms mentioned in so many tracts and official declarations actually represented the general aspirations of the social groups under study. It became evident that even when these groups attained political power, they did not implement these reforms but rather tried to become integrated into the existing social structure: what looked to some like massive social mobility turned out to be more like institutionalized social climbing. In the second place, this apparent surrender to conformity did not mean that there were no important changes, but rather that those which were obviously taking place were not the ones generally anticipated. Finally, in their efforts to discover a suitably dynamic and modernizing pressure group definitely committed to industrialization and reform, it appeared that most observers had ignored the importance of the central, paternalistic, all-embracing, and sometimes authoritarian state, which had meanwhile been steadily regaining its traditional position as the dominant factor in national politics.

In fact the reformist aspirations of these groups have been taken too much for granted: although there is a widespread belief that to bring about such drastic changes is a principal goal of the middle classes, it is enough for them to falter, hesitate, or fail to do this, for a number of other groups such as the armed forces, the progressive wing of the Catholic Church, the intelligentsia, or the peasantry to be put forward as alternative initiators of reformist movements. However, in spite of this enthusiasm, doubts about the declared intentions of all these groups arise whenever they are studied intensively: such doubts, for instance, largely dominate the companion volume of essays edited by the present writer, *Obstacles to Change in Latin America* (1965).

In this book scepticism gains ground. Moreover the framework within which social mobility takes place is also examined and Dr Richard Adams rightly demonstrates that, far from showing profound alterations, the traditional structure has suffered fewer changes than is usually thought. He concludes that, while it is possible to distinguish a growing middle-income sector, the older and basic dual structure of prestige and value systems has not changed as much as has been supposed. Rather the apparently new middle group is only an extension of the traditional upper class, both in terms of economic position and of basic values.

An examination of the political activities and motivations of groups such as military officers, university students, rural migrants, and industrialists results in a picture which will not bring comfort to the staunchly reformist. For example, though industrialists and peasants stand roughly at opposite extremes of the social spectrum, it is fair to assume that for differing reasons they should both be directly interested in changing the traditional institutional structure. It is particularly difficult to see why peasants should be satisfied with things as they are, and reasonable to think that the least satisfied are those who move into the cities to try to better their lot. But once there, their relative importance as potential supporters of fundamental change tends to decrease as they become integrated into the outer fringes of the vast urban service sector. The postwar import-substitution industrialization of Latin America is capital- rather than labour-intensive, so that the number of workers directly engaged in manufacturing industry is relatively small, their wages are high, and they mostly tend to be skilled, with the result that the chances of a peasant migrant becoming an industrial worker are slight. On the other hand the service sectors of the vast urban centres of the region afford many opportunities to the more active of the rural migrants. Even stretching the classical Marxist concept to its limits, it would be difficult to say that yesterday's peasant who today peels potatoes in a restaurant, sells newspapers, or shines shoes has changed his 'relations of production' and has become an industrial worker. In fact, the rural migrant brings with him to the large capital cities the acceptance of the hierarchical, centralized, and organic system of authority with which he feels familiar. As Dr Eric Hobsbawm points out, rural migrants and peasants understand and accept personal leadership and patronage because it alone provides a link between the political world of the hinterland and that of the city. Untouched by any other traditions, such as the anti-caudillist ones of liberalism or socialism, the new immigrants look naturally for the powerful champion, the saviour, the father of his people. And from such an eager following did Vargas, Perón, Ibáñez, and other populist—though not necessarily reformist—leaders derive their most loyal and vociferous support. As things are, the rural inhabitants of Latin America—not all of them peasants—are gradually becoming a minority in a region which is surprisingly urban in relation to its degree of industrialization. Searching for political leadership, the peasant almost inevitably finds himself supporting an urban-based populist movement with very tenuous interests in the countryside. It is probable that populist movements will pay an increasing attention to the agrarian situation, but it is extremely unlikely that the peasantry will transform itself into the vanguard of a successful reformist movement which will carry the urban political organizations in its wake. Even in those cases—like the Mexican revolution—in which the peasantry played a significant political role in bringing about drastic changes to the traditional structure, once their immediate personal demands were satisfied they lapsed easily into political passivity and even into an acceptance of some of the more conspicuous features of the *ancien régime* with which they somehow felt identified. As Professor François Chevalier points out, in his detailed study of the Mexican *ejido*, the peasants, although they occasionally burnt sugar mills and farm-houses, once their essential rights had been regained did not press for the abolition of the hacienda system as they 'apparently did not wish to abolish an institution which was as traditional · as the villages themselves and formed an essential part of their cultural horizon'.

At the other end of the spectrum, the industrialists have also proved a disappointing source of ideas or incentives for a reformist movement. Argentina offers a relevant example. More industrialized and at an earlier period than her neighbours, she boasted a significant manufacturing sector as early as the decade of the 1920s. This activity was concentrated in the urban area of the province of Buenos Aires and in the larger cities of the interior. More important was the fact that these industries were owned or controlled almost exclusively by recently arrived European immigrants. The correlation between such arrivals and the growth of manufacturing industries is as striking as the fact that at no time during this period of early growth and consolidation did the industrialists succeed in securing a corresponding representation or even a voice in the determination of national policies. Far from it, they found themselves excluded from the main political organizations, because, according to Sr Oscar Cornblit, 'the political élite discriminated against the immigrants, who promoted the great majority of the industrial undertakings'. Such an attitude was perhaps natural to the upper-class ethos reflected in conservative organizations; more interesting is the fact that it was shared by the *Unión Cívica Radical*, the dominant political party of the period, which was supported by the vast majority of the people and had the virtual monopoly of progressive and reformist ideas. An upper-class leadership and a xenophobic lower-middle-class following gave the *Unión Cívica Radical* an unashamedly anti-foreign bias which most effectively prevented the rising industrialists from influencing its policies. In fact Sr Cornblit conclusively demonstrates that, in the face of the cosmopolitan views associated with the Argentine conservatives at that time,

The Radicals tended to adopt a body of political thought which in all its visible aspects was opposed [to the conservatives] . . . in the presence of such a sizeable immigrant community . . . the phobia against foreigners was easily rationalized and transformed into an anti-cosmopolitan and anti-conservative policy.

However determined these industrialists may have been to secure the reforms they considered essential, they had no hope of succeeding unless they first obtained political representation and, in Argentina, this they could not do by forming a party consisting principally of foreigners. In any case, they were not numerous enough to do this. Inevitably, they had to try to influence existing political groupings, and during the early years of their struggle to establish themselves, this course was closed to them. It must also be said these immigrants did not bring a social, economic, or cultural outlook very distinct from the one they found in Argentina. In fact, those who were in a better position—because of their success as industrialists—to benefit from a change in government policy, were precisely the ones who had most successfully adapted themselves to the new situation. Their wealth brought them nearer the local upper strata and, after one generation, their children were educated with those of the landed aristocracy; thus the would-be reformists of the decades of 1920 and 1930 became the supporters of order and stability in 1950 and 1960.

Peasants and industrialists are not impressive as dynamic supporters of fundamental reform, and university students, in spite of their vociferous radicalism, slide with surprising ease into the well-worn channels of orthodox behaviour. The professionalizing bent of most Latin American systems of higher education is partly to blame for this but also, as Dr Alistair Hennessy points out:

> The majority of students come from the middle class . . . those from the lower [middle class] group are aspirants to professional middle class standing and see a university career putting the seal on their social advancement. For them the university fulfils a social mobility function and is the path to status and hence security. For those from the established middle class . . . the university primarily has a status-preservation function.

This may well be the simplest and truest explanation of why the energetic rioters of undergraduate days accept professional respectability so readily once they have obtained their degrees; and while an important sector of the intelligentsia—among them perhaps the most influential and creative minds of each generation—continue to uphold reformist ideas all their lives, they are few in numbers and their political commitment is not echoed by the professional classes, who are quick to profit from the social advancement afforded by their professional qualifications.

The military have a bad press in Latin America. Their notorious record of intervention has earned them the scorn of the local intelligentsia, while the inelegant way in which they ride roughshod over people and institutions makes them a natural target for popular enmity. Of late, however, probably as a by-product of disillusionment with other political formulas, they have been attracting considerable attention.

Outside observers tend to take diametrically opposite views on the subject of the military. To most, the armed forces must naturally be grouped with the most extreme conservative sectors of society: with the landowners and the right wing of the Catholic Church. The fact that many Latin American military establishments were modernized by Prussian officers at the end of the nineteenth century, thereby adopting the uniforms and the ritual of Prussian militarism as well, has helped to make even more convincing their supposedly intimate association with the traditionalist views of the landed aristocracy.

Others have shown a tendency to endow military officers with all sorts of virtues as dynamic reformers primarily interested in the rapid economic and social development of their countries in ways largely resembling those associated with President Nasser or Kemal Ataturk. As Sr José Nun aptly puts it in the first part of his essay: 'According to one . . . theory, the traditional army is a step behind the modern society which is forming around it; according to another, the modern army is a step ahead of the traditional society which is disintegrating.'

Sr Nun then proceeds to dispel both these views without much difficulty. As it happens, the officer corps of the Latin American armed forces is overwhelmingly recruited from the lower middle class. The almost direct association between the officer corps and the landed aristocracy which existed, say, in Britain or Germany before the war, is simply not found in Latin America. Moreover Sr Nun shows that the intervention of the military in politics has almost invariably been on behalf of the declared political interests of the middle class: 'Military interventionism does not threaten the middle class . . . nor is it a substitute' for it, but it represents its interests and compensates for its incapacity to establish itself in power as a well-integrated, hegemonic group.

The close identification of social attitudes and political interests between the military and a determinedly conformist urban middle class makes it unlikely that the present situation will lead to a Nasserist or 'Young Turk' revolutionary solution. Far from embracing the cause of reform as a defence against the rise of, say, a populist movement, the middle classes are much more likely to encourage strong military régimes to take over and maintain order and stability, even at the price of illiberal repressive methods and a suspension of democratic practices.

It would need a very great deal of optimism to believe that the politics of conformity, so efficiently practised by these groups, could possibly bring about the fundamental reforms considered necessary for the rapid modernization of the region. Yet to assume that, because of this, change and modernization will not take place would be a great mistake. What these studies rather suggest is that the mechanical application of the wrong models has led to the wrong conclusions.

These wrong models have inevitably been based on the successful industrial experience of some western nations only, less attention naturally being paid to the experience of those with unimpressive industrial records. Thus the countries of the Mediterranean make little or no contribution to the construction of these models of growth. For equally obvious reasons the vague identification of political and economic liberalism with the growth of industry and the reform of pre-industrial institutions has been accepted, together with the notion that the central government is at best a passive instrument in the hands of one or other of the modernizing, industrializing groupings.

But in Latin America the central government is the pressure group which has been steadily growing in power and influence during the past decades and which alone appears to have the capacity to bring about the generalized modernization of these economies. Further, this trend is very much in keeping with the character of the Hispanic political and cultural complex. If economic growth and modernization came to Britain and the United States because of the enterprise of groups of individuals outside the government, by the end of the eighteenth century economic growth in Spain—and Spanish America—was clearly identified with the zeal with which an enterprising and paternalistic central government would carry on its duties. The wars of independence which started in 1810 did not change this situation; the victors were the higher civil servants of the crown, and the very small merchant community which then existed was absolutely committed to the central authorities from which it received patronage, concessions, and privileges. The opening of the ports and general liberalization of trade which followed the defeat of Spain was not a measure demanded by the local merchants but one imposed reluctantly and only for fiscal reasons by the central authorities, against the most strenuous opposition of the local merchants. And these were right to protest, for within a few years foreign merchant communities had been established in practically every major port of the continent, effectively displacing the native trader. The entry of Latin America into the world market as a principal supplier of primary commodities for an expanding European economy resulted in a wave of prosperity which simply engulfed the economic habits and institutions of the colonial period. These were not destroyed but disappeared from view as the rising tide of prosperity transformed the traditionalist mine-owners and producers of agricultural products into wealthy exporters and keen free-trading liberals.

Although there are some exceptions, it can be said that during the hundred years between the 1830s and the two world wars the ruling groups in Latin America were prosperous enough to afford to depart from their traditional institutions and indulge in the practice of various versions of liberalism, radicalism, positivism, and the like in the same spirit with which they adopted English public schools, Second Empire styles of architecture, Victorian manners and artistic tastes. These imitative activities were not taken lightly; those who espoused political liberalism were prepared to die for it, and often did, whilst the adoption of systems of education reflected a seriousness and depth of commitment which cannot be ignored. The culture that was being imitated so eagerly was the culture of wealth, progress, and prosperity: those who resisted were unhesitatingly regarded as obscurantists and superstitious bigots. The evidence which justified such harsh epithets was close at hand: free-trading liberalism and the export of primary commodities resulted in vast and immediate wealth while every protectionist measure diminished this wealth and 'taxed the worker' in the name of an illusory future development of national industries which, even if they were ever formed, would not be able to face competition from European manufactures without protection.

This period came to an end between the crisis of 1929 and the second world war. By the early 1950s it was generally accepted that Latin America had to move on from import-substitution to fully-fledged industrial development, and the efforts of governments and international technical agencies were directed to this end. But at the time it still appeared that the only experience likely to be useful was that of the European nations which had gone through this process in the nineteenth century, and therefore a conscious attempt was made to put Latin America systematically through the 'stages of economic growth' suggested by that experience. Perhaps this could be seen at its crudest in the recommendations of the Alliance for Progress, which roughly identified economic growth with democratic control, social justice, and a specific number of fairly detailed institutional reforms. Although the directness of these recommendations is explained by their political character, it must be remembered that the Alliance was reflecting opinions widely held, not only in technical agencies such as the Economic Commission for Latin America, but also in academic and political circles.

The 'stages of economic growth' approach has not been very successful. The reforms which were considered absolutely essential have not in fact taken place; the groups which alone, it was thought, could bring about development and modernization have not even managed to achieve recognition, much less the capacity to dictate policy. (The import-substitution industrialization of Latin America was neither the product of the activities of an industrial bourgeoisie nor did it produce an industrial proletariat.) Even so industry has developed reasonably well and rates of industrial growth of 8 and 9 per cent per annum are becoming commonplace. The social reforms which were considered—possibly with un-exceptional ethical justification—absolutely necessary if widespread political violence and a communist revolution were to be avoided, have not been implemented, but this has not been followed by a repetition of the Cuban experience. Far from it, with all the guns turned towards a mythical enemy on the extreme left, the bastion of democracy has indeed been stormed—more than fourteen times since the Alliance for Progress made democratic control an absolute condition for the reception of aid from the United States—but on every occasion the attack has come from the right, and today there are more *de facto* régimes in power than anybody cares to remember. More, the trend in those countries where the military are not, nor are likely to be, in power is strongly towards centralized control. The three revolutionary movements which are generally accepted as such—those of Mexico, Bolivia, and Cuba—have resulted in two single-party systems and one military dictatorship. Such happenings may be universally deplored and action organized to try to reverse them, but it is also interesting to try to understand why it is that the whole of the region is so evidently moving in the same direction.

It appears that in 1929, with the breakdown of the system based on the free flow of exports to the markets of the northern hemisphere, Latin America started the painful road back to find her own level of economic and political awareness. This road led away both from upper-class affluence and from the pluralistic liberalism which the hitherto powerful ruling groups had embraced with such gusto. In fits and starts since 1929, the countries of Latin America have been returning to their own Hispanic, hierarchical, and more or less authoritarian political tradition. If both the United States and the Soviet Union may justly be regarded as nations with great social mobility and a generalized aspiration to become egalitarian societies, precisely the converse would apply to Latin America. If at one time it was confidently expected that industrialization would transform highly stratified, traditional societies into modern, thriving industrial societies with great internal mobility, by now these hopes should have been abandoned. At least from a social point of view, Latin America has been by-passed by the industrial revolution; it is now possible for countries like Brazil, Mexico, Chile, or Argentina to develop impressive industrial sectors incorporating the latest available technology and even modes of consumption without all this resulting in fundamental changes in the traditional social structure.

Conversely, the reforms—agrarian, fiscal, and administrative, in the Alliance for Progress version—which were considered absolutely essential if economic growth was to take place, have not been implemented, but this has not prevented industry from effectively taking root in a number of countries. Of course from every conceivable point of view these reforms are most desirable— agriculture should be more productive, peasants should be better treated, taxes should be fairly assessed and collected, and the general national and municipal business of government should be conducted with efficiency—but they are not absolutely essential to ensure a moderate rate of economic growth. Not essential, that is, as reforms, though as moderate improvements they would be useful indeed, but then how much must the delivery of mail or the collection of taxes improve before one can call such an improvement a reform? Perhaps too much weight has been given to words whose meaning is not altogether clear, and the resulting confusion has obscured the fact that in the absence of a reformist leadership coming from rising bourgeoisie, a militant industrial proletariat, a Nasserist military officers' group, or a staunchly reformist intelligentsia, the Latin American political and social cultural complex has reverted to historical precedent, vesting the central government with all the authority necessary to perform the general improvements needed. The politics of conformity which have dominated the last decade have apparently led to the return of a paternalistic centralism which has a great deal in common with the traditions of the Spanish Enlightenment. This should not appear excessively paradoxical. Few analysts of the contemporary situation in Europe, Africa, or Asia hesitate to interpret the knowledge they have of recent happenings by what is known of the historical background of these areas, often going back several centuries; the prevalence of feudal or tribal institutions in other parts of the world makes modern developments intelligible, while some of the most significant writings on English economic and political history trace—to name only two—the industrial revolution and the Labour Party to events functionally related to the Nonconformist movement.

The Latin American institutional tradition includes neither nonconformity nor those fundamental political—as distinct from social —features of feudalism which determined the relations between central and peripheral power; its history has been dominated by paternalistic centralism with the qualified exception of the hundred years after 1830. Latin America entered modern political life in the sixteenth century when feudalism had already disappeared from most of Europe; the same powerful alliance of Castile and Aragon that sent Columbus to discover a new passage to India was the one that decisively defeated the Moors of Granada and consolidated central, monarchical power over the peninsula. What the Spanish conquerors imposed on their new dominions was a highly centralized version of the authoritarian Renaissance state; there were no regional sites of political power in the new countries; the little power possessed by local landowners and military leaders was derived directly and exclusively from the goodwill of the captain-general, viceroy, or king. If the central authority went unchallenged—as it did, because even at the time of the movement of independence it was the local upper classes who challenged the distant crown of Spain—the established Church was certainly never in danger. There is nothing in the history of Latin America which could even remotely be compared to English nonconformity. Even at the height of anti-clericalism, the fundamental authority of the Catholic Church was seldom questioned; there are no Cromwells or Wesleys in Latin American history. Without feudalism or nonconformity, Latin America has none of the historical ingredients which make for an autonomous, pluralistic, liberal movement. Because of this, there is a strong tendency to emphasize the paternalistic, centralist elements which, after all, are present in any well organized, modern bureaucratic organization. Also because of this, once the prosperity of the nineteenth century came to an end, and with it the artificially-sustained liberalism and radicalism of its dominant urban groups, Latin America started slowly to find its way back into its own cultural main stream.

There is little doubt that the reforms and the accelerated economic growth suggested and so enthusiastically supported from outside Latin America are not taking place in the expected way. One of the principal reasons for this may be that neither those reforms nor the economic growth are significantly related to the present needs of these countries as they themselves understand and interpret them. If this is even partly true, then there is good reason to expect that the politics of conformity, which so evidently dominate the scene today, will soon give way to a new awareness of national interest firmly rooted in the cultural and historical traditions of Latin America; changes based firmly on such an awareness will perhaps stand a better chance of being implemented rapidly and efficiently.

Political Power and Social Structures

RICHARD N. ADAMS

THE acceptance of the emergence of a new middle class has become almost a necessity for students of Latin American development. It fills an explanatory niche so successfully that few question its theoretical significance or propose alternative interpretations. Specialists in economic development see it both as the source of entrepreneurs and as an index of progress; political historians see it as a source of leaders and new political ideologies; anthropologists have characterized it as a middle mass, and detect in it a new, emergent culture; and sociologists, seeking some additional objective index, have found the middle class amply represented in the changing occupational categories of the population census.

In spite of this, the Latin American middle sector or middle class is specially difficult to define. This is not necessarily due to the novelty of the phenomenon, or even to lack of adequate knowledge about it: exactly the same problem exists with regard to the middle classes in more advanced, industrial societies. Some have referred to this group as 'an occupational salad' while others have observed that 'the new middle class has stubbornly resisted all attempts to define its upper and lower limits'. In fact, it is obvious that the question of when salaried employees begin to be members of an upper stratum or ruling class and when they 'really' still belong in the working class cannot in general be answered.[1]

Some sociologists maintain that the crucial problem is not merely one of definition but involves an appreciation of changes in power relations and their consequences. It is, however, difficult to abandon traditional concepts, and the study of this power aspect has been hindered by outmoded interpretations in terms of horizontal strata and class. Thus, even those who have managed to break away—by the way making better sense out of Marx—sub-

[1] Ralf Dahrendorf, *Class and Conflict in Industrial Society* (Stanford UP, 1959), p. 52.

stituting power for property, still do this within the old framework of class.[2]

The position taken in this essay is that the usefulness of the middle-class concept for the study of contemporary Latin American society has been greatly exaggerated and this has in turn obscured other processes which are of considerable importance. While it is possible to distinguish a growing middle-income sector, the older and basic dual structure of prestige and value system has not changed as much as has been supposed. Rather, the apparently new middle group is only an extension of the traditional upper class, both in terms of economic position and of basic values. It is possible to understand many aspects of contemporary Latin America if one sees individuals operating in terms of one of these two major sectors (the upper and the lower); while it is quite impossible to do so by insisting on the emergence of a new middle class.

The two sectors are distinguished by having vertical parallel structures, distinctive value systems, and different bases for social mobility. The lower sector has wealth as its goal, and the recognized means to obtain this is labour. The upper sector has a variety of prestige symbols as its goal, and the means of achieving these lie in the manipulation of power. There is continuity between the two sectors, since wealth is one of the set of prestige symbols in the upper sector and may be said to be the principal prestige symbol leading to mobility in the lower. The individuals who are mainly concerned with survival occupy the lower reaches of each sector.

At the bottom of the lower sector are the destitute, and also the unskilled labourers who are principally concerned with survival; at the bottom of the prestige or upper sector is a group mainly concerned with trying to avoid returning or falling into the lower sector.[3] Although there are important individual exceptions, both lower levels are characterized by little willingness to accept innovations; a conservatism born of the need for survival.

The upper reaches of each sector contain individuals who have

[2] Dahrendorf, for instance. Bendix, on the other hand, analysing the role of governmental political power, insists on keeping separate the factors leading to social stratification (Reinhard Bendix, 'Social Stratification and the Political Community', *Archives européennes de sociologie*, 1/2 (1960), pp. 181–210).

[3] This is the group which Andrew H. Whiteford has called the 'Middle Middle Class' (*Two Cities of Latin America* (New York, 1964), p. 219).

entered that area by virtue of successful accumulation of wealth. The successful small entrepreneur who continues to do manual work himself, while employing some labour and being involved in some capital investment, stands at the top of the lower sector while the *nouveaux riches* occupy part of the upper portion of the prestige sector. In both cases the upper sections also house those who are there by virtue of having been born into a situation in which they inherited the opportunity and the necessary materials to stay on top, and have the ability to remain in that position. In the upper sector the old upper class, the 'aristocracy', occupy the highest prestige positions, and will continue to do so as long as they have any basis of power. At the top of the lower sector there is a similar traditional survival in the individual craftsman with a work-shop, a man of reasonable wealth, employing a few workers, and quite uninterested in competing for the prestige symbols of the upper sector.

Since many delineations of social strata have depended on occupation, the dividing line between the two sectors has become confused. This can be seen in the problem of placing those enter-prising individuals, skilled labourers or small entrepreneurs, who rise from the lower sector, continue to work manually themselves, and pay little or no attention to the basic value system of the upper sector. In completely independent studies from different disci-plinary backgrounds, Andrew Whiteford, an anthropologist, and Melvin Tumin and Arnold Feldman, sociologists, decided to place them within the middle class. Whiteford did so because his in-formants classified many skilled occupations in this same way; [4] Tumin and Feldman did so because 'skilled workers enjoy relatively high incomes and prestige, due mostly to the scarcity of such workers in proportion to the high demand for their services. Further, their work, dress, and attitudes toward work resemble the white-collar more than blue-collar echelons.' [5]

These kinds of essentially ethnographic distinguishing features are not descriptive of social structure and provide little insight into social development. Under these circumstances, ethnic groups and social strata are essentially the same kinds of concepts. They are descriptions of styles of life, or of the subjective allocation of

[4] Ibid.
[5] *Social Class and Social Change in Puerto Rico* (Princeton UP, 1961), p. 324.

the members. The last of these has always been an unsatisfactory way to describe and clarify social sectors for general theoretical purposes, although such subjective estimations are evidently valuable in other ways.[6]

This problem has been well described again by Whiteford in recognizing the difference between this 'lower middle class' and the rest of the middle sector. 'The cultural discontinuity which existed between the Middle Middle Class and the Lower Middle Class was obviously a reflection of the traditional Spanish disdain for hand labor.'[7] These people's only means of rising in the social scale is through labour, yet those who succeed in accumulating wealth will not be able to move into the upper sector unless they get something else besides wealth.

The upper sector can be occupied only through access to a series of prestige symbols that require some wealth, but wealth alone is not enough. Correct use of language, dress, mannerisms, and, indeed, an upper-strata culture is difficult to acquire unless one grows up in or near it. Many specific symbols are so esoteric that only the initiated can know what should be learned.

The two sectors distinguished here have specific structural differences that hold for a wide area of Latin America. Before going into the kinds of changes currently under way and their causes, a comment is in order as to the historical derivation of the dual-sector idea. It is obvious that the dual sectors are somewhat congruent with the nineteenth- and twentieth-century social structure based on the hacienda-export system and economic liberalism. All writers recognize the general nature of this system and we need not explore its variations. The delineation made here, however, is done entirely on the basis of contemporary studies, not on a forward projection from historical materials. Simple though it may be, it was arrived at only after much sifting of the various descriptions of social-strata systems led to the conclusion that the dual-sector idea was an organizing principle that seemed to hold good for almost all the data at hand.

Further, while there are important similarities between this dual division and the Marxist two-class system, there are also important differences. The upper sector contains many of the

---

[6] Bertram Hutchinson, 'Class Self-Assessment in a Rio de Janeiro Population', *América latina*, 6/2, pp. 53–64.

[7] Whiteford, p. 119.

owners and controllers of means of production, but not all, since some belong to the lower sector. Working for subsistence is a major characteristic of the lower sector, but it is also a way of accumulating wealth. Another problem lies in the allocation of white-collar workers. Dahrendorf gives what is probably a reasonable neo-Marxist view of this by allocating them to the lower sector, since they are completely without control or ownership, and live off wages. In the present analysis, however, they are unquestionably part of the upper sector, for it is by means of this classification that we can see the structural similarities in the two sectors, and note continuity of prestige as the criterion in the upper sector and continuity of work as the criterion in the lower one. We are, then, dealing with a phenomenon that was central to Marx's formulation, but its interpretation here points in a somewhat different direction. Conflict between the two sectors is not a distinguishing characteristic of the structure as a whole although conflict between individuals and small groups is endemic. Finally, analysis of the changes and processes does not lead to the conclusion that there will ever be a classless society.

The Lower Sector

Much literature on the Latin American lower sector clearly distinguishes the rural from the urban components. Not only have observed differences been emphasized, but most specific studies have focused on one or the other. Nevertheless, studies of the past fifteen years have important similarities.[8]

---

[8] Oscar Lewis ('The Culture of the Vecindad in Mexico City: Two Case Studies', *Proc. of 33rd International Congress of Americanists*, i. (1952) pp. 387–402), for instance, challenged the simplistic, contrastive, folk-urban dichotomy of Robert Redfield (*The Folk Cultures of Yucatan* (Chicago, 1939)) and the entire Maine-Tönnies-Durkheim tradition on which it was based and succeeded in describing some of the structures common to both the urban and the rural components of the society, pointing out that the convenient sociological dichotomy had been vastly overused. This trend has been supported by the work of D. S. Butterworth ('A Study of the Urbanization Process among Mixtec Migrants from Tilantongo in Mexico City', *América indígena*, 22/3 (1962), pp. 254–74), W. P. Mangin ('The Role of the Regional Association in the Adaptation of Rural Population in Peru', *Sociologus*, 9/1 (1959), pp. 23–35, and 'Cultural and Psychological Characteristics of Mountain Migrants to Lima, Peru', ibid. 14/1 (1964)), Juarez R. Brandão Lopes ('Aspects of the Adjustment of Rural Migrants to Urban-Industrial Conditions in São Paulo, Brazil', in P. M. Hauser, ed., *Urbanization in Latin America*

The picture that now emerges focuses on the increasing rural-urban migration of the past half-century and permits us to distinguish three different kinds of cultural situations: (1) people raised in a rural environment, living in that environment; (2) people raised in a rural environment, living in an urban environment; and (3) people raised and living in an urban environment. Comparatively speaking, the migrants generally undergo considerable tension on entering the urban environment, and the adjustment period is eased through maintenance of strong rural bonds. The longer they stay, the more they take on the culture of the city and, according to Germani,[9] fewer children are born, legal marriage becomes preferred over free-unions, the husband's salary increasingly provides the economic base, and the domestic unit becomes more stable, urban voluntary associations are joined, more friendships develop outside the kin network, newspapers are increasingly used, attendance at the cinema becomes a regular occurrence, and children are more likely to be in school.

The bonds of kinship constitute the major continuity spanning both rural and urban areas. Germani's samples, in which so many changes were associated with length of urban residence, did not show significant changes in this matter. The reason has been expressed by one author as follows:

What is necessary for survival within such a context is access to the subordinate roles which can provide at least some degree of physical security in a world over which the *criollo* has no control. Lacking in effective industrial answers to his problems, e.g., unions or cooperatives, he depends upon his kindred to provide the necessary 'insurance'. By increasing the number of his kinsmen, he increases the probability that at least one of them will be in a position to be of service to him in time of need. The wide lateral extension of kin terminology reflects this need.[10]

The same importance is attached to kinship in the other geographical extreme of Latin America, in the Mexican population of Texas; there individuals will be able to list the names and addresses of as many as 500 relatives, and, in so far as can be determined,

---

(New York, 1961)), Arnold Strickon ('Class and Kinship in Argentina', *Ethnology*, 1/4 (1962), pp. 500–15), and others.

[9] Gino Germani, 'Inquiry into the Social Effects of Urbanization in a Working-Class Sector of Great Buenos Aires', in Hauser, pp. 206–23.

[10] Strickon (*Ethnology*, 1/4 (1962), p. 508).

the specific utility of this knowledge has to do with the help these relatives may render if one has to seek work.

The rural-urban continuity, so manifest in kinship, is also physically visible. Marginal to all major Latin American cities are the so-called 'slum towns'—the rural migrants' response to construction materials available in the city—and a little farther out are agricultural settlements that have, over the years, become dependent on city wage labour for survival.[11]

Current evidence suggests, then, that the formation of an urban proletariat does not require cutting off rural relatives and values. Since this was not the expected result, we must ask ourselves why strong kinship ties survive the process of urbanization? One possible answer to this may be found in contrasting the experience of the United States with that of Latin America. In the United States it can be generally said that labour moved to cities in response to a call from the cities rather than because of agrarian pressures. The fact that many Latin Americans migrate because of agrarian insufficiency rather than industrial attraction means that the effects of the adjustment to industry may not be as strongly felt as in the United States. This is related to Hirschman's observation on the reasons for dualistic economic development.[12] Industrialization in Latin America, he argued, cannot readily begin in areas where handicrafts produced with cheap labour can readily compete. If rational investment is the mode, there will continue to be a large area of potential production that can only be utilized very slowly. This view ignores the continued importance of small-scale urban production and service enterprises that keep many migrants in a style of life close to that of their rural counterparts. The labour situation is similar to that of the towns and the social structure surrounding it is supported by the same factors. The same kinds of devices that provided insurance for survival in the rural area continue to operate.

The *vecindad* [writes Oscar Lewis] acts as a shock absorber for the rural migrants to the city because of the similarity between its

[11] Ruben Reina (*Chinautla, a Guatemalan Indian Community* (New Orleans, 1960) has illustrated this in Guatemala and Ralph L. Beals in Ecuador ('Acculturation; Economics and Social Change in an Ecuadorian Village', in Sol Tax, ed., *Acculturation in the Americas,* Chicago UP, 1952)).

[12] A. O. Hirschman, *The Strategy of Economic Development* (1958), pp. 125–32.

culture and that of rural communities. Indeed, we find no sharp differences in family structure, diet, dress and belief systems of the *vecindad* tenants, according to their rural-urban origins.[13]

Earlier, we suggested that wealth was the principal basis for recognizing ranking or stratification within the lower sector. Wealth or income occupies this rather special position in the structure of the lower sector because it is the only basis for cumulative prestige. In that sector prestige depends upon income because to have or to maintain it time and money must be expended. In the Central American and Andean Indian communities, the men who are recognized as community leaders must have enough wealth to take time off to handle community matters. Beyond this, however, lower-sector prestige always involves things which cannot be had by wealth or power, but which are personal skills of the individual. Quickness of mind, ability in certain tasks, selfishness or lack of it, honourableness in relations, and so on, are individual features that cannot be inherited, accumulated, or shared. Therefore, prestige in the lower sector is not something that permits social mobility in the sense that this term is generally used. Mobility can only be had by the accumulation of wealth, since that permits a person to do things which are clearly beyond the capacity of his fellows, and it can be shared by the entire family of the individual.

The central position of work in mobility hinges on the fact that it is the only means regularly available to lower-sector individuals to obtain wealth. Buried treasure, the lottery, and other devices both legendary and real, might catapult an individual into wealth,[14] but cannot be depended upon by rational and ambitious individuals. The value of work in the lower sector revolves around the role it is perceived to play in an individual's aspirations. Although they show some superficial variations, their pattern is highly consistent and it ranges from high value to disparagement. Perhaps the central issue is whether the amount of wealth that one can, in fact, accumulate within the going system is sufficient to achieve any of the valued symbols visible within the total system. In most instances it is not.

Whiteford quotes an apparently energetic, but puzzled, entre-

---

[13] *Proc. of 33rd International Congress of Americanists*, i. 400.
[14] George Foster, 'Treasure Tales, and the Image of the Static Economy in a Mexican Peasant Community', *J. Amer. Folklore*, 77 (1964), pp. 39–44.

preneur from Querétaro, Mexico, on the subject of one of his dairy farm employees:

> I have a dairy farm and I have Indian workers in charge of it. I told them, 'For every litre more of milk [you produce] I will raise your wages one-fourth of a centavo'. They said, 'Oh, si, señor, si señor', and smiled. What happened? Nothing. I know they could have raised the milk production, but they weren't interested. . . . Some of the Indians are skillful, and some of them are good workers, but they have no ambition.[15]

One needs to know little of Mexican dairy economics to recognize that the proposed rate would require an astronomical increase in milk production to produce any significant increase in wealth for the Indian. No special sociological insight is necessary to see why extra work is not popular. Since wages are judged in terms of the lower sector, and prices of most valued items are set by the upper sector, it is only under unusual circumstances that work will permit the accumulation of sufficient wealth to acquire the needed prestige symbols.

If we look at some cases in which work has been highly valued, such as among Guatemalan Indian village dwellers, it is clear that the gains available are significant within the somewhat closed value system of those villages. Achievement in the Indian cultural system is possible through the exercise of an important role in the community. Gaining these positions requires income and ability, and as it is perfectly possible to accumulate the necessary amount of wealth to achieve this, the value of labour is enhanced.

It is evident that this discussion of vertical structure makes no initial distinction between what might be called 'ethnic groups' and those that compose the general 'civil population'. The reason for this should now be obvious. Although sedentary agricultural Indians and other such distinctive cultural entities have sometimes violently divergent visible cultures, an understanding of their behaviour within the system as a whole, and an understanding of the system itself, requires that we assume that centuries of interaction have provided a common structure, and that this common structure will be reflected in behaviour.

The Upper Sector

Although Marx had to allow for failure of unification of the lower class through most of history, he did not need to do this for

[15] Whiteford, p. 166.

the bourgeoisie. In the same way, it is easier today to see the structural relations between the various components of the upper sector, even though these are not the same ones as constituted Marx's ruling class.

The upper sector comprises the entire set of upper strata and most of the middle strata ordinarily distinguished in sociological analysis and in the common view of the contemporary Latin American. In Whiteford's analysis of Popayán and Querétaro, it would include everybody from his Middle Middle Class upwards. All the people included within this range have a common mobility structure, since the goals and means for their achievement are the same. The importance of wealth to this sector lies in the fact that it provides the means for obtaining and maintaining the symbols that demonstrate the upper sector status of the individuals. So it is that the income of a white-collar worker may well be less than that of a lower-sector entrepreneur, but that he uses his income to obtain certain household appliances and equipment, clothing and brands of cigarettes, and other material items that are presumed to indicate an individual's upper-sector membership. The *empleado* takes great pains not to be confused with the manual labourer.

The structural continuity between the rural and the urban sectors exists through the direct linkage of a rural 'local upper class' [16] with the so-called 'middle strata'. The urban middle strata include bureaucratic and white-collar employees, businessmen, and probably most professional people. Government, business, and industry are operated by them, and it is generally to their advantage that these institutions be maintained. Because of this, their interests are best met when salaries and profits flow with regularity. The provincial or local upper class (including as it does the local 'importers' and 'exporters') also benefits from this kind of stability. Rural and urban elements are cemented by kinship here as in the lower sector.

The upper sector is distinctive in that there are other means besides income of rising in status within the sector that are always present and are often much more important. When Eric Wolf characterized the emergent *mestizo* population of the past century and a half as 'the power seekers', [17] he correctly identified power

[16] R. N. Adams, *Cultural Surveys of Panama-Nicaragua-Guatemala-El Salvador-Honduras* (Washington, Pan American Sanitary Bureau, 1957).
[17] *Sons of the Shaking Earth* (1959), ch. 11.

as the crucial feature of the upper sector. It is left for us to add, however, that power-seeking is not limited to the *mestizos* in the upper sector. The nature of power is something that one can seldom depend upon having; power is a process that exists as a part of many relationships, and anyone who fails to keep the process going may suddenly find himself without it. Wolf's characterization should, therefore, be extended to the entire upper sector. It would not be an exaggeration to say that the entire internal structure of the upper sector is a series of relationships established and altered by virtue of a constant concern for gaining and using power.

This structure has been little analysed, although Anthony Leeds has made a valuable sortie in his brief study of career patterns in Brazil. The reasons for our ignorance are multiple. In the first place, most sociologists and social anthropologists have become interested in examining systems only when they were aware of their boundaries. Thus we have studies of communities, kinship groups, social classes or strata, even whole societies. Since it is generally accepted in the ideology of Western social science that there is a 'middle class', it has also been assumed that the structure relating the 'middle' and 'upper' classes is less important than the dividing line between them. Unfortunately Marxist sociology, in which a firm belief in two classes dominates, has provided us with little fruitful infrastructural analysis of classes.

In the second place, as a field exercise, an adequate exploration of this sector of society requires social relationships at a financial and stylistic level that is beyond the ability of middle-income sociologists and anthropologists. The sociologist who gains the knowledge and ability to enter the higher areas of the upper sector would be tempted to do just that rather than spending time in sociological research. Entrance into the higher reaches of the upper sector by marriage inevitably places the student in the awkward position of betraying his kin if he studies them.

Third, there are surprisingly few concepts in sociology for this kind of phenomenon. Most middle-level sociological concepts have developed in the Euro-American tradition in which this kind of mobility has not been seen to be a dominant characteristic. This ethnocentric bias (that has, incidentally, diffused to the Latin Americans themselves since much of their training has been at Euro-American hands) is related to the fact that the very strange-ness of the phenomenon has led interpreters to regard it as inexplicable or irrational and as characteristic of a structure that is thought to be immature or underdeveloped. In short, what may in fact be a central feature of the upper sector of Latin American society has been characterized as an irregularity that this society will outgrow as it develops.

The activities related to the quest for power are multiple and complex. Since there is a wide variety of bases for power, the effective 'power seeker' makes full use of the particular basis that he has at hand and also extends his activities over a wide range of such bases. For instance, it is not enough to have control over the income of a set of individuals, but one must also be able to call on a wide network of kinsmen and *compadres,* to have a wide number of acquaintances through associations in sports clubs and political groups or among fellow students from university days, and to have established the pattern of many small reciprocal obligations. The exercise of power in Latin America (and presumably, in principle, elsewhere) is not the total amount of such contacts and controls that can be counted, but the ability to mobilize what is necessary for tactical advantage at a given moment. Towards this end, flexibility in organization is crucial, and consequently a major kind of organization is the background for a large number of shifting, interlocking cliques.

In a study of careers in such a structure in Brazil, Anthony Leeds holds that this is peculiar to what he considers as a transition from a 'static-agrarian' to an 'expansive industrial' society.[18] I do not think the major features of this kind of power structure are necessarily 'transitional' phenomena, or that we must expect Latin American society eventually to shift over to a structure more like that typical in Anglo-American history. The nature of demographic expansion, economic development, expansive nationalism, and international power manipulation is such that this kind of structure may well endure indefinitely in Latin America. Not only are individuals moving up within this general sector, but they are moving down. An inability to maintain the symbols of higher status within the prestige sector inevitably results in descent. With the changing base of power (to be discussed later), it becomes increasingly important to maintain a wide series of contacts.

The nature of these complex articulations is one of the many

[18] 'Brazilian Careers and Social Structure: a Case History and Model; *Amer. Anthropologist,* 66/6, pt. 1 (Dec. 1964).

things that we do not know about the upper sector. Whiteford sees the upper class as composed of sets of preferred interaction, with each set, in turn, being part of a larger set of sets.[19] The manner of the development of the Di Tella industrial operations in Argentina suggests that such a general model would also serve there.[20] Leeds describes the Brazilian *panelinha* as a 'closed, completely informal primary group, held together in common interest by personal ties and including a roster of all key socio-politico-economic positions'. [21]

One feature upon which many observers agree is that kinship ties play an important role in industrial, commercial, and governmental operations. 'As industrial families proliferate, so do enterprises', writes W. P. Strassmann. This author goes on to explain that he believes that 'family-centredness has been typical of early industrialization everywhere', and that 'as in countries outside Latin America, restrictive family control has weakened in many large enterprises'.[22] Although predictions continue to be made that family interests will decline as industrialization advances in Latin America, we find indications that such interest continues to be a central feature of the entire picture. Discussions of mobility always include marriage into the upper strata as an important alternative device. Restrictions on maximum land ownership in Mexico are reported informally to have led to the strengthening of kin bonds in order to hold together large land areas under multiple individual ownership. It is probably true that flexible industrialization can proceed more rapidly without binding kin ties, but whether true or not, it does not follow that this is the way chosen by Latin Americans to ease their industrial problems.

The individual who operates in the upper sector today manifests psychological characteristics that are entirely congruent with the structural situation as it has been observed. Raymond Vernon's summary of the character of Mexican businessmen indicates that they fall little short of the 'economic man' incarnate, a model that can hardly be unique to one period of history or one cultural tradi-

[19] Whiteford, pp. 58–60.
[20] T. C. Cochren and R. Reina, *Entrepreneurship in Argentine Culture* (Philadelphia, 1962).
[21] *Amer. Anthropologist*, 66/6, pt. 1 (Dec. 1964).
[22] 'The Industrialist', in J. J. Johnson, ed., *Continuity and Change in Latin America* (Stanford UP, 1964), pp. 168–9.

tion.[23] Latin American entrepreneurs illustrate well the generalized
description given by Kerr and others: 'They do not advance on
the wings of a rigid ideology; rather they tend to be pragmatic.
They favour a structure of economic and political rules which best
permits them to pursue their gains.'[24] And when these 'gains'
consist of what Hoselitz has characterized as 'not . . . augmentation,
but . . . redistribution of the social dividend',[25] then the manipulation of small power and the trading of influence are manifest
throughout the entire sector.

It is important to remember that the structure of the upper
sector is such that it has, in a sense, its own built-in labour force
that accepts its ideology and its prestige system. The white-collar
worker may find himself at odds with the upper class, but his way
of life is a basic—though largely ineffectual—attempt to survive
within the upper-sector system, as this is done without significant
power, the basic factor for upward mobility.

The upper sector of Latin America, containing the élites and
most of the so-called 'middle classes', still constitutes the home of
the rulers of society. This is true whether we are speaking of revolutionary Cuba or the rest of the countries. When it is said that
the 'middle classes' have taken over the ruling positions in Latin
America, this should be seen in the framework of the interrelationship between these various parts of the upper sector. For it is the
changing power relations between the diverse components of the
upper sector that account for the changes that have generally been
described in terms of class systems. These may be described as
kinds of occupational sets, although it is the relations contingent
upon the occupational positions, and not the individual himself,
that are important. Among such positions of special importance
are the military, mechanized agrarian capitalists, merchants, industrialists, expansionist bankers, the resurgent Catholic clergy,
university-trained technicians, students, and guerrilla revolutionaries. All share the common interest of gaining and utilizing power,
but all use different instruments, and base their efforts on somewhat
different elements of control.

The military, with their unique combination of organization and

[23] *The Dilemma of Mexico's Development* (Cambridge, Mass., 1963).
[24] Quoted by Strassmann, p. 175.
[25] Quoted by J. Medina Echavarría, 'A Sociologist's View', in E. de Vries
and J. Medina Echavarría, eds., *Social Aspects of Economic Development in Latin America* (UNESCO, 1963), ii, 75.

weaponry, are potentially in a position to take over a government at almost any time they wish. But they have never been able to police their own activities so as to eliminate abuses that antagonize the rest of the country. The military's position with regard to power tends to be a jealous guarding and augmenting of prerogatives within the framework of a civilian government. There is no political ideology peculiar to the military, but there is a tendency for younger officers to see their civilian support as including the lower sector, and for the older officers to assume that it lies almost wholly within the upper sector. This division, however, is far from universal, and it is often an older officer backed by younger colleagues who actually takes control of the government at a given time, thus bridging the gap between the more traditional power wielders and the newer power seekers.

The liberal capitalist who flourished as the basic element of the nineteenth-century agrarian and exporting economy has been complemented by a modern brand of agrarian capitalist whose interests turn more on domestic markets and whose activities increasingly require mechanization. The progressive labour laws that appear on many statute books in Latin America, while often evaded, nevertheless have made it increasingly advisable for the entrepreneur to reduce direct labour costs and the possible control that government can exercise through labour. The importance of domestic markets has grown with the expansion of urban populations and middle-income groups. Also, as the rural population increases, the relative amount of subsistence from agricultural land has decreased, and along with it the relative dependence of farmers and peasants on their own production. This growing demand for marketable agricultural products includes food staples and raw materials for industry. The new agrarian capitalists differ somewhat from the older exporting group. They are concerned with a mass market, and therefore it is to their advantage both to promote wealth in the lower sector and to encourage mobility from the lower to the upper sector. The first widens the market, and the second increases the variety of desired products. This reflects no newly discovered morality, but merely a rational vision of how to achieve entrepreneurial success. In contrast to the older agrarian exporter, who regarded the lower sector exclusively as a source of labour, the new domestic producer also values it as a potential market.

Essentially the same attitude is found among the merchants and industrialists. Their relationship with the lower sector has an additional quality that varies with their specific businesses. The increase in production and the widening of the range of industrial consumer goods require not only a wealthier lower sector, but also the adoption of the tastes and prestige system of the upper sector. It is to the advantage of the industrialists and merchants to change the prestige system of the lower sector from an emphasis on wealth to a desire for the wider variety of items that characterize the upper sector. The widening of the industrial market thereby entails fundamental cultural changes in the population.

The need for credit to develop production and the internal market has resulted in the emergence of a new attitude on the part of banks. Older banking policy tended to restrict credit to a clientèle defined by family background and élite social status. With the expansion of the upper sector, banks have changed their policies to provide credit to people who in earlier years would have been excluded because of their lack of social standing. In most instances this has been done through establishing new banks rather than by transforming the policies of older establishments.

The expanding internal market, and the emergence of the new entrepreneurs, has been accompanied by growing nationalism. The export capitalist's focus of interest could never be wholly local, even if his mannerisms marked him as provincial. The newer capitalists have direct and vested interest in the nation, since not only their products but their markets are located there. They manifest collective concern over foreign competition that makes the marketing of national products more difficult. While their economic policy places them squarely on the side of world capitalists, they are equally squarely in competition with those capitalists, and are active in pressing their governments into protectionist policies, and in some instances even decry the overcapitalizing that may be available from foreign sources.

Of quite a different order has been the change evident in the manners and activities of the Catholic clergy. The decline of the Spanish empire in the new world placed the Church in a difficult position. The anti-clerical liberalism of the nineteenth century hit the Church especially hard in some countries; it was everywhere increasingly poor, both in terms of financial support and of the quality of the clergy.

The new papal policies of this century have had very marked consequences in Latin America. Priests are now adopting progressive social attitudes, and senior Church officials speak openly of the evils of social suppression inherent in the conservative governments and social sectors that control them. What might be regarded as a new orthodoxy, if contrasted with the practices of the colonial period, has resulted in a new missionary zeal directed even towards the Catholic population. The new clergy is predominantly composed of foreigners, and the ideologies being introduced are competing with older more conservative tendencies still present in the Church. These progressive policies reflect a change in the policies of the world Church which does not always coincide with the local interests of the clergy.

Besides the new agrarian, industrial, and commercial capitalists, who represent a new point of view within the upper sector, of equal importance are certain power seekers who face quite different obstacles in their efforts to get power. Three instances will illustrate this variation: students, *técnicos,* and revolutionaries.

The students of specific concern here are those at the major national universities. For the most part, students at private (usually Catholic) universities often have their feet firmly on the ladder of success, and their futures are reasonably clear. The national universities, however, provide the only access to higher education for students who may come out of the lower sector, or from less successful families of the upper sector. They enter in considerable numbers, spend 70 per cent of their time in supporting themselves, and most of the rest in a mixture of classes, study, and debate. An enormous number never complete their work. Within each student population are a few who have determined that one way to power is through leadership in student activities, particularly political activities. Student politics in Latin America tend to concern themselves with national as well as university problems, and this has had from time to time an important effect on the national scene. The principal interventions have been those that challenged the activities of government and, given the traditional picture in Latin America, these were usually directed against right-wing governments.

Students tend to identify themselves with the political position of the lower sector, and try to act as its representatives, being heard where the real members of that sector are not. The students clearly illustrate many problems inherent in the aspirations of the lower sector. The overwhelming number of those who eventually graduate must be satisfied with mere scraps of upper-sector prestige. Their student challenges and objections are readily put aside. As in any case of learning, the repeated failures of students' efforts are un-rewarding and eventually lead the individual to seek some other kind of behaviour.

The graduates of the faculties of economics have been an important product of the national universities over the past few decades. The growing role of government in development planning and in the control and direction of the national economy has in-creased the demand for these graduates. Unlike lawyers, whose numbers usually exceed demand, there are not enough economists to fill available posts. The study of economics offers the student nurtured in an attitude of protest a professional situation where he does not need to drop his old complaints. Most faculties of economics have long since been deeply concerned with problems of social justice, and many have turned to the study of socialist theories. This has given a socialist flavour to these graduates, and has served to bring into the government, often to positions of importance, individuals who do not depend directly on capitalistic enterprise for their support.

The economists seldom go into professional work as pure Marxist theorists because their training is usually mainly social and political in content rather than strictly economic. These econo-mists retain a degree of interest and concern in the issues charac-teristic of university days. They challenge the economics of capitalism and demand that a different set of answers be produced. Perhaps more than in the case of any other professional group, the efforts of the economists to obtain power provide a basis for change within Latin American society.

A few of each generation of students retain the extreme political ideas of their university days. The standard response of the governments has been to exile the individuals involved, and to allow their return only after they have been tamed by age and lack of success outside their own country. Most return to sink into middle-class oblivion or to reflect cynically on the realities of their social order. It has always been the custom in Latin America to grant asylum to political exiles though inhibiting their political activities. The advent of Fidel Castro in Cuba has proved to be a turning point for the activities of the present generation of student extremists by giving them a base and a direct channel to socialist doctrine and training.   The contemporary exile need not now drift about the world; he has a place to which he can immediately go in order to further the processes that he found attractive as a student.   The emergence of guerrilla revolutionary groups in Latin America has been made possible not only by the training and supply of individuals from the outside, but by the recruitment and support that is available from the students in the universities. As a student, the individual may be little more effective in strikes and demonstrations than previously.   But as a guerrilla sympathizer, he can provide both information and services to the guerrilla that would be otherwise unobtainable.   So it is that the active revolutionaries who may be hiding in the forests and cities of Latin America have in the students an open forum, a strong propaganda voice, and a centre for recruitment in the core of the upper sector of the society.   In this way the students have found another channel into the larger society, and a more active, challenging way of expressing their need and striving for power.

Government and the Expanding Bases of Power

The popular view of structural change in Latin America holds that the old two-strata system is broken, that a middle class has wedged and pushed its way into the picture, and that this middle class is the carrier of the nationalism that is so obviously resurgent throughout the continent; that it is the source of entrepreneurs and technicians and so is central to the development process; and that it also comprises the all-important consumers for the increased production of the area.   But when we try to define and analyse this middle class, we find it is made up of rather unrelated components, and has no clear boundaries.   In both urban and provincial studies, there are groups that cannot be readily placed, and mobility is hard to characterize.   Sometimes it produces disorganization, sometimes it reinforces kinship bonds and leads to tighter groupings.

What in fact has happened over the past half-century is that a number of principal bases of power have emerged and these are being utilized—consciously or not—by elements of the upper sector to create a larger number of competitive power seekers. Individuals of the lower sector involved in this have thus moved into the upper sector.   The new power bases include the following:

a new wealth from profit-orientated agrarian enterprises; wealth and governmental action from foreign governments; new wealth from industrial enterprises; control of bureaucracies and intermediate decision-making implicit in the increased complexity of governmental and business expansion; weapons, usually supplied from foreign sources; organized labour; organized agrarian leagues, and mass political organizations. These power bases may be added to the list of other more traditional ones such as the market in specific goods, especially staples; latifundia; church social organization; local municipal or communal organizations, and the influence of regional *caciques*.

It is evident that each of the power bases just mentioned provides the opportunity for not one, but many, individuals or groups to exercise power. It is not just one hacienda, but many; not merely one kind of agrarian export enterprise, but diverse ones in coffee, sugar, cotton, etc.; not just one industry, but steel, textiles, plastics, etc.; not just the Catholic Church, but a variety of Catholic orders and Protestant sects; not just arms for the military, but arms for the revolutionaries too.

It is therefore misleading to think that only a 'middle class' is involved in this apparent fragmentation: it is the entire upper sector that is involved. New means to power have proliferated the varieties and modes of power. The multiplication of control areas has made analysis in terms of horizontal strata almost impossible because of the continuing emergence of a number of fluctuating vertical structures. The prestige system similarly does not fall readily into horizontal strata, but rather into a complex set of interrelated cliques, each manifesting slightly more or less prestige at any given moment.

The central government is emerging as the principal operator in this field. Government in Latin America simultaneously plays two roles. To run itself, it must maintain a degree of control that is tactically superior to that of any of the constituent parts: it must at the same time be able to utilize this superiority so that it can lend this power to other entities when they are threatened by some third party. Of Mexico, Vernon writes: 'The important point is that the private sector operates in a milieu in which the public sector is in a position to make or break any private firm.' [26] Strassmann

---

[26] Vernon, p. 26.

also notes that to the industrialist 'most frightening in Latin America appears the unpredictability of the tax assessor, the labor-court judge, the foreign exchange allocator, the representative of the power or water authority, and a variety of official inspectors'. [27] And no matter how it is seen, the dependence of every enterprise in Latin America on government is not matched by the government's dependence on any single firm. The same holds true for agrarian enterprises, foreign companies, municipal organizations, indeed almost every entity that depends upon credits, land tenure, imports, and governmental inspection.

Tactical balance exists with those entities that operate as a part of the government, but that, because of their specialization, could threaten the workings of the government. The most important and, in most cases, the only actual instance of this is the military. Latin America has, obviously, long had armies but the emergence of a professionally trained and technically advanced military—with some notable exceptions—is the product of this century. Also, following the second world war, the United States Department of Defense became such a source of armaments that the military is now placed in a completely unique position. Almost every country in Latin America has within its midst a trained organization, well equipped for the exercise of power. Compared with other controllers of power, the military is well organized, always partially mobilized, and highly self-contained.

Even though they must generally obtain these armaments from abroad, and the government must allocate funds for their purchase, most Latin American governments have discovered that the best way to live with the military is either to keep it happy and satisfied or to disband it. The latter requires a self-confidence and tactical legerdemain that only a few statesmen have been able to exhibit.

With few exceptions, the military is the only element powerful enough to take over the government. Aside from keeping up its organization, education, training, and preparedness, it may have nothing to do. The military itself takes its potential political role so seriously that it is, in a number of countries, making strides in moving in on traditionally civilian functions of government. The medical branch of the army is extremely active in some areas, and

---

[27] In Johnson, *Continuity and Change*, p. 172.

it can be argued that it is often more effective in public health work than the civilian ministries. Engineering work, particularly road and bridge building, carrying on important literacy programmes, agricultural work, and many other areas have become direct fields of action for some branches of the military. It is at least debatable whether the money might be as well spent if allocated to the civil agencies rather than to the armed forces,[28] but it is perfectly clear that in every area in which the military builds up competence, it strengthens its ability to exercise independent power.

The operation of the military in government may be contrasted with that of the bureaucracy, another entity that could cripple the operation of government. Modern Latin America increasingly teems with educated bureaucrats and technicians, especially economists. Collectively, their activities, preferences, and decisions amount to an extraordinary degree of power, although it is seldom mobilized. Anyone who has tried to carry through a simple official procedure with the support of these disenchanted bureaucrats can testify to their extraordinary power. Entire government ministries can, and frequently do, fail to carry out necessary programmes which they oppose. At a lower level, the school teachers, who are usually government employees, may well provide a given government with a peculiar political environment. It is common to find quite liberal school teachers working for highly conservative governments. A major problem faced by governments undertaking action requiring rapid change is that the bureaucracy is often either uninterested or unable to push through such changes. Compared with the power of the central executive, the power of the bureaucracy is seldom mobilized; it is usually only partially and inadvertently exercised.

The major difference between the bureaucracy and the military in their possible tactical positions with regard to control of the government rests on the military's access to force and on its organization. The bureaucracy is totally decentralized in ministries, offices, general directorships, and such agencies, and although it includes many highly trained and educated technocrats and is in a good position to arrive at intelligent decisions over the handling of many governmental matters, it cannot organize collective political action; it has power, but in practice it cannot exploit it.

In many countries there has traditionally been a tactical balance

28 Lyle N. McAlister, 'The Military', ibid. p. 144.

between the stronger components of the upper sector and the government. This is well illustrated by the case of Chile, where the progress of industrialization was blocked in the nineteenth and early twentieth centuries by the combined power of the north Chilean mining interests, the southern agriculturalists, and the large importers of the central cities. These entities successfully opposed the tariffs that would have protected the development of new industries.[29] More recently, a similar situation holds in Brazil where, within a decade, one President committed suicide and another resigned under the stress of being frustrated by the traditionalist pressure groups of the country. The relationships within the upper sector are of central importance in determining much of the policy of a government. The actual situation varies, however, from those cases where the government is largely a pawn of upper-sector interests, to those in which it exercises strong control over those interests. But because the government itself is multi-facetic, and the components of the upper sector multiple and competitive, the precise situation at any one time may be very complex. The most effective control of government under these circumstances lies in the actual placing of upper-sector individuals in the government. There is some reluctance, however, to do this because acting directly in a government capacity often involves undesirable obligations.

Naïve proponents of socialist revolution assume that the elimination of large parts of the upper sector would lead to a control of the government by members of the lower sector. This is not the case, simply because as soon as individuals or groups from the lower sector assume enough control to become competitive for power, they begin to act like their upper-sector predecessors. The relations between the government and the lower sector, therefore, are not similar to those with the upper sector. Instead, the government utilizes its power to control the lower sector directly. In those areas where the upper sector dominates, this governmental control is actually exercised through business enterprises, haciendas, and other organizations.

Although trade unionism and syndicalism were imported into Latin America from Europe, during the past half-century they have increasingly been utilized by governments as a means of con-

[29] Claudio Veliz, 'La mesa de tres patas', *Desarrollo económico*, 3/1–2 (1963).

trolling labour, and through them, landowners, industrialists, and businessmen. The history of the Mexican trade union movement follows ups and downs that coincide with the government's interest at any given point in time. Under Perón, Argentina's labour organizations became a direct power base for the executive. Labour unions, during the Arévalo–Arbenz period in Guatemala, directly served the interests of the government. Under such circumstances, the government has simply become, as many observers have testified, the new *patrón*, the new boss.

This role of government is well complemented by the expectations of the lower sector. Countrymen and urban labourers are equally aware where they must turn if they need help. Andrew Pearse notes that the migrant to Rio de Janeiro tried to find a *patrão*, and preferably one who would defend his interests decisively.[30] R. W. Patch cites the situation in Bolivia where '. . . the pattern of paternalism persists in the relations between *campesinos* and the government. The *campesinos* believe their problems will be resolved promptly if they can only set them personally before "Don Hernán (Siles)" or "Don Victor" (Paz Estenssoro).'[31] They believe that special personal loyalty may be legitimately expected of them by any leader in a position to benefit them. Even in Puerto Rico, the fact that a union existed on a government-owned sugar plantation led to the perpetuation of the paternalistic dependency that had been even more pronounced in older-style haciendas.[32]

Attempts to spread the government's power bases into the rural areas have proved difficult for a number of reasons. In the first place, the rural population is more scattered, and it is easier for regional bosses and landowners to retain local control. Secondly, without a specific reform programme, it is difficult to convince the *campesino* of his own potential power. The governments, however, are gradually succeeding in extending their power to the rural areas. One device has been found in the rural labour unions. In Brazil and Peru, and for a brief period in Guatemala, these

---

[30] 'Some Characteristics of Urbanization in the City of Rio de Janeiro', in Hauser, p. 201.
[31] 'Bolivia: US Assistance in a Revolutionary Setting', in Council on Foreign Relations, *Social Change in Latin America Today*, [CFR, *Social Change* in later references] (New York, 1960), p. 141.
[32] R. N. Adams, 'Rural Labor', in Johnson, *Continuity and Change*, pp. 63–67.

unions promised to be increasingly important. Less common, but equally important, have been the attempts to gain the loyalty of community or locality groups. The Mexican *ejido* programme established such a pattern over many parts of that country. The Vicos project in Peru enabled the government to expropriate the land of the Vicos hacienda and give it to the Indians, thereby gaining some control over that population.[33] Although still not widespread, probably the most important relations between government and the rural population have been established through peasant leagues. These have been especially important in Brazil, Bolivia, and Guatemala. In Brazil Benno Galjart sees

the *Ligas Camponesas* and the rural syndicates as the transformation of the old following of the landowner into the following of a politician or a government. The peasants have less possibilities than other categories of workers to extort concessions from their employers, and therefore depend more than others on the influence they have with the state and federal government.[34]

In Bolivia the peasant leagues were formed before the time when the revolutionary government undertook to support them.[35] Until 1962 the Bolivian government had little if any control over the countryside, so that the relative importance of these peasant groups to it was vastly greater than it was in Brazil. Not only did the central government support them by ratifying the agrarian reform they had instituted, but they in turn reciprocated in later years by helping it in its struggles against the miners. The Arévalo–Arbenz period in Guatemala also saw the development of a peasants' union. While important in rural organization at the time, it was dissolved with the revolution of 1954 and has not been re-formed.[36]

The rural population has been everywhere more difficult to organize than urban dwellers. Frank Bonilla has pointed out that in the United States the labour movement has also been spectacularly unsuccessful among the 'unskilled, uneducated, ethnic minorities, inhabitants of the most economically depressed regions'. [37]

[33] Allan Holmberg, 'Changing Community Attitudes and Values in Peru', in CFR, *Social Change*, pp. 63–107.
[34] 'Class and "Following" in Rural Brazil', *América Latina*, 7/3 (1964), pp. 21–22.
[35] Patch, in CFR, *Social Change*.
[36] Stokes Newbold, 'Receptivity to Communist-Fomented Agitation in Rural Guatemala', *Econ. Development & Cultural Change*, 5/3 (1957), pp. 338–61.
[37] 'The Urban Worker', in Johnson, *Continuity and Change*, p. 205.

For his part, the rural inhabitant with a predisposition to change may find a move to the city environment an easier solution than trying to organize locally. Butterworth's study of Mixtec migrants in Mexico City noted that in the city they lose their 'fear'; the rural area provides a combination of 'extortion, political persecution, economic exploitation, banditry, and blood feuds', plus an un-predictable climate, that keeps the population in a state of constant fear of 'losing what they possess, material and non material'. [38] The success of the rural organizations depends heavily on the support the government is willing to give, and this, in turn, depends upon how badly the government thinks it needs rural support.

The relations between the government and the rural leagues and labour unions offer a good illustration of paternalism. This paternalism combines two rather different elements; first, it is the recognition and expression of a power relationship that exists within a dual-sectored society when the upper sector individual is perceived (whether correctly or not) to have unique control over the environment of the lower sector individual. Second, it involves attaching to this relationship the symbolism of a father-child relationship of an unusually authoritarian variety. Such paternal-istic relations have often been described in Latin America and, as was observed earlier, there has even been a shift from the paternalistic dependence on the old landholder or local boss to dependence on the central government. What has still escaped some analysts is that the substitution of the state for the private *patrón* is a part of the relationship mentioned a moment ago, where the labour union now stands in a somewhat similar relation to the state that labourers did formerly to the *patrones*. Structurally, the two situations are similar; both find the labourer controlled by a single, central power, and in both we find the symbolic use of the father-child relationship.

Summary

The central governments of Latin America are successfully striving to control the principal positions in their respective domains. They are doing this through strategic control over the increased power that has become available. The direct control over this power is in the hands of business, industry, agrarian

---

[38] *América indígena*, 22/3 (1962), pp. 270-1.

enterprises, and in the organization of labour, countrymen, and other individuals. The proliferation of power bases marks a change from the nineteenth century when the governments exercised their power through unique entities that controlled their own power bases to a situation in which the government can control the same population through a number of different intermediate organizations. The important result here is not an increase in control over the population (which tactically is largely the same), but that multiple controls are available to the central government.

Whereas before, the government could control the hacienda populations only through the hacienda, or the industrialist only through monetary or tax efforts, now it is possible to exercise power over farmer and industry through the new control that the government exercises over labour. The same kind of control is now possible through peasant leagues which neutralize the power of the regional bosses (who are often also landowners).

The increase in the number of power bases and the emergence of the government as a major power have tended to perpetuate the old two-sector structure. Through the increase in power bases, and through the allocation of derivative power from the government to the organizations of various lower-sector populations, the relative and absolute number of holders of power has increased, and power has continued to be the major means of access to prestige. As a result, the upper sector has expanded. At the same time the lower sector, although in a somewhat better position through its ability to turn to the government for aid and support, is in fact still completely dependent upon work as a means of obtaining a better life, and upon wealth as the specific objective to make this better life possible. The government is tending, in its view, to replace the private boss, so that much paternalism continues.

The major structural change in Latin America has been an expansion and centralization of a vertical structure that already existed. The importance of the multiplication and separation of lateral structures, whether called strata, classes, or something else, has been so much emphasized by Western observers that this continuity has been obscured. This analysis applies as much to Cuba as to other countries, although in Cuba it has gone to an extreme, and the government has entirely replaced the older power holders with directly controlled governmental agencies. While in most countries the government rules by virtue of strategy, the dependence upon arms as an important tactical element in this strategy has brought the military to a position of increasing importance.

Peasants and Rural Migrants in Politics

E. J. HOBSBAWM

I

For the economic and social historian and the student of contemporary politics, the crucial dates in the history of Latin America do not occur in the first quarter of the nineteenth century, when most of the continent won independence from Spain or Portugal, for this did not substantially alter their economic and social structure. They occur in the late nineteenth century, when these countries entered the world economy in their now familiar roles as mass exporters of certain primary products, whose balances of payment depended in the main on such exports. This phase lasted until 1930, when the simple, hitherto expanding export monocultures collapsed and the societies based on them fell into crisis, though the basic orientation remained. In the middle of the 1950s all but three Latin American states (Mexico, Peru, Paraguay) relied for more than 50 per cent of their exports on one, or at most two, of the following commodities: coffee, bananas, sugar, cotton, meat, cereals, wool, copper, tin, and oil. Eight relied on coffee and bananas, two more on coffee and sugar or cotton. Yet before the last decades of the nineteenth century bananas were an economically negligible crop, and the phrase 'banana republic' would have been meaningless. Coffee and Brazil were indeed beginning to be synonymous from the middle of the century, but the period of maximum growth (production almost trebled) occurred in the 1890s, and it was then that coffee became synonymous not only with Brazil but with São Paulo, which had hitherto lagged a long way behind Rio and Bahia. (In Colombia, now familiar as the world's second-largest coffee-producer, the crop was insignificant before the 1870s.) Cuban sugar production shows a similar pattern. The island's share of world production was huge, but it was the even vaster increase in world demand which multiplied its output, particularly in the early twentieth century, and brought new areas under cultivation.

In a word, before the last decades of the last century a great part of the rural area of Latin America was not seriously oriented towards the world market, or often towards any but the purely local market. Another part relied on older and declining staples (like sugar in north-east Brazil), or on temporary 'boom' products. Large areas which we now associate with the characteristic products of their countries, such as the Cuban provinces of Oriente and Camagüey, had a quite different economic complexion.[1] By modern standards most regions of Latin America were not even colonial or semi-colonial economies, but simply underdeveloped areas.

Again, we think of Latin America today as a continent of headlong urbanization and immense cities. Yet though the old colonial society encouraged the development of capital cities and export ports, their size was modest by modern standards, and they were both socially and demographically isolated from the hinterland. Salvador-Bahia in 1872 had not much more than 100,000 inhabitants, and even the giant metropolitan cities—Rio and Buenos Aires—were then still under control, with perhaps half a million and a quarter of a million inhabitants respectively.[2] The rise of the international export economy gave a powerful, if selective, impulse to urbanization. Salvador, for instance, grew fairly fast but then remained static at less than 300,000 from 1920 to 1940, while Recife remained quite static until 1900, at about 100,000 inhabitants, and then began to grow fairly fast to overtake the more southern port by 1940. Of course other cities grew far more dramatically, especially in the temperate southern part of the continent. Buenos Aires had reached 2 million by 1930, São Paulo—

[1]

Output of Sugar by Cuban Provinces
(000 tons)

	1906	*1924*
Pinar	25	134
Havana	164	336
Matanzas	344	500
Santa Clara	480	893
Camagüey	38	1,187
Oriente	178	1,067

Source: Ibero-Amerikanisches Archiv, 2 (1927–8), p. 210.

[2] 19th-century Latin American censuses are largely guesswork and even 20th-century ones have some admixture of imagination.

a provincial town of 25,000 in 1874—was a city of 600,000 by 1920. Yet by the standards of the past twenty-five years even these impressive examples of urbanization, or perhaps rather metropolitan concentration, seem comparatively modest. What is more, in some cases—most obviously Buenos Aires, but also to some extent São Paulo, a state which received $1\frac{1}{2}$ million overseas immigrants between 1886 and 1936—urban growth was largely due to foreign influx. The essential separation of city from countryside remained, so long as the influx from internal migrants remained moderate enough for the newcomers to be readily absorbed into the old urban framework. Where there was foreign immigration it might even be accentuated, as in Buenos Aires, where the mass migration of Europeans reduced the percentage of national immigrants from the late nineteenth century.[3]

The rise of the export economy was bound to have the most far-reaching effects on the society and politics of the continent. However, so long as it took the form of a headlong, though fluctuating, expansion into apparently unlimited North American and European markets, the full extent of these effects was not widely realized, for they were largely absorbed and assimilated by the existing social and political systems of the Latin American republics, dominated by the traditional controllers of their politics, the owners of large estates and the vested interests of administration and the export-import trade of the capitals and ports.[4] In the urban and non-agricultural sectors change was indeed visible, especially in the southern part of South America (Argentina, Chile, Uruguay, South Brazil) where economic development was most rapid. In Central and South Mexico the effects of the new agrarian economy were already strong enough to create a revolutionary situation, for in these regions the new market-oriented

---

[3] S. Bagú, 'Evolución histórica de la estratificación social en Argentina', *Seminario interdisciplinario sobre el desarrollo económico y social de la Argentina* (Buenos Aires, 1961, typescript in Fac. of Sociology, Univ. of BA). There are, however, cases of provincial urbanization due entirely to local immigration, e.g. Tucumán.

[4] The fact that the men who controlled them were sometimes newcomers, hardly changed the systems. Thus in the Valle de Chancay (Peru) almost three-quarters of the haciendas changed ownership between 1901 and 1926, but the actual haciendas were the same as had existed since the 18th century, or even earlier. Cf. José Matos Mar, 'Las haciendas en el Valle de Chancay', in *Problèmes agraires de l'Amérique latine* (Paris, Centre National de la Recherche Scientifique, forthcoming).

hacienda was not merely an adaptation of an older pre-existent latifundist economy, but expanded at the direct expense of a dense Indian population living in autonomous village communities.[5] But, by and large, change remained below the political and social surface. What precipitated it was the 1929 depression, i.e. the sudden and almost total collapse of the world markets on which Latin America had relied.

The immediate effect was to produce a continent-wide crisis in the finances of governments, and consequent political crises. In 1930–1 régimes toppled, peacefully or by military coup, in Argentina, Brazil, Chile, Ecuador, Peru, Bolivia, Colombia, the Dominican Republic, and shortly afterwards in Cuba. However, this short-term crisis would have been of little but local interest, had it not indicated a more profound and long-term change in the affairs of the continent. It is true that neither the basis of so many Latin American economies—export monoculture—nor that of so much Latin American social structure and politics—the oligarchies based on large estates, import-export trade, and government—were fundamentally altered as yet. But neither did they return to the old dispensation. The economy of massive primary exports and free capital and commodity imports no longer functioned automatically; the one had to be buttressed by manipulating the other, and behind the temporary walls of restriction and control new economic and political interests, notably those of Latin American industrialists essentially supplying the native market, grew up. The centre of gravity shifted between states: the main beneficiaries of the age of liberal (i.e. British-dominated) imperialism—Argentina, Chile, and Uruguay—exchanged an age of expansion and prosperity for one of stagnation and uncertainty from which they have not fully recovered, while poorer, less advanced, but historically less specialized economies like those of Brazil and Mexico began to forge ahead. But, above all, the masses of ordinary Latin Americans began to enter—and in due course to dominate—the politics of their countries. Before 1930 they can be left out of account everywhere except in Mexico and (in the somewhat specialized form of 'little men's' Radical Parties on the model of Latin Europe) in the southern tip of South America. After 1930 even the tradi-

---

[5] The Andean regions, in which estates and communities coexisted in a similar manner, were much slower to enter the economy of the world market except through the rather specialized products of mining.

tional Latin American *caudillo* was often tinged with unaccustomed demagogy: the *plaza* became as important as the *cuartel*.

'In 1930 the Middle Ages ended.' The phrase of an intelligent Brazilian observer has more than local significance, even though the most radical and striking changes did not begin to make themselves felt until the 1940s and 1950s. The subject of this paper is the entry of the mass of ordinary—i.e. poor or non-white or both —Latin Americans into the politics of their countries.

II

The great bulk of these new entrants were countrymen, since in 1930 the city population formed only a modest minority in all countries except Argentina, Chile, Uruguay, and Cuba:

Percentage of Urban Population (in Centres of over 20,000 Inhabitants) in Selected Latin American Countries

Country	Year	%	Country	Year	%
Argentina	(c. 1930*)	c. 45	Cuba	1931	30
Brazil	1940	17	Peru	1940	14
Chile	1930	36	Venezuela	1936	19
Colombia	1938	15			

* Assuming even growth between the 1914 and 1947 censuses.

Source: P. M. Hauser, ed., *Urbanization in Latin America* (Unesco, 1961), pp. 98–99.

Since foreign migration ceased to be important, except in Venezuela, and the rate of population growth of the native urban inhabitants was quite insufficient to account for the expansion which has taken place since then, rural immigration provided the only available source for it. In fact, it is currently estimated that this accounts for half, and in some cases for two-thirds, of the rise in urban population, the lowest figures (26 per cent) being the Cuban (almost certainly an underestimate), the highest (65 and 70 per cent) the Colombian and Venezuelan.[6]

---

[6] Hauser, pp. 108–10. This source gives calculations only for ten countries, and omits Argentina, Chile and Peru among major states.

Those who took the most obvious part in politics were hence-forth the millions who had newly flooded into the cities, and especially into the handful of giant cities. They came overwhelmingly from the country, and remained, at least for a time, displaced peasants. Hence, though the actual political changes in the rural areas were, and have in general remained, less striking than those in the cities, we must begin with a brief analysis of them.

The economic structure of the Latin American countryside was one of export agriculture or subsistence farming, though the fantastic expansion of the cities since the 1930s added an increasingly important sector supplying the rapidly growing domestic urban market. Broadly speaking, we can say that it was dominated by the two phenomena of the transfer of land from subsistence or extensive light use to market production, and the increasingly precipitous flight of manpower from the land. The social or legal structure was overwhelmingly one of large estates, sometimes with a landless, sometimes with the attendant 'minifundist' peasantry, or of a coexistence of large estates with independent village communities, as in areas of solid Indian settlement. The thinly populated frontier regions (mainly on the fringes of the Amazon basin) into which a growing population began to filter were no exception to this, for in so far as they were not beyond the range of all administration or even knowledge,[7] they too were normally owned or claimed by some form of latifundist. The transfer to a cash-crop economy put an inevitable strain on this latifundist structure; whether it took the form of the transformation of the old extensive latifundio into an *hacienda capitalista* (to use the convenient distinction of Colombian agrarian reformers) or plantation, development through various forms of tenant farmers or sharecroppers, the substitution of urban or foreign entrepreneurs for the old *hacendados*, or some other pattern. The change from an older to a newer staple product, or the diversification of production, had equally disruptive effects. The subsistence sector was less affected by such changes, but in its turn suffered the increasing pressure of a rapidly growing population on fixed—and deteriorating—land,

[7] Thus the 1940 Peruvian census gives one-third of the population of the province of La Convención (Cuzco) as 'estimated settlers in the *selva* beyond the reach of the enumerators'. Actually this is almost certainly an exaggeration.

or indeed often on land diminished by the encroachments of the estates.

The political structure of the Latin American countryside was (except for revolutionary Mexico) that of formal or informal power exercised by local families of estate owners—sometimes in rivalry with others of their kind—each at the apex of a local pyramid of power and patronage; controlling, or seeking to control against local rivals, both the local parts of government administration and the local influence in national government. There was—and still very often is—no government power in the countryside except by the agreement of such magnates and patrons. In so far as political 'parties' existed, they were—and still to some extent are—merely labels tied on to local families and their clientèles, whose votes (if they had any) went, like their armed support and their loyalty in general, to their *patrón* or lord.[8] So far as the mass of the peasantry was concerned, there was no such thing as 'national' politics, but only local politics which might or might not have national labels attached to the local persons of power.

This structure has persisted to a considerable extent, partly because of the persistence of its social base, partly because of the separation of town and country which is so characteristic of under-developed regions and which both excluded many countrymen from the political process as conceived in the city and made the politics that came from the city appear incomprehensible, irrelevant, or unacceptable. To take an example. In Brazil (and in several other countries) illiterates are excluded from the vote, i.e. in a region like the Brazilian North-East a minimum of 75 per cent of adults as late as 1950.[9] The traditional parties hesitated to inter-fere between the politically influential *fazendeiros* (landowners) and 'their' people, so that for practical purposes nobody other than the extreme Left asked the peasants for their opinions, and the con-stitution provided little scope for hearing their answers. This does

---

8 We may, for the sake of simplicity, neglect the exceptions to this generalization which had already begun to develop by the 1950s, notably in the southern tip of the continent, but also in Colombia, where 'Conservatism' and 'Liberalism' had genuine, if quite 'unmodern', roots among the masses, in Peru, where APRA had begun to win independent mass support, and elsewhere.

9 The 1950 census gives 74 per cent as the illiteracy of all inhabitants over 5 years of age, i.e. it includes the presumably less illiterate younger population of school-going age. The definition of literacy is far from stringent anyway.

not imply that the rural masses were uninterested in politics, or unprepared under certain circumstances to oppose the political *status quo*. However, their traditional movements often took forms incomprehensible to the urban politician, as in the messianic movements which found a fertile soil in the Brazilian North-East and parts of the South between 1890 and the 1930s,[10] all the more so as these sometimes claimed to be monarchist. They were political, of course, even in the narrowly accepted sense of the word. The famous prophet Padre Cicero of Juazeiro became the virtual boss of the state of Ceará from 1914 to his death in 1934, and, as a man of influence, received the same consideration from the federal government as any other grandee. Yet the movements which stood behind men of his kind, and were able to give them the equivalent of patronage and influence, were themselves unable either to enter official politics or to change its character.

Urban-based movements which did sometimes attempt to reach the peasant, normally failed—or had only localized success—like the labour and socialist movements of European pattern. Why this was so is not altogether clear. The anarchists, whose capacity to mobilize rural masses is proved in Europe, appear to have had negligible success in their propagandist activities, except among the equivalent of urban and industrial workers (such as the Bolivian miners). The communists, lacking serious strength everywhere except in Chile, Cuba, and Brazil, undoubtedly established pockets of agrarian strength here and there—as in parts of Cuba, or one or two places in Colombia—but remained essentially an urban or industrial workers' movement with a few attached intellectuals. The socialists, negligible except among immigrant European communities, seem hardly even to have tried. It may be that the cultural gap between city and countryside was too wide, or that the Left failed to find the slogans which would move the peasants, or to formulate them in an acceptable way.[11] It is certain that the Left only slowly learned to search for the specific language accessible to peasants, and the specific forms of demand likely to

[10] For an analysis and bibliography of these, cf. Maria Isaura Pereira de Queiroz, 'Messiahs in Brazil', *Past & Present*, July 1965.
[11] Thus I was told by a Chilean communist militant, himself a peasant, that the *general* slogan of agrarian reform is not usually very effective, whereas peasants can be readily moved by the demand for their specific land, especially when they feel they have a legal or prescriptive 'right' to it.

mobilize them, and probably did not do so systematically until the 1950s.[12]

There are evidently exceptions to this generalization. The peasant-based revolutions of Bolivia (1952) and Cuba (1959) are the most obvious ones. The first is less of an exception than it seems, for the Bolivian revolution was made essentially by a combination of dissident officers, urban intellectuals, and one of the rare powerful industrial-labour movements (the Miners' Union), and the peasant movement as a whole emerged after its victory. (There was, however, a significant local movement in the valley of Cochabamba, among a rather less traditional and isolated peasantry, under Marxist influence and led by José Rojas, a local peasant who had seen something of the world.) The decisive step in the mobilization of the peasants lay rather with the non-peasant revolutionaries who (correctly) decided that agrarian reform and the granting of rights to the Indians were the indispensable conditions for maintaining a new régime.[13] The Cuban revolution was much more obviously peasant-based, at least in its guerrilla phase, though curiously enough the movement found its centre not so much in the areas already partly mobilized in earlier communist agitations, but in the Sierra Maestra, where it was brought by the urban guerrillas.

Two less successful examples of peasant mobilization may also be mentioned: Peru and Colombia. There is little doubt that APRA's mass basis,[14] especially in the northern departments of Peru which are its stronghold, reflects some success in appealing to rural strata, especially in the agriculturally proletarianized zone of sugar and cotton production. To what extent it does, cannot be said with any certainty, for APRA's past successes at elections are irrelevant: the literacy qualification excluded from the vote the bulk of the Indian peasants, whose spokesman APRA claimed to be. Nevertheless, and though both the structure and ethos of APRA in its days of glory were much more those of an urban or

---

12 F. Julião's *Que são as Ligas Camponesas* (Rio, 1962) contains an acute discussion of the problem.

13 They were right. After 1952 Bolivia, which previously counted its military coups by the hundred, acquired a dozen years of unprecedented political stability before the régime was overthrown in November 1964.

14 There is as yet no satisfactory study of the social basis and political clientèle of APRA. Cf. H. Kantor, *The Ideology and Program of the Peruvian Aprista Movement* (Berkeley, 1953).

labour movement than a peasant movement, we may allow it a modest degree of peasant political mobilization in its time. The case of Colombia is more interesting, because there is nothing modest about the peasant mobilizations which, between 1948 and 1963, may have put a peak total of some 30,000 armed guerrillas and bandits—almost exclusively peasants—into the field, and which cost the lives of a number of Colombians estimated, on the most conservative calculations, in six figures.[15] A full discussion of this, the greatest of all Latin American agrarian movements outside the Mexican revolution, is impossible in this context, but a few conclusions about it may be—perhaps somewhat baldly—stated.

The Colombian *Violencia* of 1948 and later is best regarded as a mass social revolution which, for want of effective leadership and organization, aborted into a disoriented civil war and anarchy. It involved the peasantry to so exceptional an extent, because of the somewhat unusual political traditions of that country. Colombia has been long, and with relatively few breaks, dominated by a two-party system of Conservative and Liberal factions among the oligarchy. There is evidence that, unlike the equivalent dualisms in other nineteenth-century Latin American states (e.g. Brazil), these 'parties' represented not merely labels—admittedly with certain general ideological implications—tied to grandees to distinguish them from their family rivals, but deep-rooted attachments among the peasantry, generally symbolizing local or regional, as well as feudal, loyalties. A man was a Liberal or a Conservative, not merely because his *patrón* voted that way, but because his *vecindad* (neighbourhood) was Liberal or Conservative. As so often in Latin America, the historical reasons for this state of affairs await investigation, though it may be suspected that they helped to make even past Colombian civil wars a great deal bloodier than they might otherwise have been.

In the 1930s the Liberal Party, always theoretically connected with ideologies and programmes of the Left, tended to evolve into a socially and democratically oriented 'New Deal' party, and to provide a common umbrella for traditional Liberals and more popular and socially-minded politicians. There is some evidence

[15] G. Guzmán and others, *La Violencia en Colombia* (Bogotá, 1962–4) contains a mass of invaluable material. For a brief English discussion, E. J. Hobsbawm, 'Anatomy of Violence', *New Society*, 1963, and 'The Revolutionary Situation in Colombia', *World Today*, June 1963.

that the new social appeal made by Liberal-revolutionary tribunes and demagogues had some echo in the countryside—where, of course, Liberalism was already something that peasants took seriously and identified with themselves. The growing appeal of Liberalism to the poor threatened to turn it into the permanent majority party, thus destroying the basis of the stable and symbiotic rivalry of the oligarchic 'Liberal' and 'Conservative' factions.

The great spontaneous urban Liberal uprising of April 1948 ('*Bogotazo*') had some rural echoes; but, more important still, it led to a systematic attempt by the Conservatives, hitherto hard-pressed in the countryside by the transformed and strengthened Liberals, to shift the political balance in their favour by armed force. The clash and counter-clash of the two factions produced both local mobilizations in self-defence, and a confused set of risings, counter-terror against rural Conservatives, &c., in which the long-suppressed frustrations and tensions of the peasantry found an unusually savage and bloody expression. The resulting anarchy, and in some areas the fear of possible social revolution, was such that the entire political system appeared in danger. The Liberal and Conservative grandees agreed to end the civil war, eventually devising the formula of peaceful party coexistence under which Colombia is still—though with increasing difficulty—governed, and by which Liberal and Conservative presidents succeed each other in regular succession. But the genie had been let out of the bottle. All the attempts made since 1953 to put it back again have never quite succeeded in inserting the stopper.

Broadly speaking, we may therefore say that, until the present, the growing dissatisfaction and unrest of the Latin American peasantry has not found an expression commensurate with its importance; except perhaps in the headlong avalanche of rural migrants who have voted against the *status quo* with their feet by moving into the city slums. Nevertheless, and especially since the middle 1950s, signs of agrarian unrest and agrarian political mobilization have been multiplying, and it may be useful to survey them briefly. With the possible exception of Colombia, none of them has been organized by the traditional parties of the continent (which is not surprising), or to any extent by the populist movements which became so characteristic of the continent in the early 1950s.[16]

---

[16] APRA's part in the very widespread Peruvian peasant unrest of 1961–3 was small and confined to its traditional northern fiefs.

Leadership and inspiration have come largely from the Marxist Left (communist, socialist, Maoist, Trotskyist, Castroite, or whatever the label), and this may account for its comparative localization.

Four types of peasant have proved most susceptible to such agitation. The first, and least typical, consists of independent peasant pioneers seeking to evade the advances of the market economy and the growing encroachments of lord and state by pushing into the unsettled and unknown frontier regions surrounding the Amazon basin. Communist nuclei of this sort are known to exist in inland Brazil (Goias and Mato Grosso) and in the Amazonian regions of Colombia (Meta, Caquetá). Land is not normally a problem for such men, for there is plenty of it. Freedom is what drives them inland, freedom that they associate with the only ideology that comes to them with the message that peasants are men with rights. In numerical terms this frontier communism is negligible. The second type, numerically far more important, consists of peasant (i.e. normally Indian) communities claiming, or rather reclaiming, their communal lands since the late 1950s, and often doing so by direct occupation. Such occupations of common lands are of importance in the Indian parts of Chile, in the Andean region in general, and especially in Peru, where they reached large and national proportions in 1961-3. Here again the object of the peasantry is to return as far as possible to the traditional subsistence agriculture of the community, though population growth and the deterioration of lands are likely to make this impossible even after the recovery of alienated common lands. However, it would be a mistake to regard such movements as simple traditionalism sailing under the red flag for want of any other. The mere fact of collective and positive peasant action is proof of political self-discovery and the desire for change. It is a revolutionary act for peasants, especially Indians, to behave as if such terms as right, freedom, and justice applied to them just as to other men, even when it is a question of something as obvious as the legal right to specific pieces of land alienated within living memory by trickery or force. Moreover, there is evidence that this political self-discovery is also a burning desire for a share in *modernity*, which finds expression in the passionate and universal drive for education and enlightenment. Almost the first thing any peasant community does when it can, is to build a school. (This has been very striking in Bolivia since the revolution of 1952.)[17]

The third type of restless peasantry is even more interesting. It consists of the most dynamic, modern-minded and market-oriented elements—one might almost say the future kulaks of Latin America. The peasant movements of the eastern slopes of the Peruvian Andes (which include the most militant and successful of the communist agitations, that of La Convención) are very good examples of this. They consist of Indian farmers who have individually migrated into hitherto unexploited territories now being rapidly opened up to cash-crop agriculture (coffee, tea, &c.). The movement of La Convención is essentially based on the agitation of a limited number of prosperous colonists (*arrendires*) for tenant rights against the latifundists, which at the peak of the agitation passed naturally into the demand for the expropriation of the *hacendados*. These *arrendires* are men who received insecure tenancies on vast estates for labour rents—so many days' work on the lord's demesne[18]—which they in turn subcontracted to *allegados*, who in fact performed most of the labour service. It is fairly evident from areas where such colonization does not occur on land already parcelled out among latifundists, that it is likely to produce a stratified peasant society without a special tendency towards collective political radicalism, at least at present.[19] What gives rise to an agrarian revolutionary movement is the oppressive rigidity of the latifundist straitjacket in which the new farmers find themselves constrained.

There remains a mass of less readily classifiable peasant occupiers and tenants in conflict with the latifundist system which dominates them and the unpredictable hazards of the new or the changing

---

[17] A communist peasant organizer put it as follows: 'There are three things you have to do to get anywhere with peasants. The first is, you must live exactly as they do. If you can't stand the food, you can't organize peasants. Second, you have to talk to them not just about *the* land, but about this land, which used to belong to them in their grandfather's day but was taken over by the Hacienda X. Third, you must always be teaching them something. I'm not an intellectual, so I teach them football. But learn something they must—they insist on it.'

[18] For La Convención see Hugo Neira, *Cuzco, tierra y muerte* (Lima, 1964) and Hobsbawm, 'Problèmes agraires à La Convención' (for publication in *Problèmes agraires de l'Amérique latine*).

[19] Cf. H. Martínez, *Las migraciones altiplánicas y la colonización del Tambopata* (Lima, Ministerio de Trabajo y Asuntos Indígenas, 1961, mimeo).

market economy. It is neither possible nor necessary to analyse all the complexities of Latin American agrarian problems here, but a few general observations may be made. The first is that the actually landless group, the rural proletariat, is normally among the least politically-dynamic or readily-organizable agrarian groups, except perhaps in regions of advanced plantation labour, by the quasi-urban methods of trade unionism.[20] It is the peasant—and not necessarily the peasant with insufficient land—who provides the most immediately explosive element. Second, mere minifundism or poverty is not sufficient to produce agrarian agitation. It is normally the juxtaposition of the peasant and the hacienda (especially the *hacienda* with changing economic functions and structure—e.g. shifting from extensive to intensive exploitation, or from direct plantation to exploitation by tenants or sharecroppers) which produces the politically inflammable mixture. Thus in Colombia, the Department of Boyacá, where small and medium holdings predominate, has remained politically conservative, whereas the Department of Valle del Cauca, where large and small properties coexist, has been notably more rebellious.

Land Tenure in Boyacá and Valle del Cauca
(per cent)

Size of holding	Boyacá		Valle del Cauca	
	Occupiers	Area	Occupiers	Area
0·5 ha.	74·4	17·2	51·3	3·7
5–100 ha.	25·2	51·7	43·4	37·2
Over 100 ha.	0·5	31·3	5·3	59·7

Third, it is the increasing involvement in a monetary and market economy which, whatever its form, produces particular tensions found neither in the traditional subsistence economy nor in old-established and unchanging market economies.[21]

---

[20] Cf. Julião, pp. 50 ff.

[21] 'The introduction of a monetary economy into the countryside produces commercialization of property. When money becomes the medium of exchange, this results in the appearance of credit. Because of indebtedness, the process of sale quickens, so that an ordinary drought or poor harvest means that land passes into the hands of the creditors and

All this provides an ample basis for the political awakening, or even the revolutionizing, of the Latin American countryside, and Mexican experience shows that the mere fact of past land reform is no bar to it, so long as the process of economic development in the countryside continues.[22]   It is delayed by the political and cultural lag of the country behind the city, its inaccessibility, and the usual inability of peasants to take more than local or traditional initiatives without outside leadership.   Possibly in areas of mass emigration the lowering of economic pressure and the loss of the most dynamic peasant cadres may also maintain the social temperature below boiling-point.   On the other hand the increasing absorption of the rural zones into national politics tends to work in the opposite direction.

III

Whatever the effect of rural emigration on the countryside, it is as nothing to its effect on the cities, which have been flooded—indeed drowned—by an influx of peasants which has no real parallel in the demographic history of the world.   The figures are extraordinary:

Population Growth of Some Latin American Cities

	1940	1960
Salvador–Bahia	348,000	656,000
Recife	290,000	798,000
São Paulo	1,776,000	4,000,000
Lima	520,000	1,700,000
Santo Domingo	70,000*	350,000
Mexico City	1,448,000	4,500,000

* 1935.

The rate of growth is consequently unprecedented—as high as 9 per cent per annum (Cali, Colombia)—and so is the general rate of

moneylenders' (R. Stevenson and others, *La planificación agraria* (Bogotá, 1960), pp. 53–54).
[22] Thomas F. Carroll, 'Land Reform as an Explosive Force in Latin America', in J. J. TePaske and S. N. Fisher, eds., *Explosive Forces in Latin America* (Ohio State UP, 1964), p. 118.

urbanization.   Around 1960 Argentina, Chile, Uruguay, Cuba, and Venezuela already had an urban majority, and so possibly had Mexico.   By 1970, on present trends, they will have been joined by Colombia, Peru, and even Brazil.

Inevitably such an influx was bound to destroy the older social and political structure of the cities.   So far as the masses of the urban poor were concerned, these had always participated to some extent in the political life of the cities and republics.   At the very least the long and self-contained existence of the city—which might well be a white or *mestizo* enclave in a coloured countryside—had allowed certain permanent patterns to be established.   Politicians sought the support of townsmen.   The common people might live in their accustomed symbiosis of riotous parasitism with the urban grandees; labour movements might develop and flourish, on the basis either of an essentially immigrant European proletariat (as in Buenos Aires and São Paulo) or of a traditionally metropolitan labour force (as in Havana).

The process of dilution and structural change can be illustrated by the example of São Paulo.   The following two tables are self-explanatory:

Birthplace of São Paulo Metal and Building Workers who entered their industries 1936–60

Date of entry	Percentage born in					
	Foreign		City		Other parts of Brazil	
	Metal	Bldg	Metal	Bldg	Metal	Bldg
1936–40	60	45	12	10	24	45
1941–5	29	25	23	12	45	63
1946–50	22	21	28	10	47	70
1951–5	14	11	37	9	48	80
1956–60	11	8	31	9	58	82

Source: Azis Simão, 'Industrialização e sindicalização no Brasil', *Rev. bras. de estud. polit.*, 13 Jan. 1962, pp. 87 ff. Based on samples of 68,000 and 32,000 workers respectively. The place of origin could not always be ascertained.

Grades of Skill of Workers in a São Paulo Factory by Place of Birth, 1960

(*Percentage of workers holding grade*)

Place of Birth	Unskilled, Semi-skilled	Skilled, Supervisory	Technical	Sales	Admin.
Bahia & NE	96·5	1·2	0	1·2	1·2
Rest of Brazil	84·3	5·8	0·5	1·6	7·9
City	47·9	14·6	0	8·3	29·2
Foreign	52·1	26·1	16·8	1·7	3·4

Source: Glaucio Ary Dillon Soares, ' Desenvolvimento econômico e radicalismo politico', *Bol. centro latinoamericano de pesquisas em ciências sociais,* May 1961, pp. 117 ff.

They may be summarized as follows. Foreign-born workers, a majority until the second world war, fell to about 10 per cent of the labour force within twenty-five years. Their place was taken partly by the city-born (i.e. largely their own children), but mainly by internal immigrants, especially in the less skilled occupations. The foreign-born retained their hold of the skilled and technical jobs, the city-born advanced rapidly into the white-collar jobs, the internal immigrants remained overwhelmingly unskilled and semi-skilled. It will be evident that this influx was likely not only to burst the bounds of any already existing labour movements but also to destroy much of the unity of background and style of the smaller and older proletariat. And this is indeed so. In São Paulo, as in Buenos Aires, the older unions were swamped by new government-sponsored and sometimes government-controlled bodies, while the traditional socialism, anarchism, or communism of the early proletariat retreated into the higher ranks of skill [23] or on to the fringes of industry.

It may be—but there are no studies on this difficult subject— that the same process of dilution or depolitization affected also

[23] The typical communist voter in São Paulo in the last free elections (1947) was a male—aged 18–40—skilled worker, born in the capital or resident there since before the war, mainly in the older industrial area (Simão, 'O voto operario em São Paulo', *Rev. bras. de estud. polit.,* Dec. 1956, p. 139).

60   *The Politics of Conformity in Latin America*

the unorganized activities of the labouring poor, such as riots. At all events it is remarkable how few riots—even food riots—there have been in the great Latin American cities during a period when the mass of their impoverished and economically marginal inhabitants multiplied, and inflation as often as not was uncontrolled. Thus the last great riot of the unaided poor in Bogotá (student-initiated riots are another matter) occurred in 1948, since when the population of the city—and it is fair to say the body of misery it contains—has risen from less than 650,000 (1951) to over a million (1964).[24] Or rather: there is unrest and violence. What is missing, unless the direction comes from students, from old nuclei of left-wing leadership (as in Niterói, opposite Rio de Janeiro), or from governments above, is the old-fashioned city 'mob' with a knowledge born of experience of what are the strategic and politically vital points of the city, where riot will have the maximum effect.

It need hardly be added that the rural influx also (and most directly) affects the pattern of political parties and votes. It may be argued that the characteristic populist leaders and parties of the 1940s and 1950s, whatever their claim to national and rural interest, represented primarily movements based on the urban poor, and hence increasingly on the new internal immigrants. This is particularly clear in the case of Argentina, where Perón deliberately made himself the spokesman of the creole up-country immigrants, the *cabecitas negras*, against the European and cityfied natives of Buenos Aires.

The political attitudes of the immigrants are naturally dictated by their poverty, the insecurity, the appalling living conditions, and the hatred of the rich of a gigantic and constantly expanding proletariat and sub-proletariat. Yet this is a population with no prior commitment—or even potential commitment—to any version of urban or national politics, or indeed to any beliefs which could form the basis of such politics. Unlike most nineteenth-century transatlantic migrants, they lack even a potential nationalism, for they are not foreigners. Unlike the East and South European migrants of the early twentieth century, they lack a native tradition of socialist/anarchist or labour movements which could hold them together in the strange land. What they do possess, the habits and

[24] Banco de la República, Bogotá, *Colombia, a Guide for the Investor* (1964).

reactions of rural kinship and communal life, doubtless help them to make themselves a little more comfortable in the big city by settling in groups from the same village or province, by transferring peasant mutual aid to the building of slum shacks or modest houses, and in other ways; but it does not, as it were, reach up far enough socially to be a political guide. They understand personal leadership and patronage alone.[25]   It alone provides a link between the political worlds of the hinterland and the city. Untouched by any other traditions, such as the anti-caudillist ones of liberalism or socialism, the new immigrants look naturally for the powerful champion, the saviour, the father of his people.

The politicians, with or without parties or movements, who have succeeded in gaining the support of the urban masses vary widely in their personalities or political attitudes. They might be old-fashioned oligarchs or generals, who gained a reputation for helping the people by lavish patronage, or the provision of work, or the right kind of building, or who were merely lucky enough to coincide with a period of exceptional prosperity. In Lima General Odría (the objects of whose Odriist movement are adequately expressed in its title) has gained the largest body of support in the *barriadas* (shanty towns) against the competition of APRA, Acción Popular, and the various Marxists.[26]   Vargas and Perón were old-fashioned political officers or oligarchic bosses who transferred to a deliberately populist programme; Batista in Cuba (whose early populism tends to be forgotten because of his later tyranny) was that somewhat rarer phenomenon, an actual man of the people— a sergeant, not an officer. All these, however, were leaders who established themselves by their action as rulers, past or present,

[25] It is often argued in Latin America that the new immigrants transferred the sort of loyalty they had given to their feudal superiors to any person of power and influence who could give them benefits in return for their support. This is a considerable oversimplification, though it has some truth in it. There are deeper reasons, both in the rural tradition of politics and the social situation of the urban masses, for a natural tendency towards *caudillismo*. Even in Europe it emerged clearly in early labour movements in the transformation of certain individuals into heroes and charismatic leaders; and this in spite of the deliberate discouragement of such a tendency by the early socialist parties, and the extremely poor natural equipment of some of the leader-figures with charisma.

[26] For the politics of the *barriadas*, see F. Bourricaud, 'La place de Lima dans la vie péruvienne', in *Les problèmes des capitales en Amérique latine* (Paris, CNRS, 1965), pp. 138–58.

i.e. by performance and not promise. This is also true of the revolutionary father-figures like Paz Estenssoro in Bolivia or the much greater Cárdenas in Mexico, whose reputation rested on their actual achievements. Governing is clearly by far the easiest way to become a populist leader in Latin America.

Cases of leaders who made their way from opposition to power for the first time by the support of the urban masses are much rarer, and not only because of the comparative rarity of governments coming to power by the votes of the masses or by their insurrections. Jorge Eliécer Gaitán of Colombia is the clearest example, though in fact his crucial step to the power that would have been his if he had not been assassinated was to capture the leadership of the Liberal Party, which implied the presidency. This is rather easier to do with a strong but minor following than the capture of national office directly.[27] The rise of Jânio Quadros in Brazil appears to be an even clearer case, for he owed nothing to any pre-existing machine, but since he rose not simply as a champion of the poor, but also (at least in São Paulo) as the standard-bearer of 'clean government' in the interests of the rich and the middle classes, he was not quite the political barefooted boy that he seemed. It was not until his attempted come-back in 1962 that his vote was overwhelmingly proletarian and poor.[28] Equally rare is the politically most mature form of populism, the combination of a leader with a strong and permanent movement or organization once again preceding power. Examples may be sought—with varying degrees of lack of success—in the Aprista types of party, in the Chilean *Frente de Acción Popular* (FRAP), perhaps in the new Christian-Democratic Parties, but not, curiously enough, in the Communist Parties, whose relative lack of success may well be partly due to their systematic refusal to accept this pattern of popular politics. Their leaders, throughout Latin America, have normally been

---

[27] Gaitán, a Liberal by origin, formed his own National Revolutionary Leftist Union in the 1930s, but had sense enough to return to work within his old party, demonstrating in 1946 that he could lose the party any presidential election by withholding his sizeable personal vote.

[28] Dillon Soares (*Bol. centro latinomericano, &c.*, May 1961) for conclusive evidence of this greater attractiveness of Jânio Quadros to those identifying with the upper and middle classes. It ought to be added that (in São Paulo) his chief rival, Adhemar de Barros, though a member of the 'good' families, is passionately disliked by the local Establishment, if only for the really sensational corruption of his administrations.

functionaries or intellectuals; and the one obvious example to the contrary, Luis Carlos Prestes, proves the rule convincingly. For this gifted man, who spontaneously moved into the role of a Latin American revolutionary people's champion through his career as an insurrectionary officer and the myth-producing adventures of the 'Prestes Column' which traversed the hinterland in the 1920s, did his best, as soon as he actually became a communist, to conform to the stereotype of the party secretary as then established in the Communist International. He nevertheless retained a substantial charisma for the limited area of the working-class movement.

We may therefore conclude in general that the experience of populism reflects the relative passivity and lack of initiative of the urban masses, much more readily mobilized by an existing ard sympathetic power from above (or by a former holder of power seeking to regain it) than capable of carrying a man or movement to the top. The only clear case to the contrary is that of Colombia, where Gaitán's assassination was followed by a formidable and entirely spontaneous rising of the Bogotá poor. But the situation which developed in Colombia between 1934 and 1948 was so clearly one of potential—and not merely urban—social revolution from below that normal criteria hardly apply to it. The immaturity of the masses is also clearly reflected in the instability of the 'movements' which grew up around many of the populist leaders, whose essential relationship with their followers was that of the orator facing the people on the *plaza*. Gaitanism died with Gaitán; Jânio Quadros's fortunes, even in his period as the poor man's champion, owed little to the memory of that earlier Father of the Poor, Getulio Vargas. Even the socialist sector of the Chilean FRAP showed a great deal of electoral instability.[29] Examples of solid and permanent popular movements are not unknown: APRA is one. Yet the most striking example of a populist movement which survived the disappearance of its leader is Peronism; and this because it transformed itself into a typical labour movement organized by and based on the (Perón-sponsored) trade

---

[29] The solid core of the Chilean labour movement passed to the Communist Party in 1922. It has remained a typical working-class party, not exceptionally strong in the capital. Support for the Socialist Party, which reappeared in the 1930s—generally in alliance with the communists, but as their more dynamic and often radical partner—has oscillated sharply since then.

unions; but the industrial development which could provide the
base for such a transfer is rare in Latin America.

A further factor diminishes the explosiveness of the rural immigration into the city: the obvious superiority of city life, even in
the most purulent *favela* or *barriada*, to the countryside. This is
not merely a matter of statistical fact: nowhere is the gap between
the average income and consumption of city dwellers and countrymen wider than in Latin America: average incomes in Caracas,
for instance, are ten times as high as in rural areas, a by no means
unusual figure.[30] Nor is this advantage merely that of the industrial
or regularly employed workers, in the strict sense of the word,
who tend to form an aristocracy among the poor which is not
without its bearing on the political attitudes of their labour movements, socialist or otherwise. It affects the bulk of the migrants.
Of the immigrants into Buenos Aires one-fifth say that they have
sometimes regretted their decision to migrate, but two-thirds are
satisfied with it.[31]

This is not due to any preference for the city over the country:
the proportion of immigrants who considered it 'better in Buenos
Aires' was very small, and in Santiago 62 per cent of a sample
thought it was 'bad' that young people should migrate to the city.[32]
But if the city is bad to live in, the country is infinitely worse.
Nevertheless, the poverty, overcrowding, insecurity, social disorganization, and the other troubles of city life are such that the
vast and inchoate masses who keep pouring into them cannot but
remain a potentially explosive force. It takes little enough to
submerge men and women whose normal fate is to have at best
their nostrils above the waterline. The governments which operate
from the presidential palaces in the midst of these growing rings
of misery and hate do not look out upon them with any sense of
comfort. There have been few urban insurrections of late, but
the events in the city of Santo Domingo in May 1965 prove that
the urban masses may have lost nothing of their potential power.

We can now summarize this discussion of the impact of the
rural and ex-rural masses on the politics of Latin America. At

[30] ECLA, *The Economic Development of Latin America in the Post-War
Period* (1964), p. 55.
[31] Gino Germani, in Hauser, p. 228. This volume contains other
material on the question.
[32] A. Girard and R. Samuel, *Situación y perspectivas de Chile en
Septiembre 1957* (Santiago de Chile, 1958), pp. 18 ff.

first sight it has been comparatively slight, though in the cities it has produced a new electorate and a new clientèle for political leaders and movements—often of the populist kind—which has transformed the official political scene in many of the republics. One might go so far as to suggest that, while in the early stages of the post-1930 social changes—say from 1930 to 1950—it may have produced a radicalization of Latin American politics, reflected in various successful and abortive revolutions and changes of régime,[33] in the later stages it may well have led to an apparent lowering of the social temperature. That lowering is only apparent. The explosive potential of the countryside may be diminishing, because of its rapid relative depopulation, but not its possibilities as a base for guerrilla action. The explosive potential of the cities would be diminishing only if the industrialization of the republics were capable of providing employment at the rate of migration, or if alternative employment became available. Neither is so far the case.

The countries of Latin America are, socially speaking, a broad-based, rapidly tapering pyramid, exceptionally poor at the bottom, exceptionally rich at the top, and not very much in between. Half the population (taking a hypothetical average) earn about $120 per year (or 16 per cent of personal incomes before taxes), 45 per cent earn $400 a year (or 51 per cent), and 5 per cent earn $2,400 a year (or 33 per cent).[34] It is improbable that this situation provides the foundation for stable social and political systems. It is more than probable that the comparative lull in the mass politics of Latin America—a lull which even the Cuban revolution did little to disturb—will prove temporary. When it ends, the observer may fervently hope that it will produce some sort of a solution, and not one of those relapses into anarchy which have been by no means unknown in Latin American history, and of which Colombia since 1948 provides so tragic an example.

---

[33] The Cuban revolution of 1933, the revival of the Mexican revolution in the 1930s, the Bolivian revolution (whose roots go back to the period well before 1952), the remarkable advance of Colombia towards spontaneous combustion, the rise of Acción Democrática in Venezuela, of Getulio Vargas in Brazil and Perón in Argentina, are some examples; as are the Chilean 'socialist republic' of 1932 and Popular Front government of 1938.
[34] ECLA, *Economic Development of Latin America*, p. 53.

The Middle-Class Military Coup

JOSÉ NUN

UNLESS a distinction is made between the structural and the circumstantial factors of military intervention in Latin American politics, important differences between countries are apt to be ignored. Table 1 (p. 68), for instance, shows that the number of successful coups varies independently of the degree of economic development: there were as many in Argentina as in El Salvador and fewer in Honduras than in Brazil. Evidently the intervention of the military in politics represents a different phenomenon in a country with an income per capita of $500, 70 per cent of its population living in cities, and with a large middle class, than in one where less than one-third of the population lives in cities, income per capita is only $150, and scarcely 8 per cent of the population can be classified as belonging to the upper and middle classes.[1]

Interpretations which tend to ignore these differences have generally been influenced either by traditional liberal anti-militarism or by the advocacy of militarism as a dynamic force for economic development.[2]

---

[1] Intentionally, the data given in this example correspond approximately to those of Argentina and Guatemala. In a recent study of Latin American militarism, the case of the latter country was considered as a paradigm of events in the rest of the continent. See Fedro Guillén, 'Militarismo y golpes de estado en América Latina', *Cuadernos americanos*, 140/3 (1965), pp. 12–16. Lieuwen makes equally far-sweeping generalizations in his examination of the coups that occurred between 1962 and 1964. See Edwin Lieuwen, *Generals vs. Presidents— Neo-Militarism in Latin America* (New York, 1964).

[2] For a critical commentary on the literature dealing with this subject, see Lyle N. McAlister, 'Changing Concepts of the Role of the Military in Latin America', *The Annals*, 360 (July 1965), pp. 85–98; and my study 'A Latin American Phenomenon: The Middle Class Military Coup', in *Trends in Social Science Research in Latin American Studies* (Berkeley), Mar. 1965, pp. 55–99. For a typical expression of the liberal theory, see Edwin Lieuwen, *Arms and Politics in Latin America* (New York, 1961); the best exposition of the developmentalist theory is John J. Johnson, *The Military and Society in Latin America* (Stanford UP, 1964).

The *liberal model*, based on the experience of Europe in the eighteenth and nineteenth centuries, envisaged the army as the bastion of traditional and feudal values. Its officer corps was drawn from the aristocracy, and was antagonistic to the liberal bourgeois state. From 1815, with the Pax Britannica contributing to a decrease of militarism and the state taking deliberate measures to ensure civilian control over the armed forces, there ensued a professional revolution which reached its peak by the end of the nineteenth century. The developmentalist model conceives of the army as an intelligentsia in uniform, dedicated to progress and development and peculiarly suited to achieving them. It is based on the experience of the Afro-Asian countries, where the officer corps was mostly drawn from the popular sectors. There is a Nasserist version of this model which will be discussed later (pp. 113–18). Finally, the socialist model, which, from a rejection of militarism similar to that espoused by the liberals, has progressed to an acceptance of the integration of the military in the body politic as a means both of strengthening it and of lending additional prestige to the civilian leadership.

These three ways of approaching the problem imply that the armed forces are an independent sector, or at least that they are hardly at all integrated with the rest of society. Thus, according to one such theory, the traditional army is a step behind the modern society which is forming around it; according to another, the modern army is a step ahead of the traditional society which is disintegrating. In fact both these theories presuppose an inverse relationship between militarism and the consolidation of the diversified social structure typical of a developed country. As one writer asserts: 'Army officers in politics are typical of pre-industrial nations lacking a strong middle class.' [3] How then is one to explain the military coups in countries such as Argentina or Brazil, which have strong middle-class sectors, and such a high degree of industrial growth that in the former country one-third of the labour force is employed in manufacturing industry or construction, while in the second domestic production accounts for two-thirds of the capital goods the country requires? [4]

[3] James H. Meisel, *The Fall of the Republic—Military Revolt in France* (Michigan UP, 1962), p. vi.
[4] Cf. ECLA, *Problemas y perspectivas del desarrollo industrial latino-americano* (Buenos Aires, 1964), p. 21.

TABLE 1

Armed Forces in Latin America

	(a) % of urban population (1960)	(b) % of illiterates (1961)	(c) % of labour force engaged in manufacturing & construction (1960)	(d) % of upper & middle classes in total population (c. 1950)	(e) % of urban upper & middle classes in total urban population (c. 1950)	(f) GNP distributed per capita (US $ 1960)	(g) Total regular armed forces	(h) Ratio of armed forces to population	(i) % military budget of total budget	(j) No. successful military coups (1920–1966)
Argentina	68	14	29	36	38	466	108·500 (1963)	0·51	13·2	7
Uruguay	82	15	28	(33)			13·110 (1963)	0·49	1·0	2
Chile	63	20	24	22	30	439	45·710 (1965)	0·62	18·0	4
Cuba	55	22	18	22	36		79·000 (1963)	1·21		4
Venezuela	62	48	15	18	27	885	22·240 (1962)	0·33	8·0	1
Costa Rica	38	21	15	22	31	310	1·230 (1964)	0·09	1·0	
Panama	41	30	10	15	32	363	3·439 (1964)	0·32		3
Mexico	54	43	15	17	37	272	52·850 (1964)	0·15	1·0	
Brazil	39	51	17	15	37	168	263·100 (1960)	0·37	11·4	5
Colombia	46	38	17	22	35	250	22·900 (1964)	0·15		2
Ecuador	35	44	25	10	28	161	13·280 (1963)	0·30		9
Peru	36	53	18		21	190	44·940 (1963)	0·41	18·0	4
Bolivia	30	68	13	8	26	86	11·010 (1960)	0·31	11·0	9
Paraguay	34	34	17	14	27	129	9·100 (1962)	0·50		7
El Salvador	33	61	14	10	25	200	6·650 (1961)	0·25	12·0	6
Nicaragua	34	62	13		23	229	4·100 (1963)	0·25		1
Dominican Rep.	29	57	11			207	17·200 (1963)	0·57	26·0	4
Honduras	22	65	9	4	25	186	4·200 (1965)	0·21	7·0	2
Guatemala	31	71	10	8	16	156	8·500 (1965)	0·22		6
Haiti	13	89	7	3	14	98			23·0	5

Sources and Explanations

(*a*) and (*c*): Centro Latinoamericano de Pesquisas em Ciências Sociais *Situação social da América Latina* (Rio, 1965).

(*b*): Unesco, *Freedom of Information* (New York, 1961). For Peru and Uruguay, id., *World Illiteracy at Mid-Century* (Paris, 1957).

(*d*): Gino Germani, *Política y sociedad en una época de transición* (Buenos Aires, 1962). The figures for Uruguay correspond to 1958 and were taken from Carlos M. Rama, *Las clases sociales en el Uruguay* (Montevideo, 1960).

(*e*): Based on Germani figures elaborated by Torcuato S. Di Tella, *El sistema político argentino y la clase obrera* (Buenos Aires, 1964).

(*f*): Annual average of the period 1950–60 (Charles Wolf, Jr., 'The Political Effects of Economic Programs: Some Indications from Latin America', *Economic Development and Cultural Change*, 14/1 (Oct. 1965)).

(*g*) and (*i*): Irving L. Horowitz, 'The Military of Latin America', in S. M. Lipset and A. E. Solari, *Elites in Latin America* (New York, forthcoming). Figures for Costa Rica refer to civil guard. In Panama officially armed forces are under the control of the police.

(*h*): I estimated these figures only as a rough indicator of the different magnitudes. Up-to-date data on adult male economically active population were not available to calculate Andreski's 'military participation ratio'.

(*j*): This column is to be taken as merely indicative in view of the difficulties involved in trying operationally to define a successful military coup. I have therefore limited myself to registering events between 1930 and 1966 in which the head of the government in power was deposed by force. Obviously, this criterion leaves out the military interventions which, without deposing the government, have modified its policies, as happened for instance in Uruguay in 1933 under President Gabriel Terra. For a discussion of some of the conceptual problems involved, see my 'A Latin American Phenomenon', in *Trends in Social Science Research in Latin American Studies* (Mar. 1965).

Note

By way of quantitative illustration, I have estimated the Spearman coefficient to determine the possible rank correlation between columns (*e*) and (*j*) and between columns (*h*) and (*j*). The main limitation of this procedure is that while (*j*) quantifies events along a period of 47 years, (*e*) and (*h*) measure their respective variables at one point in time. In any case, for (*e*) and (*j*) the coefficient is 0·02 and for (*h*) and (*j*) 0·39. Therefore, in both cases there is *no* correlation.

An objective analysis shows that Latin America is lacking in two of the basic elements of the liberal model: in the first place, its armies were generally formed after the professional revolution; and, secondly, the greater part of their officers are recruited from the middle class and not from the aristocracy.

Merle Kling has proposed an interesting modification of this model. His argument may be summarized as follows: in Latin America, the oligarchy and foreign capital maintain a rigid control over the conventional bases of economic power and prevent the rise of other social groups; the government therefore appears as the only base of economic power, the ownership of which can change; and from this situation there arises the privileged position of the military in the ruthless struggle to take possession of this coveted source of potential power; instability is therefore 'a function of the contradiction between the realities of a colonial economy and the political requirements of legal sovereignty among the Latin American states'.[5]

Even if one ignores the economic emphasis of this theory and concedes that the personal ambition of military leaders is the basic driving force behind military interventions, it is obvious that this interpretation is only valid for very undeveloped countries, characterized by a bi-polar social structure (oligarchy/masses), and a very low degree of mobility and institutional differentiation—conditions which can hardly be said to be prevalent in the more advanced countries of Latin America.

Similar objections can be raised to the 'developmentalist' model—largely based on the experience of the Afro-Asian countries —which analyses 'the political implications of the army as a modern institution that has been somewhat artificially introduced into disorganized traditional societies'.[6] It is applicable, in other words, to countries of very recent formation, where the civil and military bureaucracies are the only alternatives, in almost entire absence of modern institutions. It is unnecessary to emphasize the difference between such societies and those of Argentina or Brazil.

This lends added interest to an examination of instability in the more-developed countries of Latin America. In the two already

---

[5] Merle Kling, 'Towards a Theory of Power and Political Instability in Latin America', in John H. Kautsky, ed., *Political Change in Under-developed Countries* (New York, 1962), p. 201.
[6] Lucian W. Pye, *Aspects of Political Development* (Boston, 1966), p. 173.

mentioned—Argentina and Brazil—military coups are features of the present-day situation. In the other three [7]—Uruguay, Chile, and Mexico—the last quarter-century has been marked by political stability. Is it possible, by means of an analysis of the experience of these countries, to isolate structural factors capable of explaining interventionism in situations remote from those envisaged in the traditional models? Over twenty years ago it was observed that 'a government which cannot rely upon its middle classes will, almost certainly, be unable to rely upon the unbroken loyalty of its army'.[8] Is this the situation? And, if so, why?

This essay attempts to analyse certain structural elements that have not generally been considered in previous interpretations of this phenomenon. For at least two reasons it makes no claim to be exhaustive; first, it excludes the very important circumstantial factors, which cannot be dealt with here; and, secondly, because a model of this nature does not claim to be an exact reflection of reality, but only to place some emphasis on certain important aspects that are not immediately obvious.

The Middle-Class Professional Army

To understand the problem of political instability, one must look behind the military façade (just as, to understand Latin American inflation, one had to look behind the monetary façade). With this end in view, both the social basis of the officer corps and some of the consequences of its recent professionalization must be considered.

(a) *Social Basis.* Although statistical information on this subject is still scarce, most authorities are agreed in admitting that,

---

[7] I have omitted Cuba from this analysis both because of the incongruence of its indicators of development and because of the exceptional situation resulting from the Revolution. Together with Mexico—as we shall see later—and Bolivia, it provides the only case in Latin America illustrating the socialist model of civilian-cum-military rebellions. Thus, Article 6 of the law establishing the new Bolivian army lays it down that 'military academies must be constituted fundamentally of elements of the middle class, working class and peasantry, which in addition to the technical training relating to the military art, will be educated to respect and protect the national sovereignty and the aspirations of the people, and to defend the riches of the country against the ambitions of the oligarchy'. See McAlister, 'The Military', in J. J. Johnson, ed., *Continuity and Change in Latin America* (Stanford UP, 1964), p. 146.
[8] Katharine Chorley, *Armies and the Art of Revolution* (London, 1943), p. 78.

since the end of the nineteenth century, the majority of Latin American officers have been recruited from the middle class.[9]

In his study of generals, brigadiers, and admirals in Argentina, José Luis de Imaz found that only 23 per cent of the sample examined were descended from the traditional families. He estimated that 73 per cent of the brigadiers and generals interviewed came from families belonging to the wealthy bourgeoisie, 25 per cent from the lower middle class, and only 2 per cent from the working class.[10]   Although the category 'upper middle class or wealthy bourgeoisie' is excessively large, and includes everybody from landowners to professional men, and even supposing that all the fathers concerned who were landowners, businessmen, or industrialists belonged to the upper class—which is certainly an exaggeration—this survey does indicate that two-thirds of the officer corps is of middle-class origin. Moreover, contrary to what is generally believed, the data provided by Imaz indicate that '[Argentine] generals, today just as much as formerly, come from an urban background, half of them from the capital and the Greater Buenos Aires area'.[11]

John Johnson reached similar conclusions with regard to the middle-class origin of Brazilian officers,[12] even though in this case the greater part came from the small towns in the interior. For the purposes of this study this difference does not appear to be of decisive importance in view of the relative homogeneity of the system of values prevalent throughout urban Brazil. It has, for example, recently been asserted that 'those who leave the small towns to take up residence in the big city find there an atmosphere that is familiar to them, and it is not so difficult for them to adapt themselves to it as might be thought'.[13]

In Chile, where the officer corps represents a more typical cross-section of the urban population as a whole,[14] there has been,

---

[9] Cf. McAlister, in Johnson, *The Military & Society*, p. 145; Johnson, ibid. pp. 102 ff. For a discussion of the same tendency in Europe, see Morris Janowitz, 'Armed Forces in Western Europe: Uniformity and Diversity', *European J. of Sociology*, 6 (1965), p. 232.

[10] José Luis de Imaz, *Los que mandan* (Buenos Aires, 1964), p. 58.

[11] Ibid. p. 56.

[12] Johnson, *The Military & Society*, pp. 235–8. Also Charles Wagley, *An Introduction to Brazil* (New York, 1963), pp. 253–4.

[13] Maria Isaura Pereira de Queiroz, 'Les classes sociales dans le Brésil actuel', *Cahiers internationaux de sociologie*, 39 (1965), p. 162.

[14] Johnson, *The Military & Society*, p. 108.

ever since the war of 1879, a continuous penetration of the military profession by the sons of middle-class families.[15]   A similar trend has been evident in Uruguay and Mexico since the turn of the century.   In the case of Mexico, it is possible that recruitment has taken place from even lower social strata: for example, an examination of the applications for admission to the Military College in 1955 reveals that 14·64 per cent of the candidates were the sons of workers and 2·98 per cent the sons of peasants.[16]

This description does not imply that the class situation of the officer corps entirely explains its political behaviour.   It does, however, restrict the field of investigation, and makes possible an assessment of the importance and relative autonomy of outside factors inhibiting or determining the behaviour of this group.[17]   It is, after all, not entirely fortuitous that the liberal model which prevailed in the nineteenth century should have paid particular attention to the basis of recruitment of those destined for military command: 'after all, their origins constitute the source of the "non-Armed Force" opinions of the armed force organizations.'[18]

In the countries under discussion, there are other factors which presumably tend to strengthen this class affiliation, owing to continual contact between the civil and military spheres.   Among these are the lack of a tradition of active warfare, which diminishes the separation between the daily life of the officers and that of the rest of the population.   Another factor that has still not been investigated is the mediating role fulfilled by retired officers: the

---

[15] Cf. Liisa North, *Civil-Military Relations in Argentina, Chile and Peru* (Berkeley, Calif., 1966), pp. 17–20.

[16] Javier Romero, *Aspectos psicobiométricos y sociales de una muestra de la juventud mexicana* (Mexico City, 1956), quoted in McAlister (Johnson, *The Military & Society*, p. 147).

[17] Cf. Louis Althusser, *Pour Marx* (Paris, 1966), pp. 85–128.

[18] Marion J. Levy Jr., *Modernization and the Structure of Societies—a Setting for International Affairs* (Princeton UP, 1966), ii, p. 595. Contrast: 'Social origins and early backgrounds are less important to the character of the professional military man than to any other high social type', C. Wright Mills, *The Power Elite* (New York, 1956), p. 192. However, Mills himself adds that 'the point should not, of course, be pushed too far' (ibid.); and, moreover, he does not offer any empirical evidence to support his thesis.   Incidentally, although the latter is expressed in such categorical terms, it is weakened by its relative nature, in so far as little is known of the importance of the social origin of the other 'high social types'.

available data do, in fact, indicate a tendency towards 'rejuvenation' among the higher ranks of the armed forces,[19] which means that the retirement—voluntary or enforced—of the officer occurs when he is still fully active and capable of embarking on a civilian career, while at the same time keeping in touch with his old comrades in arms.   Moreover, whereas in technologically backward societies the increasing technical specialization of the army tends to link the officer more closely to foreign sources, in societies of a higher cultural development, such as those we are analysing, the same phenomenon leads to increased contacts between the officer and his civilian colleagues.

Finally, it is worth pointing out an obvious fact which is too often forgotten, namely the 'civilianization' of the officers that is a direct consequence of their continual political activity.   Although one should not exaggerate the importance of such contacts, which in any case are limited to certain social sectors, this is nevertheless an argument against the traditional conception of the army as an institution completely isolated from its social context, and the consequent exaggeration of the uniqueness of the armed forces' attitudes and behaviour.   It would, of course, be absurd to deny the existence of characteristics peculiar to the army as such but so far no attempt has been made to determine how important these are in determining an officer's behaviour.[20]   Several studies devoted to this question apply to the military establishment the concept of the 'total institution' formulated by Goffman.[21]   However, such studies pay less attention to the distinctions drawn by the same writer with regard to methods of recruitment and the permeability of the institution to the influences surrounding it,[22] and ignore his assertion that 'total institutions do not really look for cultural victory',[23] which explains the relative ease with which its members are able to become reintegrated into the society outside the institution.[24]

[19] Imaz, p. 68.
[20] As far as Latin America is concerned, the only study I know that compares attitudes of cadets before and after their military training is: Mario Monteforte Toledo, *Guatemala—monografía sociológica* (Mexico City, 1959), pp. 367 ff.
[21] Erving Goffman, *Asylums—Essays on the Social Situation of Mental Patients and Other Inmates* (New York, 1961), *passim*.
[22] Ibid. pp. 118–19.
[23] Ibid. p. 13.
[24] Ibid. p. 73.

(*b*) *Organization.* While it is true, on the one hand, that the greater part of the officer corps comes from the middle class, the military establishment can, on the other hand, count on a degree of cohesion and institutional solidity which is entirely lacking in the Latin American middle class.

The tendency to consider social phenomena in isolation and in the abstract has led some writers to suppose that professionalization *per se* induces officers to withdraw from politics, by placing a barrier between them and the rest of society. Oddly enough, Mosca argued with equal conviction, and for well-founded reasons, that the contrary was true and, more recently, Finer has supported his arguments.[25] With regard to the Latin American armed forces, one observer asserts: 'on the contrary, in those countries in which they have been most highly professionalized, they seem to have become even more closely linked with the rest of society than formerly'.[26]

What happens in reality is that every system of domination attempts to internalize violence by the means most suited to its values and interests. Thus professionalism became generally accepted in European armies only at the end of the nineteenth century and as a result of deliberate government policy. The bourgeois state had experimented with various formulae for the control of the armed forces—examples of which are the unsuccessful French and American attempts to have the highest posts of command submitted to popular election—until the logic of capitalist society eventually dictated the solution. In the framework of a general tendency towards fragmentation and division of labour, the exercise of violence was also converted into a specialized field calling for high professional qualifications, and became part of a series of particular sub-systems enjoying a relative degree of autonomy. In this way 'military institutions have taken

---

[25] See Gaetano Mosca, *The Ruling Class*, ed. A. Livingston (New York, 1939), ch. 9, and S. E. Finer, *The Man on Horseback: the Role of the Military in Politics* (New York, 1962), pp. 26–30. See also Stanislav Andreski, 'Conservatism and Radicalism of the Military', *European J. of Sociology*, 2 (1961), pp. 55–58, and Philip Abrams, 'The Late Profession of Arms: Ambiguous Goals and Deteriorating Means in Britain', ibid. 6 (1965), pp. 241–2.

[26] Arthur Whitaker, 'Nationalism and Social Change in Latin America', p. 99, in J. Maier and R. W. Weatherhead, eds, *Politics of Change in Latin America* (New York, 1964), pp. 85–100.

on more and more the characteristics common to civilian large-scale organizations'.[27]   Professionalization is therefore the means by which the armed forces are incorporated into a determined place in the structuralization of society as a whole, and it is this, and not professionalism as such, that explains the apparent political neutrality of the army in the Western democracies.

This process of professionalization was bound to produce different results in Latin America, since it not only took place in armies at different stages of development but did so in the context of pre-industrial societies with structures based on the hegemony of the oligarchy and not that of the bourgeoisie.

In Europe 'military organization had established its form centuries before professionalization definitely began'.[28]   This explains in part the successful establishment of organizational controls designed to counteract the possible centrifugal tendencies which might result from increased professionalization.   In Latin America organization and professionalization take place almost simultaneously, increasing the probability of discrepancies leading to open conflict.[29]

This early professionalization had two important social consequences: first, as has been indicated above, the middle class was admitted to the career of arms through the creation of military academies; and, secondly, in contrast to its own organizational weakness,[30] this class was now allied to a sector with a remarkable degree of institutional cohesion and articulateness.   In other words the armed forces became one of the few important institutions controlled by the middle class.[31]

This relationship partly explains political instability due to military intervention but it is open to two important criticisms: first, from those who consider that the profession of arms

---

[27] Janowitz (*European J. of Sociology*, 6 (1965), p. 226).

[28] Jacques Van Doorn, 'The Officer Corps: a Fusion of Profession and Organization', ibid., p. 270.

[29] One example of this tension was provided in 1965 by the resignation of General Juan Carlos Onganía from the post of commander-in-chief of the Argentine army because of the government's failure to take account of professional perquisites in the appointment of the secretary for war.

[30] See below, pp. 98 ff.

[31] I believe it would be fruitful to reinterpret from this point of view the hypotheses of Merle Kling mentioned above, even though I would insist that I only consider them to be applicable to the less-developed countries of Latin America, which I am not dealing with in this study.

conditions its followers so thoroughly that one may ignore any other variable in seeking for explanations of their behaviour; and, secondly, from those who maintain that the middle class, by its very nature, is dedicated to the support of political stability and democratic institutions.

I have already given some of the reasons why I consider the first objection to be valid only in a relative sense. With regard to the second, it will be necessary to touch briefly on some of the factors that lead the middle class to associate with military intervention in politics.

Middle Class and Bourgeoisie

Hitherto I have deliberately used the expression 'middle class' rather than 'bourgeoisie'. G. D. H. Cole has drawn the distinction:

> Bourgeois, to any historically-minded person, calls up at once the image of a body of citizens asserting their collective, as well as their individual, independence of a social system dominated by feudal power based on landholding and on the services attached to it; whereas the words 'middle class' call up the quite different image of a body of persons who are placed between two other bodies—or perhaps more than two—in some sort of stratified social order.[32]

The same writer goes on to say that the bourgeoisie as such is not in the middle of anything, at least not consciously so.

At this point it is necessary to consider the degree of relative independence of the rural and urban sectors of the same national society; it is on this supposed independence that the hypothesis of structural dualism, so frequently met with in studies concerned with Latin America, is based. The concept of a middle class implies, by definition, a system of unified vertical stratification. But the application of the hypothesis of dualism to the Latin American situation admits of two different interpretations; in the first, the traditional and modern 'poles' are analysed as if they were relatively independent entities, with the result that some writers speak of 'two countries within the same territory'. Hence the tendency to transfer mechanically to the Latin American situation a technologically determinist hypothesis like Ogburn's 'cultural lag'. The observer 'isolates' São Paulo from the North-East, for example, and assumes that for the latter to attain the level of development of the former, all that is required is to transform the North-East without considering whether such a transformation would involve

[32] *Studies in Class Structure* (London, 1955), pp. 90–91.

equally profound changes in São Paulo. On the other hand, the dialectic interpretation finds the key to the situation in the internal unity of a historically determined system of domination. This is the unity explaining the frustration of a middle class which is prevented from fulfilling the role of a bourgeoisie. In order to analyse such an interpretation, it is necessary to distinguish between two principal stages in the evolution of the system: that of the unity of the oligarchy and that of its crisis.

The Hegemony of the Oligarchy

G. D. H. Cole's observation was based on a study of the urbanization of Central Europe which, according to the well-known theory of Henri Pirenne, was the consequence of the rise of the mercantile sectors, potentially antagonistic towards the feudal order and the power-system on which it was based. A different situation obtained in Southern Europe—a typical example being the Italian cities—corresponding more closely to Werner Sombart's interpretation: here it was the nobility that played a leading role in the formation of the new urban centres, which were thus integrated into the prevailing power-structure.[33]

The characteristics associated with the process of colonization, in the case of the urbanization of Latin America, made it from the very beginning resemble more closely the second of the processes described above, in that there was never any real dissension between the urban centres and the nascent landowning aristocracy. 'Colonization was in large part an urban venture, carried out by urban-minded people',[34] and the city represented both the point of departure and the residence of the owners of land. The difference, of course, lay in the fact that, whereas in Italy 'the power of the city becomes so strong that it becomes independent of any central government',[35] in Latin America it was precisely the urban centres which served as the instrument of colonial rule. Nevertheless, *mutatis mutandis*, a basically similar tendency was apparent: 'more typical than the struggle between burgher and feudal groups

---

[33] Cf. Alessandro Pizzorno, 'Sviluppo economico e urbanizzazione', *Quaderni di sociologia*, 11 (1962), p. 35.

[34] Richard Morse, 'Urbanization in Latin America', *Latin American Research R.*, 1/1 (1965), p. 38.

[35] Pizzorno (*Quaderni di sociologia*, 11 (1962), p. 35).

was the conflict between local rural-urban oligarchies and agents of the royal bureaucracy'.[36]

This initial 'unitary' characteristic becomes even more pronounced in the second half of the nineteenth century, with the rapid integration of the Latin American national economies into the world market. As Celso Furtado has observed, 'the entrepreneurial attitude that made the rapid development of lines of export possible had its origin within the merchant groups which operated from the urban centers'.[37] Instead of a divergence developing between the interests of the dominant groups in the cities and those in the rural areas, the urban mercantile sector consolidated its position as a landowning and capitalist oligarchy.[38]

It was thus that the great Latin American capitals became the places of residence of the privileged sectors during the era of 'outward' economic growth.[39] Beside them there developed the middle class, of the primary-products export model, composed of the exporters and importers, small industrialists, professional men, and civil servants, all integrated into the hegemonic system of the oligarchy.

This did not mean that the state was simply the expression of the subjective will of one social class, as if the underlying unity of the hegemonic structure were given by the ideology of the dominant group. On the contrary, this unity must be sought in the total structure of society, in which this ideology was only one

---

[36] Morse (*Latin American Research R.*, 1/1 (1965), p. 38).

[37] Celso Furtado, *Development and Stagnation in Latin-America: a Structuralist Approach* (Yale, mimeo, 1966), p. 13.

[38] I am, of course, giving a general outline of a long-term process. In the short term, however, there are conflicts which derive precisely from the activities of the urban mercantile sectors in their attempts to displace the pre-capitalist landowning sector.

[39] It is unnecessary to emphasize that I am greatly simplifying the discussion. Among the five countries to which I am referring, the one that most deviates from the pattern is Brazil; this country, together with Ecuador and Colombia, constitutes an exception to the Latin American rule of the unique 'primate' city. In any case, during the period we are discussing, the situation in Brazil becomes increasingly similar to that which I have described, owing to the centralization imposed from the beginning of this century onwards by the coffee-growing economy of São Paulo. Thus here too 'the leading strata of urban society were composed for the most part of members of the great landowning families' (Furtado, 'Political Obstacles to the Economic Development of Brazil', in Claudio Veliz, ed., *Obstacles to Change in Latin America* (London, 1965), p. 152).

element among many. The function fulfilled by the state—providing a framework for the oligarchy—must not be obscured by being forced into the nineteenth-century liberal model imported from Europe. In Latin America there was no question of the *status quo* being challenged; *laissez-faire* was in practice the political instrument which consolidated the economic system, and its application constituted 'a deliberate measure consciously designed to achieve specific ends and not the spontaneous and automatic expression of an economic situation'.[40] Structure and superstructure thus became fused into an extremely solid historical block, and found their expression in an advanced juridical and institutional system. Marx asserts that a particular class can only maintain its supremacy by exercising it in the name of the general rights of society. On the basis of a particular economic system, this 'conquérante' oligarchy was able to evolve a systematic justification of its dominant position by means of a normative structure which defined those general rights in terms which applied to the existing internal relationships among social groups. The fundamental reason for its success was undoubtedly the high degree of efficacy of the system itself: the bonanza arising from the export of raw materials convinced all its beneficiaries—direct and indirect —that Argentine meat, Brazilian coffee, Uruguayan wool, and Chilean minerals guaranteed permanent economic expansion. To be optimistic, it was enough to conceive of the future as an extension of the present, and the middle class enthusiastically adopted that conservative outlook which takes no account of the future or the vicissitudes it may bring. It was members of the oligarchy, not of the middle class, who were responsible for the first industrial expansion of any importance, and it was they who organized the new industrial and commercial enterprises, in which the middle class participated only as a second-rate but acquiescent partner. This is why it raised no protest when the Chilean government handed over to foreign companies the exploitation of the nitrate deposits which it had cost the country five years of war to acquire, nor when the Brazilian authorities frustrated the energetic attempts at industrialization made by Viscount de Mauá; for this reason, it neither protested nor gave support to a contrary policy when lack of protection led to the breakdown of the incipient process of industrialization

[40] Antonio Gramsci, *Notas sobre Maquiavelo, sobre política y sobre el estado moderno,* tr. J. M. Arico (Buenos Aires, 1962), p. 54.

encouraged by the first world war. Since the basic principles of the system were never called into question, commercial or industrial collapse was regarded as a problem affecting only the individual concerned, or, at most, held to be the result of corruption of a system that, in its uncorrupt state, was considered unsurpassable.

The expanding middle class made no attempt to change the system as a whole: it merely demanded recognition of its legitimate right to play a part in it. Its aspirations were limited to a desire for participation in political affairs and for revendication of its moral status.[41] The most interesting features of this process were the speed with which these aspirations were satisfied and the instrumental role of the military.

This process began in Uruguay, with the election in 1903 of José Batlle y Ordóñez. This chronological priority undoubtedly reflects the very early development of the Uruguayan middle class: at the turn of the century, it already constituted between 25 and 30 per cent of the population of the Republic, and *Batllismo* was 'the political movement which most exactly reflects [its] rise'.[42] The great leader of the *Colorados* came to power in the middle of a civil war fought against the landowning groups connected with the Blanco Party. Whereas the armed forces of the latter were basically composed of peons recruited from the big estates, the regular army gave its support to *Batllismo* and made it possible for Batlle to establish himself in power.[43]

In Argentina, a military lodge was formed as early as 1890, under the influence of the *Unión Cívica*, the immediate predecessor of the *Unión Cívica Radical*, the middle-class party which carried Hipólito Yrigoyen into the presidency in 1916. In the intervening period there were increased contacts between the Radicals and the officer corps—some of the officers played an active part in the

---

[41] On the moral outlook of the middle class—possibly a constant in Latin American political life—see, in general, Svend Ranulf, *Moral Indignation and Middle Class Psychology* (New York, 1964) and, more specifically, IBESP, 'O moralismo e a alienação das classes medias', *Cadernos do nosso tempo*, 2 (1954), 150–9.

[42] Aldo E. Solari, *Estudios sobre la sociedad uruguaya* (Montevideo, 1964), i. 119. According to the estimates of this writer—to whom I owe the figures quoted in the text—the 1908 census data make it possible to classify as middle class about 40 per cent of the active population of Montevideo, 'which is a very high percentage for that time'.

[43] Cf. Milton Vanger, *José Batlle y Ordóñez of Uruguay* (Harvard UP, 1963), p. 167.

1893 and 1905 rebellions—and this was one of the factors which eventually induced the oligarchy to allow free elections. As Puiggrós observes: 'They feared the democratic revolution, and at the same time they realized that they could not continue to monopolize political power with the immense majority of the people against them and with Radicalism increasingly influencing the army, the police and the civil service.'[44] This also explains the failure of the coup planned at the last minute by the oligarchy-dominated Senate, designed to force the resignation of President Sáenz Peña, suspend the elections, and return to the system of restricted suffrage.

In Chile, the aspirations of the middle class found expression in the *Alianza Liberal* which, in 1920, put Arturo Alessandri in the presidency. 'The "revolution of 1920" was never envisioned by most of its instigators as anything more than a program of mild palliatives; but it was unable to furnish even the palliatives.'[45] Among the most obvious reasons for its failure was the systematic opposition of the Senate, still controlled by the oligarchy. As Gil observes, 'the majority of the Chilean armed forces, composed of middle-class members in the officer corps and of men of proletarian origin in the rank and file, were sympathetic to the national cry for reform'.[46] When, after the parliamentary elections of 1924, even the new Congress—in which Alessandri already commanded a majority—postponed the implementation of the President's programme, the army took action, overthrew the ministerial cabinet and 'in an hour and without debate, the "suggestive rattling of army sabres in the congressional galleries" obtained approval of a complete program of social legislation which had been pending for years in the Congress'.[47] Although the movement was initially commanded by a group of officers identified with the upper class, 'the majority of the armed forces' officers opposed the restoration to power of a discredited oligarchy'.[48] Thus in January 1925 another coup, this time engineered by young officers led by Carlos

[44] Rodolfo Puiggrós, *Historia crítica de los partidos políticos argentinos* (Buenos Aires, 1956), p. 111. See also North, pp. 26–27.
[45] Fredrick B. Pike, *Chile and the United States—1880–1962* (Notre Dame, Ind., 1963), p. 177.
[46] Federico G. Gil, *The Political System of Chile* (Boston, 1966), p. 58.
[47] ibid. Gil's quotation is from John Reese Stevenson, *The Chilean Popular Front* (Philadelphia, 1942), p. 37.
[48] Pike, p. 179.

Ibáñez and Marmaduke Grove, eliminated the conservative faction, brought Alessandri back to the country, and drew up a new constitution which, in the words of a liberal commentator, 'although it was the work of a *de facto* government and was imposed by force of arms, has stood the test of time, and has lasted with minor modifications until our own day'.[49] Thus the armed forces ensured the establishment in power of the middle class, whose programme was put into practice by Colonel Ibáñez who, as a result of military pressure, became president in 1927. One should not forget, therefore, in considering the subsequent political stability of Chile, that 'the institutional structure that has governed Chile down to the present day was fashioned by Ibáñez between 1927 and 1931'.[50]

In Brazil, the continuous expansion of the armed forces since 1864 made them a stronghold of the incipient middle class, to which the Empire offered few occupational opportunities. 'That middle-class army, which to a certain extent formed a body outside the organizational structure of the Imperial state, would eventually overthrow it.' [51] 'Florianismo', however, marked the failure of the premature attempt of this sector to establish control over the state.[52] Although the solidarity of the Old Republic (*Republica velha*), rendered the process slower in the case of Brazil, events subsequently followed a path similar to those in Argentina and Chile: 'The middle-class revolutions that took place between 1922 and 1937 represented the efforts made by that class to achieve, by military means, a power that always eluded it.' [53] The first step towards the final achievement of this objective was the revolution of 1930, which brought Getulio Vargas to power, thanks to the decisive part played by the *tenentismo* movement. The support of the military for the régime was reaffirmed in 1932, with the defeat of the attempt to restore the oligarchy. The new groups soon realized, however, that adherence to the 1934 constitution and the

---

[49] Ricardo Donoso, *Breve historia de Chile* (Buenos Aires, 1963), p. 101.
[50] Pike, p. 188.
[51] Helio Jaguaribe, *Desarrollo económico y desarrollo político*, tr. I. Sáenz, (Buenos Aires, 1962), p. 167.
[52] 'With Floriano Peixoto, the middle class, through its élite of army officers and doctors, makes its first attempt to radicalize the petty-bourgeois revolution, installing in power a revolutionary government, infused with the ideology of that class and the possession of power by its leaders' (ibid. pp. 167–8).
[53] IBESP, O golpe de Agosto, *Cadernos do nosso tempo*, 3 (1955), p. 6.

effective implementation of the basic principle for which they had struggled—universal and secret suffrage—would result in their defeat at the hands of the paternalistic ballot-rigging practised by the landowners.

Thus the middle class found itself in the peculiar position of wishing to control the state without altering the existing social and economic structure, and of being compelled by considerations of *Realpolitik* to jettison its political principles with the anti-democratic coup of 1937 and the setting up of the *Estado nôvo*.[54]

Although several circumstantial factors make it exceptional, the case of Mexico nevertheless partially confirms the pattern outlined above. The limited nature of the political aspirations of the middle class was summed up in the well-known *Maderista* slogan, 'Effective suffrage and no re-election'. The emphasis was, above all, political : 'Madero wanted wider participation and more democratic processes in politics in an effort to end the *continuismo* of the Díaz régime.'[55] This explains the timidity of the agrarian measures contemplated in Article 3 of the Plan of San Luis Potosí, which nevertheless was enough to mobilize Emiliano Zapata and his followers :

He and his men soon threw themselves into the Revolution, not because they were excited by the magic words 'effective suffrage and no re-election', as this political document [the Plan of San Luis Potosí] suggests, but because they believed in the agrarian measures promised in Article 3.[56]

The complete ineffectiveness in this respect of the thirteen and a half months of Madero's government provoked the insurrection of the Southern leader and his proclamation of the Plan of Ayala, which gave contemporary expression to the slogan of Flores Magón: 'Land and Liberty'. It was this peasant unrest that forced the middle class to support the reforms which, albeit with great hesitation, Venustiano Carranza was introducing; so much so that the domination of the oligarchy was in fact broken only in the following decade, under the government of Obregón, whose work was completed by Lázaro Cárdenas. As for the army, its situation was

[54] Jaguaribe, 'The Dynamics of Brazilian Nationalism', in Veliz, p. 170.
[55] L. Vincent Padgett, *The Mexican Political System* (Boston, 1966), p. 22.
[56] Jesús Silva Herzog, *Trayectoria ideológica de la Revolución Mexicana* (Mexico City, 1963), p. 28.

slightly different from that described in the countries discussed above. In his successful attempts to establish control, Porfirio Díaz had considerably weakened it. Gradually he forced the retirement of a quarter of the hundred generals in the army, and dismissed about four hundred more junior officers.[57]   Also the professionalization of the armed forces was much slower than in the other cases quoted: 'Although there was a perceptible French influence and part of the equipment was German, Mexico did not invite any foreign military mission, and rarely sent officers to study abroad.   Consequently, the army was backward in both military techniques and equipment.'[58]   For this reason, as Edwin Lieuwen points out, the army was no more than a 'fragile shell' when the 1910 revolution broke out.   Nevertheless as soon as the revolution began, a number of officers, steadily increasing, 'deserted the régime and joined the revolutionary forces, impressed by their power and popular support'.[59]   In other words, in Mexico too a sizeable part of the regular army supported the attempts of the middle class to seize power.

All this highlights the relative speed with which the middle class achieved the satisfaction of its claims; and the decisive role played by the armed forces in this process.   But what must be emphasized above all is the limited nature of those claims.   Except in the case of Mexico, the political events did not constitute one of those 'cathartic' moments when the ascent to power of a new social group leads to profound structural changes.   It was the very reverse of that process: the middle class had no need of time to develop a characteristic outlook, because it merely adopted that of the oligarchy.   It accepted its heroes, its symbols, its culture, and its laws.   (It is significant that both Yrigoyen and Alessandri decided to play with 'loaded dice', assuming the presidency at a time when the parliamentary majority was in the hands of the oligarchy.) The middle class did not question the economic basis of the system, but formulated the conflict in terms of 'equality of opportunity', that is to say equality of access to the alternatives defined by that system; for this reason the two sides eventually agreed on the socialization of the political conflict, leaving the economic one on a purely private plane.   In contrast to this, the exceptional merit

---

[57] Lieuwen, *Arms and Politics in Latin America* (New York, 1961), p. 104.
[58] Ibid. p. 105.   [59] Ibid. p. 106.

of the Mexican Revolution lay in its handling of the agrarian problem.

Two points are worth making. First, a description of the integration of the middle class into a historical situation dominated by the oligarchic hegemony need not be interpreted as a moral accusation levelled against that class, on the grounds that it failed in its historic mission, since in fact its behaviour was governed by the limited framework of its 'possible consciousness', bearing in mind the conditions surrounding its formation. Secondly, this is a process and not a static phenomenon. Important political changes such as these cannot be explained simply in quantitative terms. The very expansion that was the result of the ascent and social integration of the middle class began, in fact, to weaken the hegemony of the oligarchy, making it especially vulnerable to the vicissitudes of the period that followed and leading it towards its definitive crisis.

The Hegemonic Crisis

After the 1929 depression, exports in the countries under discussion ceased to constitute the axis of the economic system, and internal investment replaced the external sector as the dynamic growth factor.

In the favourable conditions of a highly protected internal market—as an indirect consequence of measures taken to prevent catastrophe for the exporting groups—there took place a process of totally unplanned industrial development. The peculiar characteristic of this process of substitution of imports [60] was that it made possible industrialization without an industrial revolution, and without necessarily antagonizing the landowning oligarchy. These considerations are of the utmost importance in the interpretation of the behaviour of the new middle-class groups [61] that emerged during this period because the aspirations of these groups found expression within the framework of the hegemony of the oligarchy;

[60] See Maria Conceição Tavares and others, 'The Growth and Decline of Import Substitution in Brazil', *Economic B. for Latin America*, 9/1 (Mar. 1964), pp. 1–60.

[61] Although in the context of this study I keep using the term 'middle class', it is obvious that, in these circumstances, the real phenomenon implies something much wider than the concept. However, it is sufficient for the time being to draw the reader's attention to this broad group of interests delimited by the oligarchy on the one hand, and the rural and urban proletariat on the other.

the conditions of their development did not result in a fundamental conflict with that system. This is the reason for the essentially conservative nature of its political consciousness, in so far as it never transcended the limits of a corporative-economic interest and was incapable of reaching the level of 'universality' attained by the oligarchical system.[62]

This makes it easier to understand, in the first place, the apparent ambiguity of outlook manifested by these new sectors, which caused so many unfounded speculations about the emergence of a national bourgeoisie: its reformist impulses have invariably originated and exhausted themselves on the level of immediate economic interests. It is therefore quite logical, for example, to assert that 'the state that helps "my industry" has nothing to do with the more abstract state which, legislating and acting, participates in the economic life and becomes the eternal symbol of the anti-enterprise'.[63] In the same way an industrialist can be protectionist in outlook with regard to his own products, and an advocate of free trade with regard to the materials that such production requires.[64]

Moreover, it would be erroneous to consider as a lack what is a negation. The particularism of this class consciousness really means that the new group finds appropriate, or rather that it appropriates, the existing normative structure. The repeated failure of the developmental theorists, who have eventually become convinced of the sociological weakness and artificiality of their hypotheses,[65] shows that it is not just a question of supplying what is lacking but of contending with something actually in existence.

---

[62] For an analysis of the various manifestations of the collective political consciousness, see Gramsci, *Notas sobre Maquiavelo*, pp. 71–74. As this writer points out: 'Already [at the time of the extended economico-corporative solidarity] the question of the State arises, but only in the sphere of obtaining equality with the dominant groups, claiming the right to participate in legislation and administration and even to modify it, or reform it; but to do all this within the existing basic structure' (p. 71).

[63] Fernando H. Cardoso, *O empresario industrial e o desenvolvimento econômico do Brasil* (São Paulo, Tese, 1963), p. 164.

[64] Cf. Gustavo Polit, 'Rasgos biográficos de la famosa burguesía industrial argentina', *Fichas de investigación económica y social*, 1/1 (1964), p. 66.

[65] For a detailed analysis of the different variants of the Brazilian developmentalist ideology, see Michel Debrun, 'Nationalisme et politiques du développement au Brésil', *Sociologie du travail*, 6/3 (1964), pp. 235–57, and 6/4, pp. 351–80. The particular interest of the Brazilian case lies

It would be wrong to suppose, however, that the factors in this situation have remained invariable: on the contrary, the very emergence of those sectors and the growth of the urban proletariat have undermined the hegemony of the oligarchy, as happened in Brazil and Argentina after the second world war. It is interesting to examine both cases because they represent two typical variants of the model of industrialization based on import-substitution, and also because these countries have continued to be potentially Bonapartist, in so far as the crisis of the domination of the oligarchy has resulted from the action of social groups without a vocation for exercising hegemony. In such conditions there exists a basic tendency to instability, which the Roman-style [66] military coup tries unsuccessfully to correct.

The Brazilian Variant

During the *Republica velha*, federalism and parliamentarism were the principal expressions of the oligarchic political formula, which established the Federal States as the exclusive domains of various landowning groups. *Coronelismo* was its expression at the local level. In this context, national policy appeared as a mere compromise between regional oligarchies, whose rules of the game would afterwards be given formal expression as the *política dos governadores*. This system became increasingly less efficient from the point of view of the big coffee producers, who were interested in a strengthening of the central power which would facilitate the process of 'socialization of losses' described by Furtado.[67] This same economic system based on coffee provided the market for the incipient national industry. We have already seen how the middle class came into power in 1930: there followed an intensive campaign to integrate the political life of Brazil at the national level, accompanied by an increasing utilization of the urban masses as an

in the fact that rarely has an ideology been so self-conscious: an example of this is the objectives and work of the Instituto Superior de Estudos Brasileiros. See Frank Bonilla, 'A National Ideology for Development: Brazil', in Kalman H. Silvert, *Expectant Peoples— Nationalism and Development* (New York, 1963), pp. 232–64.

[66] I am referring to temporary military dictatorship, acting as an interregnum between two civilian governments. In Argentina and Brazil, the last decade has seen a number of coups of this type; the two most recent military movements have the declared aim of ending this situation.

[67] Cf. Furtado, *A economia brasileira* (Rio, 1954).

element of manoeuvre in the confrontations that ensued. The old agrarian sectors were, however, successful in preserving the federal and parliamentary structure.[68] It was evident that the Legislative Assembly had now become the arena of the bargaining between the representatives of regional *coronelismo*, the delegates of the new economic groups, and the *clientelista* politicians. As Brandão Lopes asserts,

the essential point to remember is that during this period (1945–64), Brazil became a composite state in which differing types of interests (instead of the almost unchallenged domination exercised by the agrarian interests in the past) develop agreements and compromises; and in which the 'people', in the sense of the lower and middle urban sectors (though still lacking in a definable class-consciousness and ideological outlook) must be taken into consideration, even though it in no way participates in the power structure.[69]

The Bonapartist content of the *Estado nôvo* consisted, in precise terms, of the replacement of the traditional hegemonic system by an 'adaptation of the formula of socialization of losses and division of profits to the terms of the new social reality emerging in the country and, simultaneously, its institutionalization'.[70] It is worth while emphasizing that there was no question of the middle class ingenuously falling into an ideological trap. In the first place, as I have already pointed out, the suspension of the system of political representation, caused by the establishment of the *Estado nôvo*, served its interests. In the second place, *cartorialismo* appeared to be the functional solution of the problem of its lack of occupational opportunities. Above all, however, as far as the industrial sector was concerned, there were no basic causes of conflict between it and the oligarchy.

The world depression had the practical effect of diminishing the opportunities for investment in coffee production. The resulting disposable capital, mobilized through the banking system, facilitated to the industrial sector 'an economic surplus which it had no need

---

[68] For a perceptive analysis of this point, see Furtado, in Veliz, pp. 154 ff., and Glaucio A. Dillon Soares, 'El sistema electoral y la reforma agraria en Brasil', *Ciencias políticas y sociales*, 8/29, 431–44.

[69] Juarez R. Brandão Lopes, 'Étude de quelques changements fondamentaux dans la politique et la société brésiliennes', *Sociologie du travail*, 2 (1965), p. 245.

[70] Luciano Martins, 'Aspectos políticos de la Revolución brasileña', *Revista latinoamericana de sociología* (1965), p. 398.

to expropriate, since it was spontaneously placed at its disposal'.[71]
At the same time, of course—and this is the fundamental contradiction involved in the process—this considerable volume of disposable investment capital was a function of the high level of agrarian exploitation which, by reducing drastically the purchasing power of the majority of the population, would prevent the development of an internal market which this same industrial expansion would subsequently require.[72]

It should be noted that this problem is not a new one: we need only recall the differing interpretations by Gramsci and Rosario Romeo of the Italian *Risorgimento*, the failure of which was attributed by the first writer to the lack of an agrarian reform, whereas, in the opinion of the second, it was precisely the absence of such a reform which made possible the use of the agrarian sector as a source for the original accumulation of capital.[73] Obviously, it is not a question here of deciding between alternatives, but of emphasizing the possibility of a rational justification, from a private point of view, for the Brazilian agrarian-industrial pact, and of indicating why the continuance and aggravation of this dualism was not solely due to the Machiavellian intrigues of the oligarchy. To this one must add that the continued existence of a large precapitalist sector in the economy meant that the process of import-substitution took place in the context of an abundant supply of labour at very low wage-levels.

For this reason, 'the success that Brazil had in the substitution process is the counterpart of the fact that it was in this country that development benefited a smaller number of people and begot the sharpest social tensions'.[74] The correlative of a high level of capital accumulation in the framework of a highly protected but limited market was a constant tendency 'to find oneself unexpectedly with idle capacity and to divert investment into new channels, a situation which resulted in the dilemma expressed by the slogan:

[71] Ruy Mauro Marini, 'La dialéctica del desarrollo capitalista en Brasil', *Cuadernos americanos*, 25/3 (1966), p. 137.   See also Tavares and others, p. 11.

[72] Compare Ignacio Rangel, *A inflação brasileira* (Rio, 1963), pp. 25–49.

[73] See Antonio Gramsci, *Il Risorgimento* (Milan, 1949) and Rosario Romeo, *Risorgimento e capitalismo* (Bari, 1959).   For an analysis of this controversy, see Alexander Gerschenkron, *Economic Backwardness in Historical Perspective* (New York, 1962), pp. 90–118.

[74] Furtado, *Development & Stagnation*, p. 36.

"Grow rapidly or perish!" ' [75] The first of these alternatives was possible as long as the dynamic impulses underlying the import-substitution process were maintained, but these have exhausted themselves without the country being able to find a pattern of self-sustained development. The result is the tendency to stagnation.[76]

In one sense, this might lead one to suppose that the foundations have been laid for an agrarian-industrial conflict that would transform the middle class into a genuine bourgeoisie. Such a hypothesis is now more plausible than formerly; but the course of events so far makes it necessary to introduce at this juncture two considerations.

One is the extreme heterogeneity of this middle class. I am not referring solely to the fact that in Brazil, as everywhere else, it constitutes the 'occupational salad' of which Mills wrote, but also to the already mentioned particularism of its outlook which has prevented it from transcending that heterogeneity and achieving a more general consciousness of solidarity, and which has also made it especially vulnerable to the influence of the upper class.

The other factor—intimately connected with the preceding one—has been the entry of the urban proletariat into the political arena. *Varguismo* was instrumental in establishing control over the explosive character of the first stage of this process, and Brazil's prosperity made it possible to gratify the aspirations of the new working class, a process undoubtedly facilitated by the low level of expectations resulting from the pre-capitalist background of the labour force. But what is happening now is a curiously regressive development: as the maturity of the working class increases—leaving out of consideration its evidently reformist outlook—the rate of economic growth of the country is diminishing for the reasons outlined above, and there is also a steadily diminishing possibility

---

[75] Rangel, pp. 35–36.
[76] An estimation of the distribution of income in Brazil around 1960 showed 50 per cent of the population with a per capita income of $100; 45 per cent, with $325; 3 per cent, with $1,430; and 2 per cent, with $2,850. Compare Tavares and others, p. 55. One can appreciate the magnitude of the problem if one considers that, whereas Brazilian industry faces the problem of a limited market, the 50 per cent of the population effectively outside the capitalist economy constitutes more than the combined populations of Argentina, Uruguay, and Chile. Together with the second group mentioned above, they comprise 66·5 million people out of the total population of 70 million.

of gratifying its demands without a structural transformation of the system.

It was much to Vargas's credit that in his later years he partially realized that this situation had developed, and tried to redefine the power-system of the country. But although the army had allowed him to take over the presidency in 1930 as the representative of the middle class, and to reaffirm the establishment of the latter in the government by means of the 1937 coup, that same army, in October 1945 and August 1954, expressed the fears of that same class in the face of the more popular orientation the régime was beginning to acquire.

In both cases, Getulio Vargas was overthrown by the armed forces, who acted on both occasions as the spokesmen and instruments of the Brazilian middle class. In both cases the middle class, which could no longer impose its own orientation on the politico-social development of the country, took a reactionary stand in the face of the government's looking to the proletariat for support and moving towards a Left-Wing solution.[77]

This is also the principal characteristic of the most recent military coup, which was preceded by an intensive press campaign and street demonstrations by middle-class groups demanding the intervention of the armed forces. Goulart had consolidated his position in the government thanks to the general strike of September 1962, and the labour movement 'for the first time organized for independent action, became more conscious of its power'.[78] Moreover the organization of peasant forces was progressing in the North-East. At the same time, the rate of growth of the economy was slowing down, in the midst of galloping inflation. Unable to identify the structural basis of this process and to give articulate expression to a programme capable of mobilizing the popular sectors, the middle class opted for the radical Right and, frightened by the populist measures of the government, allied itself with the traditional defenders of the *status quo* and gave encouragement to the coup.

The movement of April 1964 thus united all the property-owning classes of society: the agrarian sectors out of fear of land reform, the industrial sectors out of fear of losing their mechanisms of security, the

[77] IBESP (*Cadernos do nosso tempo*, 3 (1955), p. 4).
[78] Neuma Aguiar Walker, 'The Organization and Ideology of Brazilian Labor', in Irving L. Horowitz, ed., *Revolution in Brazil* (New York, 1964), p. 252.

middle classes panicked at the prospect of a closing of the social distance separating them from the masses, and all of these sectors were moved by the even greater fear of the emergence of a process of development diverging from the classical pattern of American democracy, to which they are all culturally linked.[79]

The Argentine Variant

A fundamental characteristic of the Argentine case—as well as of the Uruguayan—is the early absorption of the agrarian pre-capitalist sector and the consequent unification of the domestic labour market. For this reason, and viewing the problem in comparative terms, it makes less sense to refer to a dualistic structure. Another consequence of this is that the process of industrialization took place in a context of a limited supply of labour, which constituted a permanent threat to the profit margins of the rural producers, in contrast to the position in Brazil, 'making difficult their recovery when favourable conditions appear in the export markets'.[80] Despite this, and notwithstanding the presence of peculiar factors, here too the middle class has shown itself unable to break away from its tacit agreement with the landowning sector.

In order to understand the situation, it is necessary to insist on the great efficacy of the system during the era of the hegemony of the oligarchy. At the end of the last century Argentina was already predominantly urban and was undergoing a rapid process of modernization, in which immigration played an important part. The future of the land of cattle and wheat appeared definitely assured: 'A powerful tide carried everything upwards and everyone thought that the ascent would never stop until it reached the clouds, that it would never stop at all'.[81] For this reason, the principal task of Yrigoyen consisted in ensuring the participation of the middle class in the project inaugurated by the generation of 1880, not of changing that project.

So true was this that when setbacks occurred in the 1920s, it was not the middle class which blamed the raw-material-exporting system established by the oligarchy, but the oligarchy which condemned the system of parliamentary democracy defended by the

[79] Martins, p. 410.
[80] Furtado, *Development & Stagnation*, p. 36.
[81] Francisco Romero, *Sobre la filosofía en América* (Buenos Aires, 1952), p. 25.

middle class: 'the Yrigoyen government was a proof, in the eyes of many people, of the definitive failure of universal suffrage'.[82]

This remarkable subordination of the middle class—combined with the fact that it was their representatives who were in power during the 1929 crisis (in contrast to the situation in Brazil)—partly explains the oligarchical character of the coup of 6 September 1930. As Dardo Cúneo observes:

> If the military rebellion was in fact just a walk through the city, this was not due to the ability of the army conspirators; it was principally due to the weakness of the middle class, to its forgetting its historic role as a class. So great was its inactivity in this respect that, although the army was officered by members of that same middle class, it served the interests of the oligarchy against theirs. The Radical government was incapable of expressing any inspiring message or of rallying its supporters.[83]

In 1928 Yrigoyen had failed to seize the opportunity of liquidating the San Martín Lodge, the nucleus of the movement that would overthrow him two years later; once the coup had occurred, the *Unión Cívica Radical,* controlled by Alvear, refused to assume the political leadership of the officers who were prepared to rise against the oligarchical restoration.[84] Although these circumstances do not alter the fact that—to a certain extent—the 1930 coup was an exception to the pattern that I have been describing,[85] they at least serve to emphasize the fact that the military coup was not carried out against the opposition of the middle class, and the representatives of the latter did little or nothing to modify its course.

Thus, in a political climate the most salient characteristic of which is 'the weakness of all the political attitudes that are not the expression of the interests of the traditional privileged classes',[86] Argentina carried out the first stage of the process of industrialization based on import-substitution. By the middle of the 1940s

---

[82] Tulio Halperín Donghi, *Argentina en el callejón* (Montevideo, 1964), p. 23.

[83] Dardo Cúneo, *El desencuentro argentino 1930–1955* (Buenos Aires, 1965), p. 168.

[84] For an account by one of the protagonists, see Teniente Coronel Atilio Cattáneo, *Plan 1932—Las conspiraciones radicales contra el General Justo* (Buenos Aires, 1959), especially pp. 25 ff., 228 ff. Also Puiggrós, p. 321.

[85] For an analysis of the institutional antecedents of the 1930 coup, see Darío Cantón, 'Notas sobre las Fuerzas Armadas argentinas', *Revista latinoamericana de sociología*, 3 (1965), pp. 290–313.

[86] Halperín Donghi, p. 32.

the contribution of the manufacturing sector to the national product was already greater than that of the agricultural sector. After the end of the war Perón not only consolidated this industrial growth, but also gave concrete satisfaction to the political rights of the urban and rural workers. The coup of June 1943 thus led to the adoption of populist measures, to the direct benefit of the new middle-class groups, whose partial opposition to the régime revealed, nevertheless, the persistence of traditional ideological tendencies.

Peronismo marked the definitive crisis of the hegemony of the oligarchy; but in Argentina, as in Brazil, it was not succeeded by the setting up of the hegemony of the bourgeoisie, but by a series of alliances and compromises which constituted the essence of a Bonapartist system.

The prosperity of the early post-war years made it possible for the régime to concede considerable benefits to the popular sectors without doing too much damage to other social groups. Perón once said that an adversary must either be forgiven or eliminated: nothing is more dangerous than a wounded enemy. The experience of his government confirms the truth of the aphorism and reveals him as a poor follower of his own precepts. The nationalization of foreign trade and bank deposits were basically measures designed to transfer revenue from the rural sector to industrial expansion. But, in addition to being limited in scope,[87] these measures were not accompanied by a proper agrarian policy. In this respect, the ambiguity appears especially negative, in so far as the government disrupted the traditional system of production—especially through legislation protecting tenants[88]—without imposing the solutions

---

[87] Compare Juan Carlos Esteban, *Imperialismo y desarrollo económico* (Buenos Aires, 1961), pp. 44–50.

[88] For an excellent discussion of this problem, see Horacio Giberti, 'Problemas de la estructura agraria', especially pp. 29–31, in Giberti and others, *Sociedad, economía y reforma agraria* (Buenos Aires, 1965). The traditional rural economy in the Pampa region, for example, was comparatively simple: the big landowner used his land for cattle-raising; when it became necessary, after a few years, to carry out an agricultural rotation designed to improve the pasture, he would rent the land for a short period, and the tenant would be obliged to use the land for agriculture; when this, in turn, resulted in a decline in fertility the rent agreement would be ended, and the land used for cattle again. Perón, by passing emergency laws lowering rents and increasing the term of leases, modified this process without at the same time suppressing the big estates. The result was a steady decline in productivity in the rural sector.

required to supersede it; a wounded enemy, the oligarchy would wreak its revenge on a country which no longer accepted its exclusive tutelage.

As it turned out, the position of the régime became critical towards the end of the 1940s: reserves were exhausted, there was no longer any immediate possibility of another world war, and agrarian stagnation deprived the country of the resources essential for development. Its room for manoeuvre severely diminished, the government found itself faced with two alternatives: 'either to promote radical social changes, or to recognize that the prosperity of the Perón era had been the result of post-war conditions and was vanishing along with them, and to undertake the undoing of its own work'.[89] In fact, neither course of action was taken: the progressive outlook of the middle-class sectors which were represented by the system was not sufficiently developed to opt for the first choice, but it was strong enough to reject the second. An ambiguous situation therefore arose, which was resolved by the coup of September 1955 in favour of the more conservative alternative. The behaviour of Perón towards the oligarchy provides a particularly good illustration of the difficulties the middle class found in trying to play the part of a bourgeoisie. When faced with the agrarian crisis, the régime could count on an exceptional degree of popular support and had the backing of the army, and was therefore in a position to carry out a thoroughgoing agrarian reform. Notwithstanding this, it embarked from 1950 onwards on a policy still followed to this day, which consisted of trying to increase the production of the rural sector by increasing the price of its products in relation to the economy as a whole. In other words, the government was appealing to the goodwill of the landowners, producing a transfer of revenue favourable to them, by means of, first, subsidized prices—which involved the state in considerable commercial losses—and, later, by successive devaluations of the currency.[90]

In purely economic terms, the reasons for the failure of this policy are not difficult to establish. Taking into account, on the one hand, the shortage of labour and, on the other, the increasing

---

[89] Halperín Donghi, p. 60.
[90] Cf. Aldo Ferrer, *La economía argentina* (Buenos Aires, 1963), pp. 214–17. This writer estimated that, as a result of this policy, about $2,500 million were transferred between 1950 and 1960 from the rest of the economy to the rural sector (ibid. p. 215).

power of the trade unions—encouraged by the Perón régime itself—
it was natural, from the point of view of private interest, that, left
to themselves, the investment of rural proprietors would be directed
towards labour-saving and the reduction of costs, rather than
towards an increase of production.[91] For this reason—and leaving
out the problem of conspicuous consumption—price increases took
place without any corresponding increase in rural productivity;
thus there was created a chronic inflationary pressure, the chief
victim of which was that very middle class which was so afraid of
structural changes.

As a result, not only was there paralysis in a sector vital to
Argentina's development, but the effects were felt on the standards
of living of the popular sectors whose expectations had been raised
by the experience of the Perón régime. The maintenance of the
situation, however, is a current proof of the principle stated by
Gramsci: ' "civil society" has become an extremely complex structure capable of resisting the catastrophic "incursions" of immediate
economic factors (crises, depressions, etc.): the superstructures of
the civil society are similar to the trench system in modern
warfare'.[92] Frightened by the possibility of the country's political
development taking a radical turn, the middle class prefers to take
refuge in those same trenches. The process is thus a 'self-fulfilling
prophecy': the middle class is unable to assume the leadership of
the popular movement and becomes increasingly separated from it,
while that movement continues to be Peronist, and, what is more,
addicted to a form of Peronism from which certain middle-class
groups originally sympathizing with it have deserted,[93] and which
tends, therefore, to become more closely identified with Perón's
first presidency than with his second.

In these circumstances, the free elections which were once the
dream of the middle class have become its nightmare. Established
in the ideological camp proper to the oligarchy, it can interpret

[91] Giberti (pp. 42–43), describes a study carried out in the department of
Ayacucho—one of the richest zones of the Pampa region—which
revealed that 'there is an evident tendency for the value of production per
hectare to diminish as the area used increases' (p. 38). The level of
productivity of the estates of over 2,000 hectares is below the average
for the region, and even lower than that of the smallest farms investigated in the survey.

[92] Gramsci, *Notas sobre Maquiavelo*, p. 94.

[93] Cf. Torcuato S. Di Tella, *El sistema político argentino y la clase obrera*
(Buenos Aires, 1964), p. 90.

the stagnation only as a political problem; it therefore exercises constant pressure on the military to intervene, prevent the triumph of Peronism, and overthrow the government of the day which is failing precisely because it represents that middle class. This is the background of the March 1962 and June 1966 coups. It was no coincidence that, two days after the second coup, the Buenos Aires Stock Exchange showed the most spectacular rises in four years.[94] One of the *civilian* theorists supporting the movement observed with satisfaction that 'instead of electing, the people will now have the right of consenting and participating in political decisions. . . . Such consent may be either " implicit"—a passive acceptance of the new order—or "explicit", in cases where the new régime evolves towards plebiscitary forms.' [95]

The Middle Class and Democracy

It is a commonplace to compare the rapid expansion of the Latin American political arena with the very gradual evolution of the British electoral system.[96] Without underestimating the un-doubted interest of this kind of analysis, it is fair to say that 'it conveys the impression that England became a democracy primarily as a result of statutory changes in the electoral system, whereas in fact the historical process involved was a good deal more complex'.[97]

One of the decisive elements in that process was precisely the efficacy of the Victorian bourgeoisie in articulating the popular consensus. For this purpose, it skilfully utilized the deferential attitudes still persisting in the working class; it ceaselessly diffused the values associated with its capitalist, liberal and Christian ethical system; it gave enthusiastic encouragement to a complex of institu-tions 'devoted to self-improvement and self-help',[98] and, above all,

---

[94] See *Confirmado,* 2/55 (7 July 1966), p. 65.
[95] Mariano Grondona, 'Definiciones', *Primera plana,* 4/184 (July 1966), p. 11. The 'superstructural emphasis' of the coup becomes evident when, on the one hand, its representatives insist on the thoroughgoing renewal that it implies, and, on the other, the economic team selected by the 'new' government is formed by the same people who have exercised these functions for the last decade or others closely connected with them.
[96] See, for example, Gino Germani, *Política y sociedad en una época de transición* (Buenos Aires, 1962), pp. 153 f.
[97] Trygve R. Tholfson, 'The Transition to Democracy in Victorian England', *International R. of Social History,* 6/2 (1961), p. 226.
[98] Ibid. p. 232.

it proved able, from the middle of the last century, to effect a considerable improvement in the economic position of a labour aristocracy which responded eagerly to such encouragement.[99] Without this intermediate process, which made possible the ending of the original identification of the 'labouring classes' with the 'dangerous classes', the electoral reform of 1867 would be incomprehensible: the workers only began to be accepted as citizens when their conformism had extinguished the old Chartist fervour.[100] It was for that reason that the suffrage lost its disruptive character, and was able to fulfil in the political sphere the legitimizing function that the contract fulfilled in the economic sphere. In other words, the validity of the classical Marxist proposition according to which representative democracy is the form of government which most closely corresponds to the interests of the bourgeoisie depends on the previous consolidation by the latter of its hegemonic supremacy, its development of a metaphysical justification of its leading role, and its demonstration of its efficacy as a ruling class.

In the course of the above analysis, we have tried to point out some of the reasons for the failure of the Latin American middle class to achieve this position. The central nucleus of its problem is that, when it has still not succeeded in working out a stable political compromise with the oligarchy, it is already having to face the problem which Disraeli formulated a century ago: 'The Working Class Question is the real question, and that is the thing that demands to be settled.'[101]

Electoral data provide only an approximate indication of the magnitude of the problem. At the outbreak of the first world war, in a somewhat similar stage of industrial development, only 10 to 15 per cent of the population of Europe took part in elections;[102] in the countries we are considering, however, the proportion is

---

[99] For an excellent analysis of this subject, see E. J. Hobsbawm, *Labouring Men—Studies in the History of Labour* (London, 1964), pp. 272–315.
[100] Cf. Royden Harrison, 'The 10th April of Spencer Walpole: The Problem of Revolution in Relation to Reform, 1865–1867', *International R. of Social History*, 7/3 (1962), pp. 351–97.
[101] R. A. J. Walling, ed., *The Diaries of John Bright* (New York, 1931), p. 297.
[102] Cf. Stein Rokkan, 'Mass Suffrage, Secret Voting and Political Participation', *European J. of Sociology*, 2/2 (1961), 132–52. Even in Great Britain it has been estimated that around 1913 no more than 17 per cent of the population had the right to vote.

often three or four times as great, e.g.: Argentina, 43·9 per cent (1963); Uruguay, 36·4 per cent (1958); Chile, 30·5 per cent (1964). These figures are close to the most recent ones for the United States, e.g. 38 per cent in 1964.

Unable to consolidate themselves as a bourgeoisie, the most that the progressive sectors of the Latin American middle classes have been able to do has been to offer the popular sectors programmes based on fundamentally quantitative goals, mobilizing them to seek the satisfaction of their demands within the existing structural framework. This is the essential ingredient in the populism of Perón, Vargas, and Ibáñez; and it provides one of the clues to its unique character: whereas elsewhere—e.g. the United States or Canada—populist movements have had an agrarian basis and arose in periods of depression, in Latin America these movements were fundamentally urban and were associated with periods of prosperity.

For this reason economic stagnation fixes the limits of such movements, as is shown by the change of orientation of Perón's régime around 1950, and the swing of Ibáñez to conservatism which coincided with the falling-off of the Korean War boom.[103]

It has often been alleged that the Latin American middle class was progressive as long as it needed popular support to achieve power and, once established there, became reactionary.[104] Although this observation is more or less valid as a mere description of actual events, the formula is dangerous on account of the class-subjectivism to which it may lead: it can tempt the observer too easily to make a metaphorical association with a psychological 'vertigo' supposedly felt by that class when it reaches the heights of power.

If this analysis is correct, it is its internal composition and the manner in which it has achieved power within the framework of the hegemony of the oligarchy which is beginning to disintegrate that

---

[103] In the case of Brazil, observers have recently noted the tendency towards the adoption of an ideology on the part of the politician operating the patronage system, as his possibilities of immediately satisfying the demands of the electorate become increasingly restricted. It is obvious that this transition from being 'Saviour of the Poor' to being 'Saviour of the Fatherland' implies, eventually, the negation of the patronage system and as such represents a risk that the dominant groups do not seem prepared to take. See Carlos Alberto de Medina, *A favela e o demagogo* (São Paulo, 1964), pp. 95–96.

[104] See, for example, ECLA, *The Social Development of Latin America in the Post-War Period* (Santiago, 1963).

explains the behaviour of this middle class. Moreover, if we employ for a moment the hypothetical representation of history recommended by Weber, it is probable that if the process of import-substitution had been accompanied by opportunities of exploiting an external colonial market, these countries would have achieved self-sustained growth without radical internal changes and with a Fabian-style working-class participation in political affairs.

What actually happens is quite different, and tends to aggravate the instability of the middle class. In the first place, it lacks the internal cohesion of the upper class, which not only still dominates strategic sectors of the economy but has firm control over the symbols of prestige. Secondly, it can no longer fulfil the only promises it is able to formulate to the masses whose organization is now increasing dangerously, in contrast to the middle class's own institutional weakness.

It is necessary at this point to introduce a word of warning—even though this is not the place to go more fully into the matter—in view of the tendency of many interpreters to refer to the 'massification' of the Latin American societies which we are considering; [105] one must be careful to distinguish between the points of view of the observer and the person observed, even though they may use similar terminology. It is in this case that the observation of Raymond Williams is particularly appropriate: 'There are in fact no masses; there are only ways of seeing people as masses'.[106] To the oligarchies at the turn of the century, the 'masses' were the rising middle classes, just as for the latter the 'masses' are now the rural and urban workers: 'if you disapprove of the changes you can, it seems, avoid open opposition to democracy as such by inventing a new category, mass-democracy, which is not such a good thing at all'.[107]

In these conditions, and in spite of the objective indicators of 'massification' that the observer may detect, the concept of the masses does not express a general tendency towards levelling but merely identifies the proletariat, conceived as such by the propertied classes regardless of the degree of internal solidarity that those masses have been able to achieve.

---

[105] Thus, Torcuato S. Di Tella and others, eds, *Argentina, sociedad de masas* (Buenos Aires, 1965).
[106] Raymond Williams, *Culture and Society* (London, 1958), p. 300.
[107] Ibid. p. 299.

If we concentrate our attention on the low level of class-conscious-ness of the new working class, we are apt to forget that an essential ingredient in a social class, as T. H. Marshall has emphasized, is the way in which a man is treated by his neighbour. I do not mean by this that the Latin American political struggle will assume the form of the nineteenth-century conflicts: both the context and the protagonists have changed greatly. Nevertheless, as the populist atmosphere wears off, the central contradiction takes visible shape in somewhat similar terms. For this reason, even though Furtado may be right in emphasizing the differences in revolutionary potential between the urban and the rural workers,[108] it is worth remembering that the continued existence of such differences is a function of the ideological vigour of the dualistic structure as a confusing form assumed by Latin American capitalist development. On the economic plane, the underlying unity of the process is increasingly revealed by the chronic tendency to stagnation; on the political plane, it is the alliance of the middle class with the oligarchy that fully reveals that unity.

The Middle-Class Military Coup

Schumpeter maintained that 'without protection by some non-bourgeois group, the bourgeoisie is politically helpless and unable not only to lead its nation but even to take care of its particular class interest. Which amounts to saying that it needs a master.' [109] He was obviously referring to Great Britain, in view of the 'pro-tective' flexibility with which the aristocracy managed to adapt itself to the rise of the bourgeoisie.[110] Moreover, in the case of France, the disintegration at the time of the Revolution of the traditional 'protecting strata' was responsible for the high degree of instability that characterized the nineteenth century. However, in order to understand the peculiar synthesis achieved by the Third

---

[108] Cf. Furtado, 'Reflections on the Brazilian Pre-Revolution', in Horowitz, pp. 62–73.

[109] Joseph A. Schumpeter, *Capitalism, Socialism, and Democracy* (London, 1947), p. 138.

[110] So decisive was this factor, that it has recently been argued that the British bourgeoisie never succeeded in becoming a hegemonic group. See Perry Anderson, 'Origins of the Present Crisis', *New Left R.*, 23, 26–53. For a discussion of the existence of a protecting Establishment in the United States as well, see the interesting study by Andrew Hacker, 'Liberal Democracy and Social Control', *American Political Science R.*, 5/1 (1957), 1009–26.

Republic—which 'was throughout, in spirit and operation, middle class rather than either aristocratic or peasant or proletarian' [111]— it must be borne in mind that in France too there existed a 'protecting stratum', namely, the civil service, the pre-revolutionary organization of which was maintained almost intact, and which established an element of continuity which has lasted through five republics and two empires.[112]

If Schumpeter's proposition is valid for a *'bourgeoisie conquérante'*, it must be even more so in the case of a class fragmented by the particularism of its outlook and formed in a context of bargaining and compromises. For this reason, translated into the terms of this theory, my thesis is that in the Latin American countries we are considering, owing to the absence of an English-style adaptation facilitated by a remarkable economic development, and also of a French-style bureaucracy capable of absorbing the shocks originating from political conflict, it is the armed forces which assume the responsibility of protecting the middle class. It was with their support that the middle class achieved, at the beginning of the century, political recognition from the oligarchy; it was with their protection that it later consolidated itself in power; and now it is with their intervention that it seeks to ward off the threat posed by the popular sectors that it is incapable of leading.

This explains the continuous civilian pressure in favour of military intervention, which a mere chronicle of the events rarely reveals.[113] Although he does not draw all the possible conclusions from his assertion, Imaz observes:

Thus, the appeal to the armed forces as a source of legitimation— quite apart from all the other explanations given—has become a tacit rule of the Argentine political game. It is a rule that no one explicitly invokes, but from which all political groups have benefited at least once. Publicly they would all deny the existence of such a rule, but

---

[111] David Thomson, *Democracy in France* (London, 1958), p. 58.

[112] Compare Charles Frankel, 'Bureaucracy and Democracy in the New Europe', in Stephen R. Graubard, ed., *A New Europe?* (Cambridge, Mass., 1964), p. 541. See also Stanley Hoffman, 'Paradoxes of the French Political Community', in Hoffman and others, *In Search of France* (Cambridge, Mass., 1963), pp. 1–117.

[113] The reader has only to glance at the Argentine or Brazilian press in the months before the recent military coups. An analysis of the contents of such publications as *Confirmado, Primera Plana,* or *Estado de São Paulo* would be extremely revealing.

in reality it can never be ignored by Argentine politicians, who, at one time or another during this quarter of a century, have all gone to knock on the door of the barracks.[114]

The oligarchy, of course, has recourse to this expedient, and attempts to influence the military in its favour. However, the history of the coups that have taken place in the twentieth century shows that the military have only exceptionally shown a tendency to act as the representatives of the oligarchy. In other words, if the connexion between the upper class and military interventionism serves to explain an exceptional case such as the overthrow of Yrigoyen advocated also by the middle class, nevertheless, it is the connexion between the army and the interests and values of the middle class which explains most of the remaining interventions.

Thus, failure to emphasize and distinguish between the structural factors that cause the chronic instability of this class and its *penchant* for interventionism can be doubly misleading; first, because it prevents a full understanding of the peculiar characteristics of Latin American political development, and thus fails to relate to their historical context the very concepts of parliamentary democracy and of the middle class; [115] and, secondly, because it leads the observer to treat the armed forces as external factors, who interfere with the supposed normal evolution of a political process, either through personal ambition or because they have been beguiled by the upper class into serving its interests. The problem is inevitably reduced to psychological terms, and the political development of Latin America comes to be interpreted as depending less on social transformation than on a change of mentality on the part of the army officers.

Provisional Stability

We must now make brief reference to the cases of Uruguay, Chile, and Mexico. Although, as I pointed out above, the army

---

[114] Imaz, p. 84.

[115] This is the fundamental mistake made by studies which attempt to describe in the abstract the developmentalist strategy of a middle-class élite. Compare Clark Kerr and others, *Industrialism and Industrial Man* (Cambridge, Mass., 1960), ch. iii. One thus loses sight of the essentially relational nature of the notion of social class. Compare Stanislaw Ossowski, *Class Structure in the Social Consciousness*, tr. S. Patterson (London, 1963), p. 133.

in these countries supported the rise to power of the middle class, their apparent political neutrality since that event seems to constitute an objection to my main argument, which up to now has been principally illustrated by reference to the cases of Argentina and Brazil. I believe, however, that it can be seen to corroborate my argument, if we identify certain peculiar characteristics on which this a-political behaviour is based.

In Uruguay, the civil war at the beginning of the century resulted in the triumph of the middle class through a tacit pact with the oligarchy, the interests of the stock-breeders being so scrupulously respected that—although it was a country based on agriculture and stock-raising—there was no direct taxation based on land-holding which might have affected that sector.[116] Besides this compromise with a comparatively weak traditional sector, the government of Batlle embarked on an intensive process of centralization and modernization of the state, transforming it from then on into the 'common denominator' of Uruguayan life,[117] to a degree then unknown in other Latin American countries. As in the case of France, a civil bureaucracy was consolidated and became the backbone of the system. In 1961 it was calculated that 21·1 per cent of the active population was employed in the public sector,[118] which has undoubtedly created a strong complex of interests in favour of stability, and has diffused throughout the country that middle-class outlook that has become associated with Uruguay. Another contributory factor was the satisfactory rate of growth achieved by Batlle's *étatiste* programme initially, and later by the benefits deriving from a process of import-substitution accompanied by thriving foreign trade. In this context, most middle-class aspirations have been connected with the obtaining of better government employment, and the patronage system of the political parties and state paternalism have been appropriate instruments for the satisfaction of these demands.

These and other factors which have helped to make the case of Uruguay exceptional have become less operative in recent years. First, the reduced size of the internal market resulted in a rapid exhaustion of the process of import-substitution; and, secondly, as in the case of Argentina, the persistence of an agrarian

[116] Johnson, *Political Change in Latin America* (Stanford UP, 1958), p. 61.
[117] Solari, p. 167.
[118] Ibid. p. 136.

structure based on big estates has caused a fall in productivity in
the rural sector, to such an extent that since 1943 there has been
no increase in the volume of the essential exports of meat and wool.
The result is complete economic stagnation, and the gross product
per capita has remained practically stationary for the last twenty
years. This has coincided with a period of intense rural migration,
accompanied by the familiar 'revolution of rising expectations'.
Once again the public sector has tried to canalize these pressures:
the numbers of people employed by it grew between 1955 and 1961
at a rate of 2·6 per cent per year, and the private sector by only
0·9 per cent. As Solari observes, 'it is now a question of how long
the state can continue to fulfil this function'.[119]   One of the first
symptoms of the disintegration of Uruguay's *aurea mediocritas* was
the victory in 1958 of the *Blanco* Party, which replaced the *Colorados* who had enjoyed ninety-three consecutive years of power.[120]
In this decade, industrial conflicts have become more frequent,
and some civilian sectors have significantly begun to urge a military
intervention to thwart the 'Communist menace'.[121]

In the case of Chile, the expansion of the foreign-owned nitrate
and copper concerns resulted in a rapid increase in the public sector,
since owing to the system of taxation 'it was the government and
not the native owners of the exporting sector which was the agent
administering, spending and distributing a considerable proportion
of the revenue generated by foreign trade'.[122]   To these elements—
which lend the Chilean case some of the characteristics previously
mentioned of the French and British cases—there were added two
circumstances that are especially relevant to this discussion: first,
the reduced size of the Chilean political arena—until 1946, the
number of voters never exceeded 8–9 per cent of the population; [123]
secondly, and for this very reason, the fact that the system made it

[119] Ibid. p. 156.
[120] See Carlos M. Rama, 'La crisis política uruguaya', *Ciencias políticas y
sociales*, 5/16 (1959), pp. 233–42.
[121] For a significant appeal to the army from the left, see Carlos María
Gutiérrez, 'Reflexión para los militares uruguayos', *Marcha*, 16 Oct.
1965, p. 11: 'In contrast to the generals, voicing official policy and
given to political bickering, subservient to United States strategy and
fearful of the economic and social transformation for which the
people are clamouring, one observes the different attitude of the
junior officers, who realize the stupidity of the way the country is
being governed.'
[122] Aníbal Pinto, *Chile, una economía difícil* (Mexico City, 1964), p. 160.
[123] See Gil, p. 213.

possible to pass on the benefits derived from mining and the first stage of industrialization to those popular sectors which participated in political life, thus facilitating their acceptance of the rules of the game. It is worth noting, for instance, that 'Chile is probably the only country in the world that instituted a legal minimum salary long before a minimum wage'.[124] In other words, the military interventions of the 1920s consolidated the power of the middle class *vis-à-vis* a particularly flexible oligarchy; this régime integrated a limited proportion of the population into the national political system ('probably about a fifth to a quarter of all Chileans live in what we think of as a modern society') [125] and, at the same time, gave it access to its benefits.

It is not necessary to emphasize that I have pointed out only a few of the factors that explain Chile's stability: despite everything, it may be noted that every broadening of the political framework has been accompanied by the threat of its complete breakdown: between 1946 and 1952 the number of voters increased by 75 per cent, and in the latter year, in a context of open rejection of the parties of the Establishment, Carlos Ibáñez was elected; between 1958 and 1964 the electorate increased by a further 78 per cent, the entire political spectrum was displaced Leftwards, and the Christian Democrats were elected on a platform which can certainly be described as populist. Moreover, the Chilean economy has been virtually stagnant since 1954. In these circumstances, it seems safe to assume that, in the short term, stability will be maintained as long as the government succeeds in preserving a compromise with the higher levels of the urban wage-earning sector. However,

the political significance of these groups as spokesmen for the working class as a whole has . . . been small and has probably been decreasing, especially since the stagnation of the Chilean economy during the last decade began to reduce the opportunities of employment and to endanger the standards of living which these groups had gained for themselves.[126]

---

[124] Albert O. Hirschman, *Journeys towards Progress* (New York, 1965), p. 264. The law establishing minimum salaries for employees was passed in 1937, whereas this measure was extended to the workers only in 1955.

[125] Silvert, 'Some Propositions on Chile', in Robert D. Tomasek, ed., *Latin American Politics* (New York, 1966), p. 387.

[126] Osvaldo Sunkel, 'Change and Frustration in Chile', in Veliz, p. 129.

It is, therefore, probable that the pressures exercised by the lower strata of the urban and rural proletariat will become stronger in the future and—if the government fails to satisfy their demands— may cause breakdown of the stability which a limited degree of democracy has made possible in Chile. Thus conditions would again favour a middle-class military coup, the possibility of which was widely rumoured when an electoral triumph of the *Frente de Acción Popular* was feared.

Finally, with regard to Mexico, as we have already observed: 'apart from the important peasant group of Zapata's followers which remained politically marginal until the assassination of Carranza, the Mexican Revolution from the outset had middle-class leanings.' [127] The historical importance of the movement— and what made it exceptional in the Latin American context until the Bolivian and Cuban revolutions occurred—lies in its elimination of the landowning oligarchy. It thus opened the way to the formation of an authentic bourgeoisie, with an original normative structure and a collective sense of direction capable of mobilizing the politically active part of the population. As a further illustration of the difference between the form and the content of social institutions, in this case it was not a liberal state but an interventionist one that organized the hegemony of the bourgeoisie, while at the same time the atmosphere of the revolution lent a 'universality' to its particularist aspirations. This explains the misgivings expressed by a decided supporter of the movement:

This bourgeoisie has realized its potential, has become strong and becomes stronger with every day that passes, not only in the national sphere but in the international as well . . . and, like every bourgeoisie, it tends not only to become independent of the force that created it, the government, but to convert the latter into a mere instrument of its interests; the government thus ceases to be a mediator, capable of balancing the interests of the bourgeoisie against those of the rest of the nation.[128]

In this process, the armed forces played a decisive role, and their present neutrality is in fact a function of the consolidation of the

[127] Moisés González Navarro, 'Mexico: The Lop-Sided Revolution', in Veliz, p. 226.
[128] Leopoldo Zea, 'La Revolución, el gobierno y la democracia', *Ciencias políticas y sociales*, 5/18 (1959), p. 543.

hegemony of the bourgeoisie: [129] 'the military element is the permanent reserve of order; it is a force which acts "in a public way" when "legality" is threatened.' [130] The greatest problem facing this 'legality' is the fact that at least 50 per cent of the population has been denied the benefits of development: [131] 'the self-same people who made the agrarian revolution, or their descendants, have little but poverty for their reward now that the revolution has passed into the industrial stage because it has been channelled through the capitalist system.' [132] The stability of Mexico, therefore, depends much less on the good humour of its generals than on the ability of its bourgeoisie to incorporate these internal colonies into the life of the nation.

The External Factor

Up to this point I have avoided referring to external pressures in favour of military intervention because it is these internal factors that determine the efficacy of any external pressure that may be brought to bear.

I mean by this that the density of social relationships in the countries under discussion is such as to make highly improbable a military coup pure and simple, in the sense that a group of officers supported by the United States Embassy seizes control of the government at midnight. The size and complexity of the military establishment, combined with the frequent divergences of opinion among the officers themselves, tend to make relatively impracticable a *putsch* that does not enjoy a relatively high degree of consensus.

---

[129] It is interesting to note that the structure established by Cárdenas for the *Partido de la Revolución Mexicana* increased the similarity of this case to the socialist model of civil-military relations. The PRM, in practice, comprised four sectors: agrarian; workers; popular; and military. In other words, the armed forces, whose officers in any case held at that time over half the posts in the government, were considered to be an active part of the political system. However, this sector was dissolved in 1940 after three years of existence, and the officers holding elective posts were absorbed into the popular sector. 'This does not mean that the army divorced itself from politics. On the contrary, having returned to its old position behind the throne, the military's role in Mexican politics has remained strong and partisan' (Robert E. Scott, *Mexican Government in Transition* (Urbana, Ill., 1964), p. 134).

[130] Gramsci, *Notas sobre Maquiavelo*, p. 81.

[131] Cf. Pablo González Casanova, *La democracia en México* (Mexico City, 1965), p. 81.

[132] González Navarro, in Veliz, p. 228.

With this consideration in mind,[133] two points must now be emphasized. The first directly concerns the armed forces: namely, the extent to which their outlook is influenced by the strategic revolution closely linked to the development of the Cold War and the rise of national-liberation-front movements. It is in this sense that Horowitz is right when he affirms that 'United States policies of military globalism tend to make obsolete earlier efforts at a standard typology of Latin American military styles and forms based exclusively on internal political affairs '.[134] Here we are not only considering the greatly expanded programmes of military aid, but the fact that, since 1961, the United States has reappraised the basic policy underlying such aid, replacing the principle of Hemispheric defence—for which it assumes sole responsibility— by that of internal security.[135]

What is most important to remember is that, by definition, the counterinsurgency operational projects blur the distinction between the military and the political spheres of action. In the context of the *guerre dans la foule*—a permanent war, which need not be declared—there is no longer any sense in the classical distinction according to which the civil power was responsible for the direction of the war and the military power for the conduct of military operations. In such a war, since the enemy is not immediately recognizable, his identification depends on the military operations themselves; this limits considerably the sphere of civilian decision.

In other words, political intervention has now become, for the Latin American officer, a matter of professional interest. In this connexion, it would be interesting to study the probable increase of the potential conflict of loyalties already mentioned: to the

---

[133] It is important to relate this consideration to the new forms assumed by imperialist activities, especially the growing tendency to replace direct investment by various types of association with local concerns. This is even more valid in the case of the relatively advanced countries such as those we have been describing, and it is symptomatic of the internalization of the external influence to which I have referred in the text. See Hamza Alavi, 'Imperialism, Old and New', in John Saville and Ralph Miliband, eds, *The Socialist Register* (London, 1964), pp. 116 ff.

[134] Irving L. Horowitz, *The Military of Latin America* (mimeo), p. 45. Horowitz analyses in detail the incidence of the external factor, and I therefore refer the reader to his work, which will appear in Lipset and Solari, eds, *Elites in Latin America*.

[135] Cf. Lieuwen, *Generals vs. Presidents*, pp. 114 ff.

organization and to their profession. The tactics of imperialism may affect one more than the other, in so far as it may concentrate on the sending of missions to the country concerned, or on inviting selected officers for training in its own establishments. One may hazard a conjecture that the second alternative will be preferred in the case of the more advanced countries of the continent, where direct manipulation of the military establishment as such would not be so easy. This accounts for the increased importance attributed by the United States military academies to the political indoctrination of their Latin American guests.[136]

I said above that I would draw the reader's attention to two points. The second of these is, in fact, essential to an understanding of the first. I refer to the particular vulnerability of the Latin American middle class in the face of the strategies used during the Cold War. This corresponds exactly to the worsening of its relations with the popular sectors, and thus systematic anti-communism appears as the kind of rationalization most appropriate to its interests. Moreover as a correlative of the absence of any vocation for hegemony among its various component fractions, the middle class only achieves a precarious unity on the basis of negative principles. It is opposed to corruption and to communism, without realizing that the former is a function of the irrationality of the system that the middle class helps to perpetuate, while the latter is merely the name that its own fears give to the aspirations of the popular sectors. This sufficiently explains why, in the five countries under discussion, it is in those where the middle class is least stable and feels most threatened that this type

[136] 'Dr McAlister: I would like to ask a simple-minded question about it. As conceived, is this primarily done for military or for political purposes? The college, that is. [He is referring to the Inter-American Defense College, Fort McNair, Washington, where about thirty-five Latin American officers receive training every five months.]—Col. Hicks: I imagine I can respond to that. Anything that we do in the military I believe has a political overtone to it.—Dr McAlister: Right.—Col. Hicks: And we are . . .—Dr Milburn (interposing): That is one of the more sophisticated statements I have heard made at the conference. (Laughter).—Col. Hicks: So definitely there is a political connotation to the school.—Dr McAlister: But is it just a connotation?—Col. Hicks: Yes' (U.S. Naval Ordnance Test Station, *A Symposium on Military Elites in Latin America*, ed. Louis D. Higgs (China Lake, Calif., Mar. 1965), pp. 137–8). Referring to the training received by the officers at this College, Lieuwen observes: 'They are taught much about Communism here but little about democracy' (*Generals vs. Presidents*, p. 148 n.).

of outlook most flourishes. It was a Brazilian officer, General Golberi do Couto e Silva, who formulated the 'ideological frontiers' doctrine, and an Argentine officer, General Onganía, who demonstrated enthusiastic adherence to it.

Some Conclusions

Precisely because the military establishment is inseparable from the society surrounding it, it is legitimate to infer in these cases a different pattern of civil-military relations from those described at the beginning of this essay. Military interventionism does not threaten the middle class (as in the liberal model), nor is it a substitute for its absence (as in the developmentalist model); it tends to represent that class and compensate for its inability to establish itself as a well-integrated hegemonic group.

Several consequences follow from this interpretation.

1. The ideologists of the middle class—whose interests, according to one partisan observer, coincide not only with those of Latin America but also with those of humanity in general [137]—would be wrong to interpret my analysis as a justification of interventionism; I have, on the contrary, tried to demonstrate why the middle class is not in a position to contribute to the development of these countries. Moreover, in its present form military interventionism tends to prevent rather than favour the possibility of certain sectors of that class ever transcending their profoundly traditional outlook.

In this connexion, the observation of Gramsci is perfectly valid when he distinguishes between 'progressive' and 'regressive' varieties of Caesarism.[138] Despite its compromising and its limitations, the first variety does assist the consolidation of new social groups, whereas the second tries to preserve the elements of a social order that has exhausted its possibilities of development. This is the fundamental difference between a Vargas and a Castelo Branco.

Just at the moment when the loss of the dynamic impulse of the import-substitution model is creating the objective conditions for ending the agrarian-industrial pact, free elections are becoming an essential instrument of political bargaining, which makes possible the gradual union of the progressive groups. This possibility is,

[137] Víctor Alba, 'La nouvelle classe moyenne latinoaméricaine', *La Revue socialiste*, 133 (1960), p. 468.
[138] Gramsci, *Notas sobre Maquiavelo*, pp. 84 ff.

however, eliminated by the fears of the upper and middle classes; it is for this reason that both the Brazilian and the Argentine military governments have lost no time in suspending the electoral process, and are tending to search for forms of functional representation which avoid the risk inherent in normal elections.[139]

We are not concerned here with advocating territorial representation in the abstract, nor must corporativism in general be identified with one of its manifestations, i.e. fascism. However, given the present degree of development of the societies I am considering, the danger inherent in projects of this kind is that they constitute an institutional 'freezing' of a system of relationships which must be changed. For this reason, the price that is paid for reducing the electoral influence of the popular sectors is the maintenance of the self-same structure that has led to the crisis. Therefore, not only is this a transitory solution, since it does not deal with the fundamental causes of the problem, but it already reveals what it leads to in the long term: as the tendency to stagnation increases, so will popular discontent, and the corporativist system will develop an increasingly Rightwards bias. This will happen even though, in the short term, fortuitous movements of economic expansion—due, for instance, to a temporary fluctuation in the foreign market—may favour compromises with trade union organizations of a reformist outlook.

2. The other point worth mentioning is the possibility of a 'Nasserist' variant; this is a frequent theme in present-day Latin American writing.

There are, of course, two possible meanings of the term Nasserism. One of them, on an extremely vague and theoretical level, applies the term to any military group whose objectives are 'a mixture of radical independence, the reconquest of national identity and emphasis on social progress'.[140] According to this interpretation,

---

[139] Referring to the corporativist tendencies in Latin America, a writer observes: 'The major social purpose of the syndicalist approach is to find a way of subsuming the new class complications of modernism to hierarchy, preserving a kind of Latin *Führerprinzip*, leaving inviolate the privileges and powers of the traditional, and thus escaping the secularization and, to their eyes, immorality of the nation-State' (Silvert, 'National Values, Development, and Leaders and Followers' *International Social Science Journal*, 15/4 (1963), p. 563).

[140] Anuar Abdel Malek, 'Nasserismo y socialismo', in R. García Lupo, ed. 1, *Nasserismo y marxismo* (Buenos Aires, 1965), p. 186.

Kemal Ataturk and Perón were Nasserists '*avant la lettre* '. Obviously, this greatly reduces the scientific usefulness of the concept, because what it gains in general applicability it loses in precision.

The other meaning, however, is specific, and refers to one prototype of national development—the Egyptian—and is the only one that appears relevant to a concrete analysis. From this point of view, I believe that the Nasserist variant as such is inapplicable in the context of these countries. I will give briefly some of the reasons on which I base this assertion, leaving out of account obvious ethnic and religious differences between the two contexts.

In the first place—as in the Afro-Asian model in general—the degree of integration of the Egyptian army into the society around it was considerably less than in the case of Latin America. It should be remembered that, after the defeat of the precursory movement led by Ahmad al-'Urabi in 1882, Egypt underwent for seventy-four years, in one form or another, British military occupation. This not only limited the opportunities for natives in the military profession, but deprived this career of patriotic appeal. As recently as 1936 the Anglo-Egyptian Treaty reopened the Military Academy to the sons of the petty bourgeoisie—especially the rural petty bourgeoisie—and it was then that Nasser and most of the future Free Officers entered the army.[141] In addition to this lack of integration of the Egyptian officer into the context of the influential sectors in the country, there was also the impact of the immediate colonial situation and, later, the 'experience of the concrete Fatherland'[142] as a result of the disastrous Palestine campaign.

In addition to these peculiar characteristics, it is necessary to take into account the circumstances of the country. In 1952 Egypt was an essentially agricultural country, with nearly 70 per cent of the population consisting of *fellahs*,[143] a per capita income of under $120, nearly 80 per cent illiteracy, and an industry contributing only 10 per cent of the gross national product.[144] At the same time, as a consequence of underdevelopment and foreign control

---

[141] Cf. Bernard Vernier, 'L'évolution du régime militaire en Égypte', *Revue française de science politique*, 13/3 (1963), p. 604.

[142] Jean Ziegler, *Sociologie de la nouvelle Afrique* (Paris, 1964), p. 294.

[143] Abdel Malek, *Égypte—société militaire* (Paris, 1962), p. 26.

[144] Charles Issawi, *Egypt in Revolution* (London, 1963), pp. 46–47.

over important sectors of the economy, there was an absence of national bureaucratic and entrepreneurial cadres.

Finally, the degree of popular participation in the system was extremely low. Thus, one writer observes:

> It is incorrect to argue that the old regimes in Egypt and Syria were overthrown because the people ceased to accept their legitimacy. Legitimacy was not yet an issue in nations in which few classes and groups of the population had entered politics at all. In spite of the constitutional formula for male suffrage in both countries, the predominantly poor and illiterate masses did not achieve a high voting rate, and to expect from them active and discerning participation in political affairs would be absurd.[145]

It will be observed that we have here the characteristics peculiar to the developmentalist model, with the addition of the colonial factor, which tended to increase the nationalism of this first generation of Egyptian officers drawn from the popular sectors. Given this context, it is understandable that, after the 1952 movement, the army should become, in theory and in practice, 'the real backbone of the state',[146] and that the degree of mobilization of the urban and rural workers should be very limited. At the same time it explains the extreme economic liberalism which characterized the first phase of the Revolution (1952–6), when desperate efforts were made to attract foreign capital and thus encourage the incipient industrialization process.

The nationalization of the Suez Canal Company represented the watershed of the régime, and its change of orientation was further emphasized by the legislation of 1961 and 1963, which transferred 80 per cent of industry to state ownership.[147] But it is precisely now, when Egypt has succeeded in doubling its industrial production, that the future success of Nasserism depends on its ability to supersede the factors that have characterized it hitherto. In other words: the previous absence of popular participation, to which I referred above, and an especially favourable international situation—due, above all, to Soviet support—made it possible to liquidate the aristocracy and the foreign interests ' "from above", bureaucratically, without the bourgeois revolution being obliged

---

[145] See P. J. Vatikiotis, *The Egyptian Army in Politics* (Bloomington, Ind., 1961), pp. 99–100.

[146] Ziegler, p. 347.

[147] Abdel Malek, in García Lupo, p. 170.

to resolve the problem of democracy and that of the rural sector'.[148]
It is this specific development of Nasserism that establishes the
limits of the movement.   Therefore, Abdel Malek is correct in
thus summarizing the alternatives now facing the régime:

> the choice is between, on the one hand, a coalition of the two currents
> of the national movement—Nasserism and Egyptian Marxism—which
> would allow Egypt to realize to the full its potential internally, in the
> Arab world, and in the global struggle against Imperialism, and to
> take the first steps towards socialism; and, on the other hand, the
> elimination of these possibilities by the combined action of the pro-
> imperialist forces in the Arab world and the reactionary forces inside
> the Egyptian establishment.[149]

It is obvious, even from this brief outline, that there is a great
difference between the Egyptian case and that of the Latin American
countries under discussion, as regards the integration of the military
into civilian society, a much higher degree of popular participation,
and the absence of an immediate colonial experience.   The most
important factor, however, is the greatly superior level of development as compared with Egypt in 1952; in the Latin American
countries under discussion, therefore, the chief problem is not that
of introducing technical innovations but of organizing rationally
and establishing social control over those that already exist.

Whereas the slogan *enrichissez-vous* coined in the Europe of
the nineteenth century simultaneously fulfilled a social function,
creating new techniques of production and imposing on society as
a whole a growing need for rationalization, first formal and later
substantive, in the conditions of Latin American economic growth
the principle of private profit has resulted in a considerable increase
in the irrationality and imbalance of the system.   A good illustration of this is the 'over-equipment' of the modern sector of industry
by imported labour-saving machinery, that is to say, machines
which economize on what is precisely the most abundant factor.
This made it necessary to give protection to the small quasi-craft
industries which, even if they operate with very low productivity,
give employment to a considerable proportion of the labour force
otherwise threatened with technological unemployment.   This
resulted in a division of the market in the only practicable way,

[148] Hassan Riad, 'Las tres edades de la sociedad egipcia', in García Lupo,
pp. 38–107.
[149] Abdel Malek, in García Lupo, p. 188.

that of regulating the system of prices in accordance with the high costs of the least efficient concerns. These have therefore managed to survive, while modern businesses make profit margins high enough to compensate them for maintaining in idleness a part of their installed capacity; which is clearly prejudicial to the interests of society as a whole. That is why these economies have suffered all the disadvantages of a paramonopolistic market structure,[150] without enjoying the benefits of increased productivity that have resulted from such a structure in the developed capitalist countries. Moreover, this increases the dependence of industry on the traditional exports: since it is prevented by its high costs from competing in the international market, the primary sector still has to be relied on to supply the foreign exchange the country needs.

At the risk of over-simplifying the problem, it can, therefore, be asserted that these countries have already passed the Nasserist stage as far as their industrial expansion is concerned—and also as regards the degree of popular mobilization—though not as regards the confrontation with the oligarchy and the foreign interests. The immediate task facing the continent is the appropriation for social ends of the potential economic excedent, through a radical transformation of its existing structures.[151] However, both the level of development and of institutional complexity, and the vulnerability of various sectors of the army to pressures exercised by the beneficiaries of the *status quo* would appear to condemn to failure a revolution 'from above' directed by the armed forces. It must be remembered that, in order to succeed, such a movement would have to acquire a populist character; and the stagnation of the economy,

---

[150] ECLA, *Problemas y perspectivas* . . . , pp. 22–24. For a perceptive analysis of the distortions of Latin American industrialization, see Aníbal Pinto, 'Concentración del progreso técnico y de sus frutos en el desarrollo latinoamericano', *El Trimestre económico*, 32/1, No. 125 (1965), pp. 3–69.

[151] For an analysis of the concept of 'potential economic excedent', see Paul A. Baran, *The Political Economy of Growth* (New York, 1957). In this connexion, it is necessary to submit to objective examination the supposed need for foreign capital in these countries. This is generally the 'technical' pretext for operations that provide good profits for foreign investors and at the same time help to preserve the *status quo*. For a demonstration of the fallacy of the argument see among others, the excellent study of the Chilean case included in Nicholas Kaldor, *Essays on Economic Policy* (London, 1964), ii. 233–87.

the fears of the propertied classes, and the increased maturity of the urban and rural proletariat all militate against such a development.

Even if there are in Latin America groups of officers of a Nasserist outlook—which seems doubtful—and supposing that the present character of the groups in the higher command remains unchanged, their position would necessarily be very weak; and to imagine that, in the countries we have considered, such officers could come into power by means of a coup, would be to transfer into the military sphere the Utopianism that underlies advocacy of the 'Cuban way' in the civilian sphere.

It is precisely the potential existence of such a fraction among the army officers—I am now referring to the more general meaning attached to the term Nasserism—that can encourage confidence in an alternative to violent revolution, which both the international situation and internal factors (among them, the very strength of the armed forces) render, for the moment, impracticable.   In Latin America, however, the efficacy of such a progressive group cannot make itself felt *before*—as in the Egyptian case—but only *after* an intensive mobilization of the popular sectors.   It is on this, and not in any *appel au soldat*—which, thus, introduces an element of confusion—that the success of a coalition based on a programme of revolutionary reforms will depend.[152]   And it is the struggle to achieve such a programme that can lead to the organization, from below, of a new hegemonic consciousness capable of putting an end to the crisis.

De Tocqueville once said that 'it is not in the army that one can find the remedy for the ills of the army, but in the country'.[153] In this study I have tried to give a contemporary twist to this proposition in the context under discussion; the concluding reflection would be that 'neither is it in the army that one can find the remedy for the ills of the country'.

July 1966.

---

[152] The idea of 'revolutionary reformism' is discussed by, among others, André Gorz, *Stratégie ouvrière et néo-capitalisme* (Paris, 1965), and Lucio Magri, 'Le modèle de développement capitaliste et le problème de "l'alternative" prolétarienne', *Les Temps modernes*, nos. 196–7 (1962), pp. 583–626.

[153] Alexis de Tocqueville, *De la démocratie en Amérique* (Paris, 1963), Bk ii, ch. 26, p. 349.

University Students in National Politics

ALISTAIR HENNESSY

*Desgraciado el pueblo donde los jóvenes son humildes con
el tirano, donde los estudiantes no hacen temblar al mundo.*
JUAN MONTALVO

LATIN Americans have learnt to live with turbulent student activity
much as the Middle Ages learned to live with the plague. It is a
recurring phenomenon liable to burst out at a moment's notice;
sometimes dying down as suddenly as it erupts, sometimes dragging
on and exhausting all those involved. But the analogy is unjust;
what appears as a disease or as wilful irresponsibility is often the
genuine expression, in an unjust society, of a frustrated younger
generation, turning to political action with a fervour compounded
of opportunism, malaise, and genuine idealism as a means of finding
its identity. Precisely for this reason it is unrealistic to expect
students to eschew politics and embrace a new professionalism
based on the needs of a technical revolution so long as they are
enmeshed in an outworn and unreformed university system.

Cuba is still the only country in Latin America to have brought
the university system into line with the needs of a developing
economy, and the Cuban assertion that university reform is impossible without a total social and political revolution has yet to
be proved wrong. To a large number of Latin American students
this is a self-evident truth, and in order to hasten the process they
believe that universities must become more not less politicized.

The crucial issue in contemporary Latin America is education.
But this merely begs the question: education and politics are so
intertwined that it is difficult to say where one begins and the other
ends. Some universities are so politics ridden that they may justly

be described as political rather than academic institutions, but for a continent undergoing rapid social and economic change the political university is a luxury. Quite apart from the high rate of illiteracy and inadequate primary and secondary schooling, the university enrolment figures are sufficiently alarming—in 1960 only 3·1 per cent of the university age group (20–24) were receiving higher education (the United States equivalent is 34·9 per cent) and of these 522,100 students, 33 per cent were in Argentina alone.[1] This inadequacy, apart from the high drop-out rate and too many of the types of graduate that cannot be usefully employed, is striking. The economic implications of an educational system totally unable to meet the demands of economic development, and the political implications of students taking to the hills and to urban terrorism are obvious. Faced by Latin America's crisis in education we might well adapt Marx's dictum to 'a spectre is haunting Latin America'—the spectre of frustrated and wasted youth.

Perhaps the most notable gap in our knowledge of Latin American society is the lack of detailed analysis of the role of age and youth in the process of social change, and yet this society is one of the youngest in the world. Although there have been a number of surveys of student attitudes, very little work has been done on the actual mechanics of student politics.[2] Are the younger generation the key factor in the revolutionary equation, as the Cuban revolution might lead one to suppose, or are the Mexican

[1] *Tercera reunión interamericana de ministros de educación* (Washington, 1964), p. 36. Cf. also I. Rodríguez Bou, *La educación superior en América Latina* (Washington, PAU, 1963), pp. 43 ff. It might be objected that this is a false analogy, and that it would be more exact to compare figures with Asian or African countries, but not only has Latin America been independent for 150 years but the first universities were founded in the 1550s and now, in theory, state universities are open to all.

[2] The most detailed study is that on Chile by F. Bonilla, a shortened version of which is in *J. of Inter-American Studies* (1960), no. 2. General problems are discussed in E. Wight Bakke, 'Students on the March: the Cases of Mexico and Colombia', *Sociology of Education*, 37/3 (1964). An introductory discussion is S. Lipset, 'University Students and Politics in Underdeveloped Countries', *Minerva*, 3/1 (1964). See also the special issue on Student Politics of the *Comparative Education R.*, June 1966, ed. S. M. Lipset. For a bibliography see H. F. Dame and others, *The Political Influence of University Students in Latin America: an Analytical Survey of Research Studies and Related Literature* (Washington, 1965).

and Bolivian revolutions, where the role of youth was less apparent, more typical as models?

The influence exerted by student political groups is an unknown quantity. That students demonstrate, smash windows, burn buses, shoot policemen (or spit at Senator Robert Kennedy and howl down the President of Colombia) is certainly evidence of surplus energy, but is it anything more? The fact that they have been doing similar things since the second decade of the century against forces blocking change and against an uncomprehending older generation suggests that perhaps this is merely the form which their exuberance takes in Latin America. Whereas in meritocracies, affluent societies, and welfare states the frustrations of youth often take the form of aimless protest and the outrage of moral norms *pour épater le bourgeois*, in Latin America political protest is the tradition. It may be that what student movements do to prepare their members for their adult roles in highly politicized societies is more important than their revolutionary potential.[3] When one contrasts the self-confessed objectives of these protests—to remove the obstacles in the way of the march to the Promised Land—with the durability and flourishing state of these obstacles today, it can justifiably be asked—what does it all add up to? In trying to answer this question it is as well to be on guard against the students' own image of themselves. Their publications show them still to be prisoners of the reformist mythology which is, at one and the same time, a barrier to flexibility or to a change in attitude and a spur to further revolutionary effort.

Dr K. H. Silvert has suggested a fourfold division of situations governing the extent of student influence.[4] His general conclusion is that their political influence and role as an innovating élite is minimal in rudimentary social structures, increases with the rising

[3] Cf. K. N. Walker, 'La socialización política en las universidades latinoamericanas', *Revista Latinoamericana de Sociología*, 1/2 July 1965. This is based on surveys in Puerto Rico, Colombia, and Argentina.

[4] In J. J. Johnson, ed., *Continuity and Change in Latin America* (Stanford UP, 1964), pp. 222–4. The four categories are: (1) Situations of Stable Traditional Societies (Nicaragua, Haiti, and Paraguay); (2) Situations of Beginning of Modernization and Disarray (El Salvador, Guatemala, Ecuador, Peru, Dominican Republic, and Panama); (3) More Mature Situations of Temporary Resolution (Colombia, Venezuela, Bolivia); (4) Situations of Institutional Complexity and Relative Strength (Mexico, Argentina, Uruguay, Chile, Brazil, and Cuba).

complexity and disarray caused by modernization, declines with the demand for professionalism and again becomes minimal in situations of institutional complexity. But, as he himself is the first to admit, any categorization must appear simplistic unless historical conditioning factors are taken into account. It could be added that by seeking the influence on politics outside the university one may miss the crucial influence of politics inside the university and the complex interweaving of political interest with academic policy. How can students be described as a modernizing élite if their influence cannot even modernize the universities? Ultimately the interrelationship between academic matters and politics makes it artificial to try to separate these two strands; students' attitudes to political change can only be understood in the wider context of the university crisis and of the tradition of the University Reform Movement.

A major cause of student frustration is the academic inadequacy of the state universities, which are failing to cope with the demands made on them by the increasing pace of social change. At the root of this failure is the inability of universities to become fully professionalized in their teaching function. Part-time lecturers teaching irrelevant syllabuses to part-time students is not university education in any proper sense of the word. State universities often seem little more than vocational night schools geared to producing the minimal qualifications for entry into professions which the needs of the country no longer demand. Although it might be argued that developing societies can afford neither to pay full-time staff nor to lose their extra-mural services, the effect of amateur professors, however dedicated, on universities and students has been disastrous. Professors tend to skimp their teaching duties, to be out of touch with the latest developments in their subject (although this varies widely with the nature of the subject), and to have a minimal contact or relationship with their students. As comparatively little research is done in Latin American universities, they tend to be parasitic on foreign universities, dependents not explorers of the expanding frontiers of knowledge. In academic quality, as in material wealth, it seems that the rich countries are getting richer and the poor poorer. Although in the past it could be argued that industrial revolutions have occurred in spite of, rather than because of, university systems, today specialized development techniques and the urgency of unsolved problems place a great pressure on universities to produce modernizing élites—the more so as Latin American countries have been slow to produce indigenous entrepreneurs.

So far from contributing to economic and social development, universities, with a few notable exceptions, have become an obstacle to it; not only are they not producing enough good technical experts but the tensions generated within them disorient students and deflect their energies into often irrelevant and self-defeating political activities.[5]

The reasons for the university crisis are not easy to pinpoint. One of these is certainly the population explosion, coupled with rising expectations, which has already hit the secondary schools. Prejudice against technical and vocational schools has led to the overcrowding of academic secondary schools which can provide the entrée to the prestige professions. The roots of political extremism as well as of academic incompetence must be sought in these overcrowded state secondary schools where underpaid and socially undervalued teachers pass on their discontent to their pupils. Secondary school pupils are frequently politically conscious, fight elections, resort to strike action, and are often the most vociferous elements in street demonstrations.

The response of governments has been to increase the number of state universities but this is itself a further irritant. Most are on a shoe-string budget and can only raise expectations without satisfying them. Unless they are geared to serving their region they may become artificially isolated (as some older universities are already, such as Loja in Ecuador with its overblown law faculty and Bolivia's seven universities each with its own law faculty): if, on the other hand, they are too closely identified with regional interests they may become involved in the political struggle of the region against the central government. The federal university of Oriente in Venezuela is perhaps the most promising model but

[5] A general discussion of state universities can be found in Rudolph P. Atcon, *The Latin American University* (Washington, PAU, 1963); L. A. Sánchez, *La universidad en la América Latina* (Lima, 1962); A. M. Grompone, *Universidad oficial y universidad viva* (Mexico City, 1963). An interesting sociological analysis is L. Scherz García, *Una nueva universidad para América Latina* (Santiago, ORMEU, 1965). For an excellent analysis of the University of Montevideo see Aldo E. Solari (*Aportes*, no. 2, Oct. 1966).

few countries have Venezuela's resources to float an economically viable university able to attract a good teaching staff.

The Mexican case of the metropolitan university fulfilling a function of national integration is instructive. As originally developed by José Vasconcelos in the early 1920s, the university was designed to create a nationalist revolutionary consciousness, but the reluctance of students to return to the provinces after graduation has made this purpose self-defeating. The massive size of the National University (UNAM) has contributed to its academic instability. The most deplorable instance of this has been the success in May 1966 of student rioters in forcing the resignation of the Rector and deans of faculties, which shows both the difficulties facing a Rector determined to raise academic standards and the ramifications of PRI politics when the government failed to take a tough line against the rioters. This doubtless encouraged students at Culiacán and Morelia in October to try their strength too but in the latter case the government moved in troops and for the first time in many years forcibly occupied a university campus—significantly with scarcely any public outcry. Much of this provincial discontent is due to the way in which the smaller State universities are starved of talent and money but so far attempts to relieve pressure at UNAM by improving State universities have little to show. The case of the Technological University at Monterrey, with support from local industrialists, is a notable exception. Unless pressure at UNAM can be relieved and the standard of provincial universities raised, both will remain foci of discontent open to fomentation either by the extreme Left or by right-wing clerical groups.

It is too early to see how the Peruvian policy of establishing universities in remote regional centres will develop, but it is a straw in the wind that where student federations have been established they are already dominated by Peking-line communist sympathizers.[6]

---

[6] The first and most interesting of these, re-founded in 1962, is the university at Ayacucho where Quechua is obligatory and which is geared to serving the needs of the Sierra, but it has been hampered by shortage of funds and the extreme poverty of its students. The prohibition of partisan politics has been a dead letter since the resignation of its first rector, Fernando Romero, in 1962. The slow progress of Belaunde's reform programme as well as the equivocal behaviour of the APRA majority in Congress is playing into the hands of the 'pekineses' even in Lima.

Although, therefore, the emphasis in these universities is on technical training, their influence may be more significant politically. Whereas in the past the big metropolitan universities have been the main centres of political disturbances, now provincial universities, particularly where there is an awakened peasantry from whom some of their students are drawn, are becoming politically influential. In recent years there has been a growing number of disturbances at provincial universities in Mexico, Peru, Ecuador, and particularly Colombia. The sedate university of the sleepy colonial provincial city is an historical anachronism and universities like Cuzco, or the Universidad del Centro at Huancayo, the centre of the 1965 disturbances, could well become the power houses of rural revolution.

For their part, universities have responded to increased demand by stiffer degree examinations in order to prune dead wood, although the high drop-out rate seems to be caused by economic rather than academic factors. Attempts to tighten up examinations are strongly resisted by student organizations, supported by political parties, which argue that examinations and grading perpetuate class divisions by penalizing students from poor homes, who have suffered from bad teaching in overcrowded secondary schools and much of whose energy has to go into earning a living while they are studying. This playing down of academic competitiveness may also be related to the psychological fear of loss of face which poor performance entails.

Entrance examinations have also become more stringent and there is the serious problem of the failed examinee who feels himself rejected by society. This can have political repercussions. Thus in Peru, where there were four times as many applicants as places for 1965, associations of failed examinees have been patronized by political parties promising to exert influence on the examining boards, in return for political support. In the selection tests themselves politics can determine the choice of candidates, and this is believed to be the case at the San Marcos and Villarreal universities in Lima where APRA has seen its traditional dominance steadily being whittled away.

Some who fail to secure places but who have the economic resources are attracted to Argentine or Brazilian universities where entry is virtually unrestricted. The subsequent political influence of studying either in other Latin American countries or in the United States, Europe, or the Eastern bloc is difficult to determine. Spain tends to be the most popular choice because of language, cheapness, and deliberate Spanish attempts to strengthen cultural ties through the Instituto de Cultura Hispánica. Study there need not confirm conservative prejudices as Spanish universities are foci of radical agitation.[7] Nor can it be assumed that Latin American students in the United States will necessarily become wedded to the American way of life. Indeed, for those who return thence (and many of course do not) tensions caused by the contrast between an affluent and an underdeveloped society may actually foment anti-Americanism, based on the apparent hopelessness of reaching United States standards through democratic processes. Similarly, time spent in the Soviet Union need not necessarily produce dedicated communists. But whatever the political influence, a variety of differing educational experiences is not particularly advantageous for developing countries seeking their own solutions to domestic problems. Ultimately there is no substitute for domestic universities geared to serving the special needs of each country, but to blame the Latin American university impasse on the universities alone would be both unjust and an oversimplification.

The early hopes of the university reformers that universities would be the agents of social change have not been fulfilled and the gap between universities and governments is as wide now as it was when the Reform started nearly fifty years ago. It is not only that governments now resent the hostile and often irresponsible criticism from the academic sanctuaries, but they also resent the inability of universities to provide the technical experts required for development programmes. Forced to look abroad for the experts the universities cannot provide, they are then suspected of kowtowing to imperialist interests.

Academic reforms, however sensible, often run up against student opposition. Some universities have introduced a first-year general course both to offset inadequate pre-university preparation and also to try to divert students, during the first year, from over-crowded faculties like law into more socially useful technical

---

[7] Latin American students may themselves have contributed to this radicalization in the same way as the Reform Movement influenced those Spanish students in the late 1920s who spearheaded the attack against the Primo de Rivera dictatorship.

faculties. At the University of Concepción in Chile this reform has had some success; but in Guatemala, for example, it was resisted by the student federation on the ground that students could not afford to waste an extra year on studies unrelated to their chosen vocation. Changes in university structure, especially if based on a United States model, are often regarded as unwarrantable interference. 'The restrictions caused by agreements [with United States foundations]', wrote the national mouthpiece of Brazilian students,[8] 'impose changes on the curricula and programmes which alienate our education from its true objective, and convert our faculties into factories of "neutral" technicians no longer concerned with Brazilian problems'. The 'Americanization' of universities and attempts to depoliticize them are a frequent cause of student strikes.

Frustrated in their attempts to force changes in universities jealous of their autonomy, governments tend to avoid confrontation by by-passing state universities. They either establish institutes under close government control in order to produce the technicians which the traditional university syllabuses are accused of not providing, or they encourage the establishment of private universities. In both cases the government's motives are suspect, in the first because of what seems a deliberate attempt to undermine university freedom and secure pliable institutions, in the second for encouraging vested private interests.

Ten years ago there were only thirteen Roman Catholic universities in Latin America; today there are thirty-one, ten of them in Brazil compared with only four ten years ago. The express purpose of many of these new foundations is to provide an education free of the nationalist and political pressures of the state universities (although many Catholics are divided on this issue and feel that this is contracting out of the ideological struggle which ultimately can only be fought out in those universities). The social exclusivism of private universities, which are largely dependent on students' fees, is encouraging the development of a dual university system in which socially prestigious (and in some cases academically reputable) private universities compete with state universities which are now both losing social prestige and lowering academic standards. Unless state universities can be reformed and brought into line with the needs of developing economies, key posts in planning

[8] *Movimento* (Rio), no. 5, July 1963.

institutes and on bodies which make crucial decisions may be pre-empted by the graduates of private and foreign universities, and the state universities will be left stranded as ineffectual relics, the refuge of the academically halt and maimed.[9]

Poor academic standards frustrate professors as well as students, causing a brain drain either to better universities elsewhere in Latin America (economists and social scientists to Santiago, doctors to Buenos Aires, historians to Mexico), or to the United States and Europe, or even to private universities.[10] Political uncertainty and governmental interference, such as the impasse at Quito's Central University after the 1963 coup, the purge of Brazilian universities following the 1964 military coup d'état and that of Argentine universities in 1966, are contributory factors in driving away staff. A further consequence, which may have far-reaching political implications, is that governments tend to use the armed forces in development projects. The younger officers in the technical branches constitute a small but growing proportion of the technical intelligentsia. It is gratifying to see military expenditure, which soaks up one-fifth of the continent's total income, being ploughed back into road building, colonization schemes, &c., but it would be naive to assume either that this will lessen military interest in politics or that it will be an effective substitute for academic training in these disciplines. On the contrary, the more effective the Civil Action campaigns, the more the military can use them to justify intervention against inefficient civilian régimes. The revival of the Bolivian armed forces as a political force is not without its lessons. At present Nasserism in Latin America is a mood rather than a policy but the thinking behind an institution like Peru's Colegio de Altos Estudios Militares (CAEM) envisages the armed forces as the levers of a technocratic revolution.

---

[9] This point is well argued in J. P. Harrison, 'The Role of the Intellectual in Fomenting Change: the University', in *Explosive Forces in Latin America* (Ohio, 1964) and his 'Learning and Politics in Latin American Universities', *Proceedings of the Academy of Political Science* (New York), 1964.

[10] Paradoxically, the better the university the more liable its graduates are to seek out the highest quality graduate schools elsewhere, outside Latin America. The problem is then to attract them back. Chile is a case in point (see S. Gutiérrez Olivos and J. Riquelme Pérez, 'La emigración de recursos humanos chilenos de alto nivel a los Estados Unidos', *Ciencia interamericana* 6/2 (1965)). See also Glaucio Ary Dillon Soares, 'La fuga de los intelectuales', *Aportes*, 2 (Oct. 1966).

The first impulse for university reform came from the students themselves. In a matter of years after its initiation in 1918 it had swept up the university youth of Latin America in a movement which has been described as the longest continuous expression of the revolution of aspirations, dominating the political and social thought of Latin America.[11] Before the reform, universities had been strongholds of privilege and, in the words of the original reform manifesto: 'the secular refuge of mediocrity, the salary of ignorance, the safe hospital for all intellectual invalids . . . and the place where all forms of tyranny and insensibility found the chair where they could be taught'.[12] With the disappearance of aristocratic titles at Independence, the title 'Doctor' became a major status symbol and universities the means of preserving status for the established élite.

The reform movement originated in the University of Córdoba, the oldest Argentine university, where the old values were in sharpest conflict with the rapidly expanding middle class of the most developed country in Latin America. The reform was therefore a revolt against the university's status-preservation function in favour of the concept of the university as an instrument of social mobility. But it was more than an attempt to bring about changes in teaching and administration which would serve the interests of an expanding middle class. It was also the expression of a new revolutionary nationalism. The First World War had destroyed Europe's claim to be the leader of world civilization, and in consciously rejecting European models the reformists sought to develop a 'new cycle of civilization' in America, by exploring their own roots and traditions. The reform was both a reaction against cultural imperialism and a reaffirmation of the Bolivarian dream of a confederation of Latin American republics which would be strong enough to resist the encroachments of the United States. Rejuvenated universities, producing a new generation of dedicated students, would be the instrument for transforming the dreams of the early liberators into reality.

11 J. P. Harrison, 'The Confrontation with the Political University', in 'Latin America's Nationalistic Revolutions' *Annals of the American Academy of Political Science*, 1961, p. 74. This is the best short account in English. In Spanish, G. del Mazo, *Estudiantes y gobierno universitario* (Buenos Aires, 1955) is a handy distillation of his larger account and collection of documents.
12 *University Reform in Latin America* (Leiden, COSEC, 1961), p. 8.

In spite of the fact that anti-Americanism sometimes took the form of an exaggerated *arielismo*,[13] the 1920s were the seed-bed of modern Latin American nationalism when, partly under the influence of the Mexican revolution, intellectuals began to propose 'American' solutions—Vasconcelos in Mexico itself, Haya de la Torre and, more forcefully, Mariátegui in Peru. But Latin American intellectuals could never wholly free themselves from the fascination of imported ideologies, and apart from Mexico there was little practical reflection of the new nationalist theorizing. Nevertheless, the reformists believed that the new universities, freed from European and North American influences, would become a vehicle for a new Latin American nationalism.

The acceptance of the university reform in Argentina after its incorporation in the university law of 1919, which led to the golden age of Argentine universities until their emasculation by Perón, was possible because it followed the victory in 1916 of the Radical government of Yrigoyen, who represented the emerging middle and lower-middle classes and who was in basic agreement with the movement. Whereas, therefore, in Argentina reform was in part a consequence of political change, elsewhere in Latin America, where there was no dynamic middle-class party such as the Radicals, the situation was very different. There, the political element implicit in reform was given precedence over the purely academic aspect. So long as the position of the university in society was unresolved. considerations of academic excellence were subordinated to the wider political issues of control. Fierce struggles within the universities occurred between established professors, often in league with the government, and reformists. Once in control, reformists could use the university as a base from which to attack the government, and in the sharpening social conflicts during the depression years of the early 1930s universities were often in open defiance of governments. In Cuba, where the militant *Federación de Estudiantes Universitarios* (FEU) had been waging a campaign against Machado, Havana University was shut down for three years between 1930 and 1933.

Autonomy became and has since remained the most sensitive and crucial issue between universities and the state. Invasion of

[13] After the Uruguayan José Enrique Rodó's *Ariel*, published in 1900, in which the materialism of the United States is contrasted with the purer spirituality of Latin America.

the campus by police is the surest way to spark off student riots. Governments continually accuse universities of abusing their autonomy by allowing their members to use the campus for subversive activities, which may mean anything from printing opposition leaflets to manufacturing Molotov cocktails or harbouring common criminals. University authorities are understandably reluctant either to discipline students or to permit the police to enter the campus for fear of far-reaching repercussions.

Although many political leaders of the 1920s and 1930s served their apprenticeship in student movements, universities and students have, in general, failed to become the social revolutionary or regenerating force envisaged by the reformists. This has partly been because of the deep political divisions within universities, which have lacked agreement on their purpose and function in society and this lack in turn has reduced their effectiveness as pressure groups. From the students' standpoint, the reformists' concept of themselves as a regenerating élite, with its understandable overemphasis on the importance of intellectuals in societies in which thinkers have always been held in exaggerated esteem, lacked a basis in political reality. It is true that the reformists envisaged forming links with working-class groups through the extension work of the Popular Universities, but there were undertones of social romanticism in this which hampered any lasting alliance and, in any case, they were only a minor part of the reformist programme.

There was, however, a more fundamental flaw in the reformist concept of political action. Students by definition are a transitional group with a turnover of four to five years between each student generation. Ambivalence towards social and political questions is accompanied by ambivalence towards the adult world, which may often be more important in determining their behaviour. Student organizations therefore face an acute problem of discontinuity. If they were merely interest groups fulfilling a trade union function, concerned with student welfare, improving facilities, &c., problems of continuity would be comparatively unimportant, as each student generation would use its bargaining strength to obtain benefits, much as any union does. But acceptance of the concept of students as a regenerating élite, with a politically active role, led to two consequences which brought politics into the university in a way not envisaged by the early reformists. These were the introduction of the semi-professional student on to the campus and the appearance of student groups affiliated to national parties. Once the university was regarded as an instrument for promoting political and social reform the corollary was for political groups to attempt to capture it for their specific programmes.   The communists at first regarded the Reform Movement as a bourgeois phenomenon (except in Cuba, where Julio Antonio Mella was the first president of the FEU and a founder-member of the Cuban Communist Party), but soon recognized the importance of the university as a sanctuary.   Under their influence reformist ideology became impregnated with a general Marxist hue.

Professional students, often but not necessarily Leftists, and whose careers may span several student generations, came to play a vital role in student politics.   Probably of indifferent academic ability, usually on the payroll of a party, they act as political activists, recruiting agents, student election managers, and liaison officers between student affiliates and the national party.   They tend to be concentrated in the larger state universities, where there is only exiguous control by the university authorities and where lax regulations enable a student to fail and repeat examinations over an indefinite period or to restart his career in a different faculty. Attempts to tighten up the repeating rule have led to strikes, as happened in 1964 at Caracas engineering faculty, in part stimulated by professional students who saw them as a threat to their livelihood.

Most efforts to eradicate this influence have been unsuccessful and government legislation, such as the new university laws in Ecuador and Brazil, with clauses excluding all but full-time students from holding student office, is strongly resisted as an unjustifiable incursion into student freedom.

Continuity and control can also be exercised in a more formal manner through the youth secretariats of national parties.   This implies control and possibly manipulation which reduce freedom of action, limit choice, and destroy the reformist concept of students as an autonomous élite.   The clearest case of this has been the APRA party in Peru which has the longest continuous tradition of involvement in student affairs.   The *comandos universitarios* keep a tight control over *Aprista* students and policy decisions such as electoral tactics have to be cleared by the party's central committee.   The same, to a slightly lesser extent, is true of *Acción Democrática* in Venezuela, and in both these cases the disastrous drop in their student support may be partly attributed to resentment at tight control by older party leaders. Even among communist groups, the popularity of the Castroist and the Peking lines may be partly explained by resentment against control by an old-guard, discredited, Muscovite leadership.

But the effect on students of this organizational aspect of trying to secure continuity of action is of secondary importance compared with the psychological effect of the reformist mythology, which has conditioned them to act in accordance with an image which has hardly changed over fifty years.

The moment a student enters a state university he enters a 'free democratic republic', a sanctuary enjoying virtually extraterritorial rights, where free speech and free enquiry are permitted. Nor is he merely a passive recipient of the wisdom of an older generation but an active participant in policy decisions through *co-gobierno*, the system by which student representatives sit on faculty boards. This echoes the medieval Bologna-Salamanca tradition in which the university was a corporation of students, graduates, and professors, in which the latter held office only so long as they fulfilled their duties to their pupils' satisfaction.

To be a representative on a faculty board offers one of the few prestige roles open to an ambitious student. No issue of the Reform has aroused such passionate controversy. So long as professors are part-time, it is argued, there is a need for students to keep a watching brief over them. In some cases students play a constructive part, as in initiating syllabus reform; in others political issues intervene and voting follows political, not academic, lines. Professors are themselves divided on the *co-gobierno* issue; many old reformists, for example, are reluctant to criticize a system they pioneered. Others may oppose it adamantly; the professors of the medical faculty at San Marcos, rather than accept the *co-gobierno* ruling in the 1960 university law, resigned *en masse* and set up the new private Cayetano Heredia University with private funds, thus throwing the San Marcos medical faculty into the hands of the Left. This was the result of a head-on clash between the conservative professionalism of the doctors and the reformist zeal of the Rector, Luis Alberto Sánchez, the leading APRA intellectual.

The reformist conception of *co-gobierno* is rooted in the myth of the incorruptibility of youth, reflecting the glorification of youth and the spiritualized idealism of Rodó's *Ariel*, expressed thus in the Córdoba manifesto:

Youth is always surrounded by heroism. It is disinterested, it is pure. It has not yet had time to contaminate itself. It can never be mistaken in the election of its own educators. . . . From now on, in the future university republic, the only teachers must be those who truly build up truth, beauty, and goodness in the soul.[14]

Because the student movement was sometimes linked with social issues (e.g. the eight-hour struggle in Peru), the public often reciprocated the students' own conception of their function, feeling that their privileged position required them to champion those who were voiceless. It was, for example, their resistance to Batista and Pérez Jiménez which enabled students to assume the moral leadership of the revolutions in Cuba and Venezuela in the 1950s and on which they tried to capitalize after the dictators' overthrow.

This attitude has had an important corollary in that, so far from being merely the defenders of progressive causes, students began to see themselves as voicing a Rousseauistic general will. Thus university elections are assumed to represent the real will of the people which electoral fraud and corrupt politicians distort during national elections. The only clear case where national elections have echoed student elections has been in Chile, where Christian Democrat domination of all the universities except Concepción preceded the party's victory in the presidential and congressional elections in 1964 and 1965. But in general there is usually a cleavage between university and national elections and, wherever there is a literacy qualification for the vote, students claim to speak for the disenfranchised.

This feeling of trusteeship is heightened by the sense of being an inheritor and transmitter of a sanctified tradition, exemplified in a 'blood of the martyrs cult', a hagiography of students killed in the cause of freedom and a chronology of emotive dates, the annual celebration of which gives a feeling of continuity with the past and provides an occasion to renew vows of fidelity. Thus in Cuba, where such dates are religiously observed (and where the tradition stretches back to the eight medical students shot by the Spaniards in 1871), 13 March, the date of the attack in 1957 on Batista's palace, when José Echevarría, president of the FEU, and four other students were killed, is used by Castro to renew and draw

[14] *University Reform*, p. 10.

sustenance from his student contacts, and to use the occasion for major policy pronouncements.[15]

The reformist mystique has given momentum to student public protest, but their image of themselves as a regenerating élite is rarely matched by performance. However, the fact that student strike action is mostly directed against university authorities over university matters suggests a greater concern with these problems than one would gather from the more spectacular and publicized demonstrations such as those in favour of Cuba or the Dominican Republic. Organizationally, students have shown much greater solidarity when acting *qua* students than as supporters of any particular political viewpoint. Thus strikes called by a communist-dominated federation for an academic purpose may receive wide support whereas a strike called for political reasons by the same federation may be poorly supported. There is often the case of a student who will vote for a communist candidate because of his greater energy in advancing (or promising to advance) student interests but who will nevertheless resist the candidate's party line. For this reason student elections can be deceptive and are open to a variety of interpretations. So long as there is a high abstention rate it is difficult to gauge the state of student opinion, but even so it cannot be assumed that those who do vote are necessarily firm believers in the efficacy of political action.

The results of student elections in general, with very few exceptions, show a rising tide of left-wing extremism which is curiously at variance with the few surveys of student attitudes so far undertaken. From these a picture emerges of students who are non-committal, often a-political and even moderate in outlook, but above all politically confused. They want change but for the most part dislike the choices open to them. In the case of a recent Colombian survey, for example, the overwhelming popularity of President de Gaulle was in striking contrast with the lack of confidence in Colombian politicians.[16] Lack of confidence in the social

---

[15] Although at the time Castro condemned the assault.

[16] 'La universidad de espaldas al sistema', *Acción Liberal*, 1 Aug. 1965. See also the detailed R. C. Williamson, *El estudiante colombiano y sus actitudes* (Bogotá, 1962), D. Goldrich and E. W. Scott, 'Developing Political Orientations of Panamanian Students', *J. of Politics*, 33 (1961) and particularly the survey in *Caretas* (Lima), 26 July 1965, based on files in the Institute of Sociology at San Marcos. In the latter, the criteria determining the way students voted were given as: the programme offered 51·7 per cent; personal qualities, 33·7 per cent, and

values of the government in power is paralleled by disillusion with democratic socialist ideologies. Votes for extremist groups, therefore, would seem to be 'anti-votes' rather than expressions of positive support for established parties.

Nevertheless any attitude which stresses the trade union function of student organizations at the expense of their political role is strongly resisted by those who continue to see political activism as the students' main contribution to social change. Any attempt to depoliticize the university will be resisted as a betrayal of the student movement. To the reformist an a-political student who abstains from elections must *ipso facto* be a supporter of the established order. This demonstrates the point of the new Brazilian university law which makes voting in student elections obligatory in an attempt to tap the politically apathetic and therefore presumably conservative abstainers.

Although an attitude stressing specialization and professionalization may be more appropriate to social needs, and is often based on a realistic evaluation of the doubtful effectiveness of student political influence, it has so far found little organized expression. Any student group recommending 'back to our books and no politics' would cut very little ice. Even those who would like to see the influence of politics in universities reduced ruefully admit that political action will be needed to bring it about. But any attempt by a government to do this by legislation is likely to fail, as was shown by student reactions to the new university laws in Ecuador and Brazil, to the tough line of President Onganía in Argentina and to proposed tighter government control in Peru. It is only where student power is constantly abused for purely political, as distinct from student, ends that a reaction will set in, drawing in the hitherto apathetic and a-political. There are signs that this is now happening even in such highly politicized universities as the Universidad Central de Venezuela (UCV) and San Marcos. But where there are specifically a-political or 'Independent' groups they tend to consist of those who do not regard the political system as a threat to their status aspirations. It is difficult to make any precise correlation between economic

political tendency 8·7 per cent. Questionnaire surveys must be treated with caution but the findings of the Lima survey are so at variance with the public image of student attitudes as to encourage further detailed research.

status and political activism but it is clear that the politicization of the university is not the consequence of a rising flood of working-class students, as these may still be well below 5 per cent of total enlistment.[17]

The majority of students come from the middle class with an increasingly large number being drawn from the lower-middle class—artisans, shopkeepers, white-collar workers, and public officials.[18] Those from the lower group are aspirants to professional middle-class standing and see a university career putting the seal on their social advancement. For them the university fulfils a social mobility function and is the path to status and hence security. For those from the established middle class, especially professional groups whose parents are unable to afford an education at a foreign or private university, the university primarily has a status-preservation function which becomes more emphatic as they feel themselves to be threatened by the aspirations of students from the lower-middle class—reflecting a social situation where the economic basis of the political élite has not expanded as rapidly as the numbers of élite position-seekers. With rising expectations, there are too many students chasing too few prestige positions. Thus while middle-class students fear proletarianization, lower-middle-class students often find their ambitions frustrated.

[17] From his quantitative study of secondary school students in Panamá D. Goldrich concludes that there is no simple correlation of increasing emphasis on politics with decreasing rank in the social scale and rejects the hypothesis that politically oriented students of the lower strata are alienated from political democracy ('Panamanian Students' Orientations towards Democracy', *J. of Inter-American Studies*, 5/3 (July 1963).
[18] Statistics of students' social origins are only available for a few universities and these are not always very satisfactory. In the case of the Central University, Quito, UCV, and the Catholic University, Lima, the three major social occupations of students' fathers were:

	(Per cent)		
	Employees	*Professions*	*Commerce*
Quito	18	18	27
Lima	19	14	18
Caracas*	31†	17	29

* Based on 10,251 replies received out of a total of 15,595.
† 20 per cent state employees and 11 per cent private employees.
   Sources: Estadísticas universitarias (Quito, 1961); *Primer censo de alumnos* (Lima, 1962); F. de Venanzi, *Mensaje al claustro* (Caracas, 1963).

It would be tempting but over-simple to conclude that the friction between these two groups is the key to student political alignments. The situation is in fact complicated by prestige and financial considerations. Although little is known about factors governing choice of professions (e.g. influence of parents, teachers, &c.), poorer students still tend to choose shorter courses like economics and education rather than the longer ones like medicine or engineering, and graduates will then choose professions which offer most opportunities. Thus a country with a retarded agriculture and an unenterprising landowning oligarchy is scarcely going to attract veterinary surgeons and agronomists. Similarly where industry is backward the chemical and physical sciences will not be an attractive proposition. Scarcity value does not necessarily bring status or wealth in stratified societies. Faculties such as medicine, law, engineering, and architecture carry high prestige. Others like agronomy, veterinary science, or economics carry low prestige (although some individual faculties have built up prestige through academic excellence—economics at the University of Chile for example) but this does not necessarily imply a correlation with radicalism.

Apart from the sex factor, which makes low prestige faculties like dentistry, pharmacy, and education conservatively inclined largely because they are dominated by women, there is also the problem of the ratio of graduates to jobs.[19] Prestige faculties, simply because of their standing, tend to be overcrowded—a process which is related to the domination of professors brought up in traditional attitudes which perpetuate prestige ratings, who fight defensive actions against the recognition of new disciplines. Prestige has been reflected in numbers, but the drop in quality among entrants, overcrowding, and the high cost of producing doctors and engineers have led to stringent weeding out, which has the effect both of keeping these professions select and of safeguard-

---

[19] The question of women's influence on attitudes to social change in Latin America needs detailed investigation. It is not accidental that the Cubans should have devoted so much energy to women's organizations such as the *Federación de Mujeres Cubanas* (FMC). Without the support of women, especially in traditionally Catholic societies, social revolution will be a chimera. The high proportion of women who vote for the Christian Democrats may prove to be a brake on their radicalism. Womens' organizations played an important role in the 1964 Brazilian Revolution.

ing job opportunities. Academic purges of this sort in a political university can make traditionally conservative faculties more radical, as the recent events in the medical and engineering faculties at Caracas have shown.[20] Where politics play an integral part in university life it is easy for a failed candidate to allege political discrimination and to appeal to the student federation, which, in the Caracas case cited, called a strike in support of lowering the pass mark.

In spite of, or it may be because of, its high prestige, medicine has always tended to be a sensitive faculty politically. First-hand contact with diseases caused by malnutrition or bad housing can arouse the social conscience even of upper-class students (as the presence of some of these with Venezuelan and Colombian guerrillas, reported in the Cuban press, indicates). The practice which is becoming common, following Mexico's lead, of universities insisting on a year's service in a rural area before graduating, could make medical faculties still more radical. Doctors are urgently needed in rural areas, but the aim of most medical graduates in the past has been to practise in the metropolis and thereby gain the prestige and rewards of attending a hypochondriac leisure class (so much the better when swollen by North American tourists, as was the case in pre-Castro Havana). Doctors who fail to secure such posts, or who deliberately reject them, might repeat the experience of nineteenth-century Southern Europe when provincial doctors were often the leaders of radical local politics (of which the career of ex-President Illía of Argentina is a textbook Latin American illustration).

Because of the small cost of producing a lawyer, academic purges are less necessary in law faculties which, as a result, are everywhere overcrowded. Law traditionally carries high prestige, promises good financial prospects in highly litigious bureaucratized Hispanic societies, is a traditional training ground for politics, and can easily be studied part-time.[21] But it is fast becoming a profession

---

[20] Both medical and engineering students, through working closely together, often show greater group solidarity than students in social science or humanities faculties. Thus, where politicized, their influence tends to be more effective, as appears to be happening now at Lima's hitherto quiescent Universidad Nacional de Ingeniería.

[21] For Brazil, there is a useful study by L. Ronald Scheman, 'The Brazilian law student: background, habits, attitudes', *J. of Inter-American Studies*, 5 (1963).

of diminishing opportunity. Some estimates put the percentage of law graduates unable to find suitable employment as high as 50 per cent. Declining job opportunity therefore tends to be a prime factor in the radicalization of law faculties, especially among lower-middle-class students whose poor family background and lack of the all-important professional contacts for law practice put them at a grave disadvantage. Economics faculties, although lacking prestige, have expanded more rapidly than any other faculty in recent years through development demands and now tend to be the most radical of all.

Apart from these factors, a wealthy middle-class student who feels himself to be a member of an established élite may be drawn into politics because of the lack of alternative prestige roles within the university and as a preparation for a political career.[22] Those from this stratum who join extremist groups may do so for opportunist reasons, or possibly because they have a sense of guilt arising from their parents' association with a previous dictator, or as a reaction against their graft or philistinism, or simply because as university students they may have little in common with parents who did not have a university education. This aspect of the conflict between generations may account for the students from wealthy families who have been drawn into extremist politics in Venezuela and earlier in Cuba, and also for the strong middle-class student element in the Dominican 14 June Movement. The key to much of this motivation lies, of course, in intra-family relationships.[23]

The lower-middle-class student, or the middle-class student who is not so secure in his sense of belonging to a political élite, may be drawn into politics from frustration and insecurity. If he comes from the provinces this may be heightened by isolation in the city

---

[22] It is often suggested that sport would provide a prestige alternative to politics and canalize surplus energies—a reason perhaps why such emphasis is placed on sport in Cuban universities although at UCV excellent facilities seem to have little effect. A permissive sexual morality might be a more effective alternative to judge from western experience. I cannot vouch for the authenticity of a remark of Mella's told to me in Cuba, that he used to insist that Cuban students would never be an effective revolutionary force until they had been flushed out of the brothels. The moral purge in Havana University against homosexuals echoes this viewpoint: see *Mella* (Havana), 5 Apr. 1965.

[23] See, for example, O. Ianni, 'O jovem radical', in *Industrializacão e desenvolvimento social no Brazil* (Rio, 1963).

through living a fringe existence in cheap *pensions*. Student residences are rare—not only because of expense but through fear of concentrating students in one place—a view which the experience of the UCV tends to confirm. For the student from a poor background, education confers responsibilities as well as status. He becomes a provider, not only for his own immediate family circle, but for the extended family and also perhaps for his *compadres*. Hence isolation is enhanced by the ever-present dread of failure, which makes it the more pressing to have some additional insurance in the form of political contacts. Student political organizations, especially when affiliates of national parties, can give the isolated student a sense of belonging, and provide an institutionalized form of the patron-client relationship which is a pervasive feature of Latin American social life.

In addition, the conflict between generations—prompted in traditional societies by the desire to break out of an inhibiting authoritarian family structure or exacerbated in fluid societies (as in Caracas) by a breakdown in family life and a loss of parental control —sharpens the need to establish new sets of relationships which can provide guidance and protection. The absence of exclusive in-groups of the fraternity or *Burschenschaften* type opens the way for political parties to fulfil this function by promising opportunities of promotion and professional contacts. It may be that what appeal APRA still retains for Peruvian students, after the loss of its revolutionary image in the alliance with Prado of 1956, is related to its sect mentality, or mutual-aid organization, rather than to the specifically political purpose of gaining power.

Any attempts by governments to rationalize administration, to prune their bureaucracies, and to replace a spoils by a merit system must serve only to exacerbate the job mania of unenterprising and risk-avoiding middle classes unless, at the same time, alternative avenues are opened up through an expansion of the economy, industrialization, or agrarian reform. It is the lack of confidence that these avenues will be opened up that is a major incentive to political involvement. The inability of governments to satisfy insatiable demands for posts in the bureaucracy leaves little alternative to the disappointed but to plot the overthrow of the political order. But there is no guarantee, as countless Latin American 'revolutions' have shown, that this will involve any fundamental social changes. To satisfy this job mania, the share-out of offices is sometimes institutionalized, as in the case of Colombia and Uruguay. Such arrangements rarely work, and *continuismo* remains a major cause of political upheaval in Latin America. But the revolts of job-hungry conspirators solve nothing, as there is nothing to prevent those thrown on to the labour market in economies which cannot absorb them from starting a new cycle of plotting. To students faced with the prospect of a marginal existence in political systems dominated by traditional power groups the Cuban revolution seemed a way out of the impasse. Not only did it break down the structural barriers and open up new avenues of advancement but it also showed how students and radical intellectuals, acting as leaders of rural guerrillas, could actively play the role of a revolutionary élite that had eluded them for so long.

In any discussion of students' attitudes towards political change the Cuban revolution occupies a central position. Whatever the disillusion among older age-groups, Castro's image can still effectively rouse a large section of Latin American youth.[24] The sense of purpose and total commitment of the new régime contrast with societies lacking a dynamic vision. Cuba is often seen as a genuine Latin American revolution in which communists have been captured by Castroists, not vice versa. The charismatic appeal of Castro, his nuisance value to the United States, and the enhanced importance of Latin America in world affairs as a result of Cuba have a compulsive attraction for the younger nationalists. Admiration for Castro is an example of generation rather than class solidarity. Analysis of the revolution in terms of class structure alone, such as the 'middle-class-revolution-betrayed' thesis, miss the point that Cuba is the one clear case where the post-war clash between generations has taken a politically revolutionary form. No one over forty, Castro remarked, can understand what the revolution is about.[25]

[24] A quantitative but unilluminating analysis based on students of the National University in Bogotá is K. N. Walker, 'Determinants of Castro support among Latin American University Students', *Social and Economic Studies*, 14/1 (Mar. 1965).

[25] This is curiously reflected in an analysis of an occupational and age analysis of Cuban exiles between January 1959 and October 1962 in R. R. Fagen and R. A. Brody, 'Cubans in Exile—a Demographic Analysis', *J. of Social Problems* (Spring 1964), where the average age is 40·3.

Particularly important in its impact on students has been the way in which Batista's overthrow seemed to confirm and justify the students' conception of themselves as a revolutionary élite. The revolution is seen as the climax of a struggle against Machado, after the foundation of the FEU in 1923, and then later, against Batista after he overthrew the students' government of Grau San Martín in 1934. A novel feature of the resistance to Batista in the 1950s was that students and radical intellectuals became guerrilla leaders, whereas in the 1920s and 1930s they had been urban terrorists. One factor in the success of the Cuban revolution was thus due to a modification in traditional methods of student activism. If Che Guevara was right in maintaining that in Latin America a revolution to be successful must be based on the rural masses, then the traditional methods of student political activism— demonstrations, riots, etc.—can only be of marginal importance and, although urban terrorism might play a part, it must always be subordinated to the guerrilla campaign in the rural areas.

Temperamentally the heroic role of the guerrilla leader is more to the taste of the young Latin American revolutionary than the more moderate popular-front tactics of official communist parties.[26] But although it is unlikely that there will be any sudden mass exodus of students to the hills, so long as the educational system is unable to absorb and satisfy the expanding student population and so long as the economy cannot expand rapidly enough to offer opportunity, there will be a fertile recruiting ground for guerrillas among alienated students who face bleak prospects as underemployed intellectuals or underpaid bureaucrats.[27]

[26] For a communist view see R. Dalton, 'Student Youth and the Latin American Revolution', *World Marxist R.*, Mar. 1966.

[27] This is not to imply that this is the only source for guerrilla recruitment, as can be seen from the case of the gifted young Lima poet, Javier Heraud, of good Catholic family and education, who was killed being infiltrated into Amazonian Peru in 1963, around whom a martyr-cult has grown up and after the date of whose assassination a Trotskyist group, the M15M (*Movimiento 15 de Mayo*) is named. From a preliminary breakdown of early Cuban Castroists I have the impression that students (or ex-students) from the many fringe private colleges may have been a more significant factor in the 26 July movement than students from the University. The University itself was closed down from late 1956 to early 1959, thus releasing students for political activity. With minimal prospects they had 'nothing to lose from revolution but their rootlessness' in Boris Goldenberg's phrase.

But the Cuban revolution is attractive for another and more fundamental reason. Radical intellectuals have despaired of either organized labour or the urban poor as revolutionary groups. Organized labour tends to be a labour aristocracy and is often reformist in outlook and open to manipulation by party bosses. The urban poor are even more unpromising material. Family solidarity, which fills the gap left by the deficiencies of organized institutions, together with *compadrazgo*, which with its interlocking mutual obligations serves as a counter-revolutionary social mechanism, have combined to make lower-class urban groups impermeable to rational ideologies. The politics of the slum, so far as they exist, are those of the *patrón* type—reduced to the search for a boss—a Vargas in Rio, Perón in Buenos Aires, Odría in Lima, Gaitán in Bogotá, even a Larrazábal in Caracas.

Revolutionary theory therefore sees peasants as the only untapped mass force. In the past, however, although peasants have thrown up able leaders they have rarely been interested in national politics, except in so far as these affect the region—even Zapata, the greatest of these leaders, was only really concerned about Morelos. Radical intellectuals now see themselves as the link between the formless protest of rural revolt and the directed revolution of workers and peasants. But there is no *narodnik* tradition in Latin America: *indigenismo* is often no more than an intellectual stance. The big state university, in the same way as the metropolis, has contributed to drain the provinces and the rural areas of talent, thus widening the gap between town and country and reinforcing the Spanish colonial legacy. In the Andean countries there is the further linguistic and cultural division. It is scarcely surprising, therefore, that the Castroist student groups which have tried to raise the peasants have had little success. The *Movimiento de Obreros Estudiantes y Campesinos* (*MOEC*), in Colombia, the *Unión Revolucionaria de la Juventud Ecuatoriana* (*URJE*) in Ecuador, the *Febrerista* and Communist youth in Paraguay, the 14 June Group in the Dominican Republic (which switched to urban activity after the fiasco of its rural rising in 1963), the Uturenko group in Northern Argentina, and Francisco Julião's Peasant Leagues in Brazil (although these do not really fit into the same category) have all collapsed through inexperience, lack of discipline and of understanding of peasant mentality, and the inability to stand up to harsh conditions.[28]   Enthusiasm and the heroism of the barricade are not enough.

To establish the *focos revolucionarios* of Guevara's thesis, where the lessons of guerrilla warfare are slowly absorbed and where revolutionary consciousness is acquired through living with and depending on peasants rather than on theoretical reading, will require a far more protracted effort than that of the 26 July in the Sierra Maestra, where the cultural barriers were comparatively easy to overcome, although even here, on Guevara's own evidence, the peasant response was not the spontaneous uprising of the myth-makers.[29]

Only in Venezuela, where conditions approximate to those in Cuba, have the guerrillas in the FALN [30] had anything approaching success; and even in this case there are now deep divisions within the *Partido Comunista Venezolano—Movimiento de Izquierda Revolucionaria* (PCV/MIR) coalition over the tactics of violence. In Colombia efforts to exploit the endemic *Violencia* by canalizing it into constructive guerrilla activity seem now to be meeting with more success.   Partly because of the realization of the difficulties involved and partly also perhaps because Cuban support for these Peking-fomented movements has had to be muted to meet the Russian view, the Cuban model is losing some of its appeal.   But this is only happening where there is a radical alternative.

The only effective challenge seems to be coming from the newly emerging radical Catholic groups or, as with Peru's *Acción Popular*, a new populist party.   In Chile the Christian Democrats

[28] Guerrilla groups are also active in Central America, especially Guatemala, where one leader, Yon Sosa, is an ex-army officer who learnt guerrilla techniques from the US counter-guerrilla school at Panama. (For Guatemalan guerrillas see A. Gilly, *Monthly Review*, May and June 1965.) Young Latin Americans going to Cuba for training in the guerrilla schools must now travel via Prague.

[29] Régis Debray in 'Le Castrisme: la longue marche de l'Amérique Latine (*Les Temps modernes*, Jan. 1965) argues convincingly that only through rural guerrilla activity can the *déraciné* middle-class urban radical be effectively proletarianized and become a genuine revolutionary. The university with its inviolable campus, he suggests, is the urban counterpart of the rural *foco*. It could perhaps be argued that in Cuba the main difference between the 26 July Movement and the student *Directorio Revolucionario*, which led to disagreements between the two in 1959, was one of revolutionary experience not social origins.

[30] *Feurzas Armadas de Liberación Nacional* which in addition to PCV and MIR militants includes disaffected right-wing nationalist officers.

have already dominated the universities for the past seven years. In Venezuela the *Comité Organizador por Elecciones Independientes* (COPEI) is the main challenger to the extremist Left; in Argentina the *Humanistas*, although divided, are a growing force: until the 1964 Revolution in Brazil, *Acão Popular* was sharing power in a curious alliance with anti-Peking Brazilian communist party students, although in both these latter cases student strength contrasts with the weakness of the national parties. Elsewhere too smaller dynamic Social Christian-Christian Democrat groups are beginning to contest student elections.

The emergence of radical Christian Democrat student groups and the gains these are making at the expense of the secular democratic Left are striking evidence of the failure of the latter to retain the support of their student movements. In Venezuela and Peru, the two strongest parties of the democratic left in Latin America *Acción Democrática* and APRA, have lost a large proportion of their student following to Castroist movements.[31] These movements, called in both countries the MIR, have become the supporters of violent revolution. In Peru the explanation for student alienation from APRA is clear: the alliance with the conservative Manuel Prado in 1956, its pro-United States and anti-Castro line after 1960, and its deliberate slowing up of Belaunde's reform programme by means of its majority in Congress disappointed the expectations of students who had come to look on APRA as a revolutionary party. However, APRA's failure to capitalize on its anti-communism is striking; elections at San Marcos, which APRA must hold for prestige reasons, are conditioned by anti-*aprismo*, not anti-communism. Non-communist students resent APRA students' strong-arm tactics and the power of APRA professors.[32] In the provincial universities, where APRA is

31 The same was true of the *Frente Universitario Radical Revolucionario* (FURR), the pro-Bosch group in the Dominican Republic which only obtained 66 votes in the 1964 elections compared with the *Fragua* group's 1,452 and the Catholic *Bloque Revolucionario Universitario Cristiano* (BRUC)'s 1,157 (*Hispanic American Report*, March 1964). They did little better in 1966, only gaining 6 per cent in comparison with *Fragua's* 53 per cent and BRUC's 41 per cent.

32 In 1958 APRA won with 41 per cent; in 1959 APRA (49·7 per cent) lost to communists, CD, and AP (50·3 per cent); 1960, APRA (35 per cent) lost to AP/communists (49 per cent); 1961, no election; 1962, APRA/ CD (44 per cent) lost to AP/communists (55 per cent); 1963, APRA (35 per cent) lost to AP/communists (43 per cent); 1964 APRA, (35·9 per cent) won against CD (9 per cent), AP (19 per cent), and communists

weaker, other parties sometimes ally themselves with them but even in the once solid APRA area of Trujillo in Northern Peru their hold is now tenuous.

The loss of APRA's revolutionary dynamism is paralleled by the growth of *Acción Popular's* student group, which won 19 per cent of the votes in San Marcos the first year it fought on its own, although in 1965 it abstained from the San Marcos elections in order not to split the vote and thus prevent the communist group from defeating APRA. The government's imaginative campaign of *Cooperación Universitaria Popular,* by which 500 students each year do vacation work among the peasantry and which APRA predictably condemns as inviting communist subversion, is one of the first examples of a government deliberately canalizing student idealism into constructive channels.   Similar activity is also an essential part of the Chilean government's efforts to associate students with development projects.

The reasons for *Acción Democrática's* failure are more complex.   Besides the political reasons for the split between the old guard and its student activists, rooted in the disagreements of 1958, students are disillusioned because the Venezuelan revolution did not move as fast as that in Cuba and resent that they themselves were unable to capitalize on their role as a revolutionary élite immediately after Pérez Jiménez's fall, in the same way as the Cubans were able to.   However, the explanation of the Venezuelan situation seems to lie in social and psychological factors associated with the febrile, get-rich-quick atmosphere of Caracas and the breakdown in the structure of the family.   This, combined with an overloaded educational system in which secondary school and university enrolments have trebled in six years, has created tensions which AD has been unable to resolve.   But with 50 per cent of the population under twenty it seems likely—to judge by the drop in the AD vote

(35·7 per cent).   Note how *Acción Popular,* seeing APRA as its main rival in implementing similar policies, allies with the communists to keep APRA out.   The attempt by Luis Alberto Sánchez, APRA's leading intellectual, to retain the Rectorship of San Marcos in 1963 after being elected senator, when according to the university statutes, the two posts were incompatible, was a particularly blatant piece of politicking. For an interesting analysis of the 1960 San Marcos elections see R. W. Patch's two articles, 'Fidelismo in Peruvian Universities', *American Universities Field Staff* (West Coast: South America series, 8/2 and 3). As political groups are officially forbidden in university elections, the parties are masked by using different names.

at the last presidential election from 49·2 to 32·8 per cent (which can be partly explained by the influx of young voters)—that demographic factors will remove AD from power unless it improves its standing with the younger generation. At present, COPEI, with an affiliated student group which claims to be the largest single party in UCV, seems better placed to achieve this.[33]

An important question for future Christian Democrat development is the extent to which their student groups, which have a mystique and discipline unusual in non-communist groups, will be able to radicalize the national parties.[34] In Venezuela differences between an older, conservative Catholic generation and the radical youth movement may widen now that COPEI has been freed from its inhibiting coalition with AD. But it remains to be seen how long a radical student group, planning to recruit members from Marxists who have been disillusioned by violence, can coexist with a party whose electoral strength is drawn from the conservative Andean provinces, the stamping ground of the army's Táchira clique. At present COPEI's gains in UCV have been so striking that the national party have given it its head, even though its students' support of the 1964 'non-repeating strike' in defiance of party leaders is an illustration of the sort of friction which may recur.[35]

In Chile the problem is not so acute, as the Christian Democrat government is already committed to a radical programme. But Christian Democrat students there are in a unique position as the only student group in control to be affiliated to a party in power. As the natural habitat of student groups is in opposition, it may mean that they will have to adopt a very critical line towards the

[33] COPEI claimed 33·8 per cent of the total vote in the 1964 student election compared with PCV's 25·1 per cent, MIR's 21 per cent and AD's 11·8 per cent (*El Mundo* (Caracas), 12 Feb. 1965). Among secondary school students AD claims second place: PCV/MIR, 41·1 per cent; AD, 33·5 per cent; COPEI, 11·6 per cent. COPEI's poor showing here is due to its not yet being strongly organized in the public secondary schools (*La República* (Caracas), 5 May 1965).

[34] ORMEU (*Oficina Relacionadora de Movimientos Estudiantiles Universitarios*) with headquarters in Santiago, trains Catholic student leaders from all over Latin America.

[35] There is some evidence to support the view that possibly the majority of COPEI students were opposed to the strike but that the leadership overrode them. There are COPEI students who are much nearer the conservative national party line than the radicals at present in control of their student affiliate.

national party if they are to continue to hold their own against opposition within the university. Some Christian Democrat student leaders dislike becoming too involved in the government's development schemes as they feel that the government's unpopularity with the Left (as in the case over the La Salvadora strikers who were killed) will compromise their position in the university.

In Brazil the Christian Democrats are a small Right-of-Centre party who have no connexion with the extreme left Catholic student group, *Acão Popular*, which was founded in 1961 by militants who wanted greater independence of the Church than the original Catholic student group JUC permitted.[36] AP's independence until the 1964 revolution reflected the peculiarity of Brazilian student politics. The artificiality of the party structure in its post-Vargas form has meant that student groups (except for the communists) have not been organized along strictly party lines. This certainly makes it seem as if Brazilian students have more freedom of manoeuvre than those in other Spanish American countries and is one reason why left-wing Catholics could co-operate with the PCB in the *Frente Único* from 1959 to 1964.

Acão Popular did not see its role limited to student politics but had as its long-term aim the capture of political power throughout the country, and although it had probably only between 2,000 and 3,000 members it had penetrated into many key positions. Paradoxically, since Brazil does not share the reformist tradition (and has still to win *co-gobierno*), students there are probably nearer the original reformist idea of a regenerating elite than elsewhere. Brazilian parties have little to offer youth and hence AP hoped to use UNE, the national union, as a pressure group to mount a campaign for structural change throughout the country. In this they were prepared to work with the communists, but the April 1964 military coup d'état forced both groups to go underground. Student effort is now geared to challenging the new university law and to resurrecting UNE, which that law abolished.[37]

[36] *Juventud Universitaria Católica* had been founded in 1951 as the a-political student section of Catholic Action. It had come into conflict with the hierarchy when it allied itself with the communists to win control of UNE in 1959. There is an interesting analysis of AP in Leonard D. Thierry, 'Dominant Power Components in the Brazilian University Student Movement prior to April, 1964', *J. of Inter-American Studies*, 7/1 (Jan. 1965).

[37] The Lacerda Law of November 1964 abolished the government subsidy to UNE and provided for the creation of a new Union, the *Directorio*

The opposition faced by the present Brazilian government in its attempts to establish a new student organization highlights the inescapable fact that right-wing groups, whether based on traditional Catholic conservatism or linked to business interests, are unlikely to attract more than a marginal student attention. Any hint of United States support for a student group is likely to be the kiss of death. Anti-Americanism, together with violation of autonomy, are the two sure causes of student demonstrations. Although students demonstrate about many other issues, these demonstrations often turn, or are turned by *agents provocateurs*, into nationalist expressions of anti-American feeling.

The fact that demonstrations are the most frequent and dramatic way in which students express their political views leads one to ask what their purpose is and what influence they exert on public opinion and national politics. Where the tradition of parliamentary opposition is weak the *manifestación* often performs an important function in expressing viewpoints which would otherwise be ignored. But the difficulty has always been to keep these demonstrations under control. This is what tends to give them their importance and to make governments sensitive to them—the more so in sections where violence is still regarded as a legitimate means of securing political change. The notorious inability of the police to control unruly crowds often leads to shooting, deaths, martyrdoms, and subsequent snowballing of public indignation. Rough handling by incompetent police can bring enough discredit on a government to force its resignation. Hence the vested interest of some opposition groups in provoking riots and raising the level of violence. The younger the demonstrator the more difficult control becomes, and the younger the victim the better the martyr. Often the failure of police to keep order forces the army to intervene and then to exact a price for incurring public odium.[38]

Nacional de Estudantes (DNE). AP, in exile and underground, refuses to form a broad front in the DNE with students it suspects of being too moderate. The PCB does not seem to be so inhibited.

[38] Anyone caught up in a secondary-school riot will realize just how difficult the police's task is. Too little attention has been paid to the structure and function of Latin American police forces. We also know remarkably little about the composition of street demonstrations or their motivation. A detailed historical and socio-psychological study of crowds and mass behaviour of the type engaging the interest of historians in Europe is a major research need. The role of violence in Latin American politics is now attracting the attention of political scientists. Apart from the

Students demonstrate to arouse sympathy for their own demands, to express sympathy for and solidarity with the demands of others, to protest against injustice, either at home or abroad, and with the specific intention of toppling a government. A strike over academic matters is usually confined to the campus, but if this looks like failing it may widen into demonstrations to rally public support. This is most likely to succeed when a political issue is also involved, such as the desire to remove a professor for his political convictions. Intimidation of this sort, particularly after a change of régime, can be most unnerving. The traditional independence of faculties within universities and the possibility that a professor's colleagues may themselves welcome his removal for political reasons mean that professorial solidarity is often weak in the face of strike threats. Deliberate provocation of the police to compel them to violate the university's autonomy is another tactic frequently used to rally public opinion.

Recent demonstrations which have roused public sympathy are those which drew attention to the government's inadequate allocations to the universities, as at Buenos Aires in the autumn of 1964 and again in the summer of 1966 or at the new University of Ica in Peru, where local workers called a general strike in sympathy. The ubiquitous demonstration against increases in public transport charges is usually spearheaded by students. The case of Christian Democrat students counter-demonstrating against a communist demonstration in Chile to exploit a bus-fare increase is a recent and unusual variation on a well-worn theme.[39]

The effectiveness or otherwise of demonstrations is linked to the siting of universities. Thus the situation of a university campus on the outskirts, as in Mexico City, makes it difficult to mount demonstrations, while in Peru the reluctance of some San Marcos students to move out to the new site on the Callao road is partly because of the strategic position of the old down-town buildings. But effectiveness is finally related to institutional complexity. Where there are alternative organized pressure groups, student importance will diminish. Thus the numerically most powerful

studies of the Colombian *Violencia* see J. Payne, 'Peru: the Politics of Structured Violence', *R. of Politics*, 27 (1965) and his *Labour and Politics in Peru* (Yale UP, 1965).

[39] K. H. Silvert has an interesting analysis of the 1957 bus-fare riots in Santiago de Chile which got out of hand, in his *Reaction and Revolution in Latin America* (New Orleans, 1961), pp. 183–95.

union in Latin America, the Argentine FUBA (the Buenos Aires Federation, which is more active than the national union, FUA) is now one of the weakest in terms of influence in Latin America in spite of its importance in the revolt against Perón. Its last big demonstration of strength, in 1958, failed to prevent government legislation allowing the establishment of Catholic universities and its opposition to Onganía in 1966 though vocal was ineffectual. The factionalism of national politics reflected in the student groupings has contributed to this decline in political influence, but the size and complexity of the university has also made it difficult to form a strong national union.[40]

Where there is a disposable mass and the leader to harness it, as in the case of the *peronista* and *varguista* brands of populism in Argentina and Brazil, or even with the *Movimiento Nacionalista Revolucionario* (MNR) in Bolivia, the role of students within the movement tends to be minimal. Where, however, unions prove impermeable to populist cajolement, or where the masses are isolated from the political leadership by cultural or even linguistic barriers, student groups can assume a crucial importance in a party's early organizational, educational, and proselytizing phases, but this importance diminishes as the process of bureaucratization and unionization increases.[41]

Thus the 'democratic Left' which grew out of student groups now has declining student support, whereas nascent Christian Democrat groups derive considerable impetus from student enthusiasm. It is comparatively easy to enlist students for opposition roles but very few parties have succeeded in carrying their student groups with them in the transition to becoming a ruling or even an established party. This is the problem which AD and APRA have failed to solve and which the Christian Democrats in Chile are now facing.

Unless a party's leadership remains sufficiently flexible and open to younger-generation pressures it will be in danger of atrophy and

---

[40] For the complexity of student groupings see *Análisis* (Buenos Aires), 7/29 (Nov. 1965). Colombia is another case of the failure to create a strong national union as distinct from a number of highly active local ones.
[41] The case of *Acción Popular* in Peru is unusual in that it only began to attract a student following after Belaunde came to power. Mexico is the striking example where student movements have exercised minimal political influence and where prominence in student politics is no guarantee of later political advancement in the PRI.

of forcing its student group to break away. The transitional process is made more difficult where the party's previous activities have taken the form of armed opposition, because of the psychological adjustment necessary in switching to a new type of activity. Even in Cuba the government is experiencing difficulties in creating a new type of heroism acceptable to a generation which nostalgically regrets being the heirs and not the initiators of the guerrilla struggle.[42]

Once a party is established in power its student branch can develop in one of two ways. (1) It can accept its new role as a prop for the establishment either (*a*) because of improved government employment prospects for its members; or (*b*) because the instruments of governmental control give it little choice; or (*c*) if the party, once in power, retains its revolutionary dynamism and succeeds in projecting a new vision. These factors need not necessarily be mutually exclusive: in the case of the Cuban FEU all three were operative. (2) It can break away to become a new opposition group either (*a*) because of disappointed expectations over promotion possibilities; or (*b*) because of the party's loss of revolutionary élan; or (*c*) if the party's leadership fails to respond to younger-generation needs; or (*d*) if there is an obvious modification of party ideology to appease foreign interests.

In societies where alternative pressure groups are weak or dispersed, as in Bolivia, students can continue to play a significant role—but as a catalyst, not as a major revolutionary force. Although they may spark off political revolutions, their narrow base as a social group precludes them from making any profound social impact unless they are accepted by mass organizations in a leadership or auxiliary capacity. The most striking example of students failing to consolidate their power as a revolutionary force was the students' government of Grau San Martín in Cuba in 1933 which, because of the absence of links with any mass organization, collapsed before Batista's armed coup.[43] Armies, not universities, expand to fill a power vacuum. Bolivia afforded the most recent illustration, when student riots in Cochabamba sparked off

---

[42] Two articles on current attitudes of Cuban youth appeared in *Bohemia* (Havana), 20 and 27 Dec. 1963.

[43] For the interesting views of Cuba's present foreign minister, Raúl Roa, who was a student activist in the anti-Machado struggle, see the reprint of articles in his autobiography, *Retorno a la alborada* (Las Villas, 1964, i. 15–22, 60–67, 73–77.

sympathetic riots throughout the country, giving General Barrientos the opportunity and the justification to overthrow Paz Estenssoro in November 1964.

However ineffectual or otherwise students may be once a government has been overthrown, they are still an important pressure group which no government can afford to ignore. The Central University at Quito was the focus of opposition to the Ecuadorian military junta between 1963 and 1966. Within hours of an ill-advised invasion of the campus by the military, roused public indignation compelled the junta to resign. Nor can a revolutionary government afford not to have the support of its universities, as the Bolivian case amply illustrates. Not only have Bolivian universities failed to produce the technicians required for the government's development plans but they have also become foci of opposition to the revolution. La Paz presents the strange spectacle for Latin America of student demonstrations spearheaded by right-wing students.

In Bolivia, early in the revolution, attempts had been made by students (spurred on by the unions and with the tacit support of the MNR government) to reconstruct the universities in the 'University Revolutions' of 1954–5, when a number of campuses were physically occupied by radical groups.[44] This movement failed, largely because the students were themselves divided, and ended in a compromise whereby university autonomy was retained and students achieved 50 per cent *co-gobierno* (Honduras is the only other country where there is similar equal representation). This failure to force universities to co-ordinate their plans, to develop technical faculties, and to foster 'popular universities' as a preliminary to widening entry, meant that the MNR government could not rely on universities either for political support or for making a contribution to economic development.

The difficulty experienced by the right-wing nationalist *Falange*, the main opposition party, in penetrating the unionized peasants, or the miners, forced it to concentrate on the universities, especially in La Paz where its main strength lies. Working alliances with other opposition groups, including at times the communists, have enabled *Falange* students to dominate La Paz University, which

[44] M. Bautista Gumucio, *Revolución y universidad en Bolivia* (La Paz, 1956), pp. 102–22. Cf. M. Duran, *La reforma universitaria en Bolivia* (Oruro, 1961).

is politically the most important. Basically hostile to the revolution, they were consequently not interested in pressing for academic reform to bring the universities into line with the country's needs, and consequently these remained geared to producing a proletariat of needy lawyers from whom the opposition recruits its staunchest supporters. In this way 50 per cent *co-gobierno* has only served to perpetuate outworn attitudes. In a country dependent on mining for its economic survival only 210 engineers of all types, including mining and petroleum, graduated between 1953 and 1962. In spite of the fact that Bolivia has inaugurated one of the most ambitious agrarian reforms in Latin America, only 71 agronomists and 14 veterinary scientists graduated in this period compared with 1,261 lawyers from the law faculties in each of the country's seven universities.[45] The MNR failed even to change the mentality of its own followers. These continued to adopt the prestige professions, with the result that the governing party could not even satisfy the job mania of its own supporters—one of the causes of its bitter internal factionalism and of its failure to retain student support—and even its own group the *Avanzada del MNR* was openly Castroite, to the chagrin of many party leaders.[46]

In order to produce the technical experts it required, the government finally set up its own technological university in 1962, with no *co-gobierno* and, by Latin American standards, a draconian academic discipline. It was one of the first casualties of Paz Estenssoro's fall from power in November 1964, when it was absorbed into La Paz University as its technological faculty. The Bolivian Revolution stands as a salutary warning that a social revolution which cannot reorganize its universities may be strangled by them.

Equally, government interference, as with the *peronista* intervention in Argentina, can turn universities and students into a régime's most formidable enemies. Autonomy by itself solves nothing, but where autonomy is threatened, confrontation between university and government is inevitable. In Cuba the issue could only be resolved by the university purges of 1959 and 1960, thus effectively destroying the university as a focus of opposition, and

---

[45] *La situación de la educación superior en Bolivia* (La Paz, 1963), p. 53.
[46] *Conferencia nacional de Avanzada del MNR* (Cochabamba, 1962). For the self-admitted failures and complete disorientation of communist students see the PCB paper *Unidad* (La Paz), 15 May 1965.

by dropping all the cherished reformist concepts. But even in Cuba the cautious handling of students is evidence of concern at the dangerous potentialities of their opposition.[47]

The idea that students are a political élite dies hard, and tempting though it may be to think that the solution to their malaise and the university crisis lies in the adoption of a new work discipline and the repudiation of politics, it is perhaps premature at a time when military intervention in politics is again on the increase. Faced by the gap between the ideals they have been taught and the reality they find, students will continue to react in a way which has been hallowed by tradition. Those students who feel, like the Cubans, that piecemeal reform is only a palliative, and that no genuine changes can occur without a total social and political revolution, may be right. The onus to prove them wrong is on their teachers and the holders of power, many of whom are now content to pay only lip-service to the reformist ideals they imbibed so eagerly in their student days.

Postscript

Since 1965, when this essay was originally written, the university crisis has sharpened throughout the continent. In Mexico, where the government is usually meticulous in respecting universities' autonomy in spite of frequent provocation, troops intervened in the University of Morelia in October 1966. In Chile, there has been a general student strike against new teaching methods at the University of Concepción, which was forced to close temporarily. In Colombia, disturbances at the University of Medellín sparked off other disturbances and led to a confrontation between the government and the student national federation over autonomy. Most dramatic of all, the campus of UCV at Caracas was forcibly occupied by the military, stung into action by terrorist attacks of which they had been the main target.

[47] For the Cuban University Reform see *La reforma de la enseñanza superior en Cuba* (Havana, 1962) and C. R. Rodríguez, 'La reforma universitaria en Cuba', *Principios* (Santiago de Chile), July–Aug. 1962. On the continuing need to purge counter-revolutionaries in Havana University see F. Crombet, president of the FEU, in *Hoy,* 14 Mar. 1965. It is puzzling that the first cell of the PURS in the university should only have been established in May 1965—four years after the party began to be set up.

Meanwhile the Brazilian and Argentinian governments are wedded to the view that the 'university problem' can only be solved by drastic government action. Perhaps it can, but so far the results have been counter-productive, provoking massive student demonstrations, decimating many faculties, and exacerbating the brain drain, already a serious enough problem. Ironically, some professors, regarded by their governments as dangerous leftists, are now working in the United States.

The new wave of student activism coincides with the formation, at the 4th Congress of Latin American students in Havana in August 1966, of the Continental Latin American Students' Organization (OCLAE) with the specific aims of 'promoting the fighting solidarity of Latin American students in their struggle against imperialism', of 'fighting to strengthen students' links with the peasantry and working class' and 'to develop solidarity between Latin American students and those of other continents' (for which purpose a Tricontinental Students' Conference is planned). Whether there is any connexion or not between the new student militancy and the Havana organization, the latter is evidence of growing communist emphasis on the revolutionary potential of students. The battle lines have now been drawn and there is every indication that 1967, like 1966, will be a vintage year both for violations of university autonomy and for student martyrs.

The *Ejido* and Political Stability in Mexico

FRANÇOIS CHEVALIER

THE Mexican revolution seems to have centred in the provincial and rural areas rather than on the capital, and Mexico City appears to have played a passive rather than an active role in events— although it is also true that important rural attitudes and beliefs have been linked with ideas originating either directly or indirectly from the capital. Since the beginning of this century political revolutions which have led to deep social changes in Latin America (with the exception of Argentina) appear to have taken place, if not always outside the capitals and important cities, at least without decisive assistance from these centres: one might quote Bolivia and Cuba as examples, subject to the same reservations as would apply to Mexico.

Because of the development of centralization in Mexico and the considerable urban growth of Mexico City (and to a lesser extent of its industry), the capital is clearly assuming a new position of exceptional influence. Certain statistics attempt—perhaps rather too eagerly—to project the image of an urbanized country by making a practice of classifying separately from rural areas localities which census returns show to have a population of between 2,500 and 5,000. While it is true that those with less than 5,000 inhabitants—representing, in 1950, 65·4 per cent of the total population—contain a certain number of people who only make their living indirectly, if at all, from the land, it must also be remembered that agricultural labourers and families who derive part of their living from the land also inhabit the larger units.[1]

[1] Mexico, DGE, VII *Censo general de población, 1950 Resumen general* (1953); cf., for example, J. Durán Ochoa, *Población*, 1955, p. 14; VIII *Censo general de población, 1960 Resumen general* (1962). I should like here to express my thanks to Claude Bataillon, *agrégé de géographie*, for sending me valuable information on various points from Mexico at a time when the results of the Mexican census of 1960, which was not published until the end of 1965, were not available.

Since then this percentage has decreased; and in 1960, by the same reckoning, the peasants constituted no more than 57·8 per cent of the population.[2]

It is therefore still true to say that, while they have lost their former dominance, rural areas still have an important influence on the life of the country. An essential and typical element in the post-revolutionary rural society is the *ejido*, which holds the most prominent position from the social, if not the economic, point of view, by virtue of the great number of people who live or depend on—or are connected at least to some extent with—such units. Not enough is known about the *ejido*—in spite of certain important and classical works (by Eyler Simpson, Whetten, etc.)—while our knowledge of individually-owned smallholdings is certainly even more limited.

But first a brief definition of the *ejido*. It consists of a unit of cultivated land held as communal or collective property but distributed in small individual or family plots. Thus the beneficiaries have only the usufruct of their plots, which are run by an ' *ejidal* committee' of three members, which in principle they elect. In 1960 the communally-farmed *ejidos* represented only 3·2 per cent of the total. The purpose of this essay is to examine the origins of the *ejido* and the environment in which it arose (for it still bears the impress of its origins), then to consider the renewal of the *ejido* under Cárdenas (who extended the concept to the whole country and closely linked it with the government), and its diversification and slow evolution since that date, with special emphasis on the poorer sectors, which still represent the vast majority of the *ejidatarios*. It then proceeds to discuss the extent to which the agrarian revolution, the *ejido*, and relative fulfilment of peasant aspirations have modified rural modes of thought, in the sense that progress has been achieved, but at the same time it considers the effects of new agrarian policies, caused in particular by rapid demographic growth. Lastly, it investigates the part played in Mexican politics by the rural interests working through organizations and associations whose real function has not hitherto been sufficiently clarified.

One is faced with highly complex phenomena, reliable study of

[2] Mexico, DGE, IV *Censos agrícola ganadero y ejidal, 1960: Resumen general* (1965), pt. 43, p. 561 (percentage calculated by the author).

which may seem extremely difficult or almost impossible.[3] However, a knowledge of economic and social structures in the perspective of their historical development and of the cultures involved can be combined with direct observations in order to throw some light on the modes of thought and influence these complex phenomena have had on the life of the country, even though it may not be possible, in the present state of sociological knowledge, to make a full analysis.

These social and economic structures and their evolution are not adequately reflected in statistics (not that there is any lack of statistics as such), although this fact does not seem to have been sufficiently recognized by many economists and sociologists. Indeed, even when statistics are reliable, they are principally concerned with theoretical legal situations which do not always coincide with the real position.   The main body of statistical information is contained in publications issued by the Dirección General de Estadística: first, the first Agricultural and Livestock Census (*Ier Censo agrícola-ganadero*) of 1930 and the first Ejidal Census (*Ier Censo ejidal*) of 1935, then the combined censuses (*Censos agrícola-ganadero y ejidal*) of 1940 (no. II), 1950 (no. III), and 1960 (no. IV), the last appearing in 1965 (an improvement of the preceding ones).   There are also statistics published by the Departamento Agrario and entitled *Memoria del Departamento Agrario*, the first edition covering the period 1915–40, and appearing in 1933–4, while the most recent edition covers the period ending in 1958.[4]   Unfortunately reliable comparison is impossible, because the statistics are not systematically compiled on the same basis.   To quote one example: on the allocation of land to the *ejidos*, the figures are sometimes confined to allocations which have actually been made, while in other cases they include those still subject to confirmation.   In the same way the figures quoted for the total number of *ejidatarios* sometimes include those who are only entitled to receive land in the future, as has finally been established by a great authority on the' rural world of Mexico, Moisés de la Peña, who has made an extremely interesting critique of the

---

[3] Robert Scott tends to hold this opinion, cf. *Mexican Government in Transition* (Urbana, Ill., 1959), further discussed by H. Cline in his important *Mexico; Revolution to Evolution, 1940–1960* (London, 1962), p. 156.

[4] It was not possible to examine all these statistics at the time of writing.

available statistics.[5]   While it is true that a large number of statistical publications have also been compiled by American institutes or international organizations, as far as the rural areas are concerned these statistics are usually derived from data which sometimes contain fundamental errors, and are even less reliable since the phenomena under investigation are more social than economic in nature, and consequently more complex and difficult to express in figures.   General statistics are therefore only of partial value for the purposes of a study such as this.   Consequently this essay has also been based on historical sources and on a few relevant monographs interpreted in the light of personal observations made in Mexico.

The Ejido as a Development of the Traditional Village Community

A fundamental distinction must be made between the central-southern areas of Mexico, generally characterized by the presence of a large number of village communities based on sedentary, native peasant populations—which were given a new structure under the Spaniards—and the vast northern provinces, where independent villages were much less numerous and usually much looser in structure.[6]

Faced with the vast expansion of large estates in the nineteenth and early twentieth centuries, the communities of the central and southern areas of the country found a new impetus towards the unity and personality which until then they had been rapidly losing.   This was the age in which the governments of liberal or Positivist tendencies—in particular that of Porfirio Díaz—were breaking down the traditional barriers, especially by building railways.

This expansion of the haciendas was certainly of value in the virgin areas—bush, forests, and steppes—which were opened up in

---

[5] M.T. de la Peña, *El pueblo y su tierra; mito y realidad de la reforma agraria en México* (Mexico City, 1964).

[6] After this essay was written, I saw for the first time Dr Alfonso Caso's article 'Renaissance économique des communautés indigènes du Méxique (*Diogène*, 1963) which briefly emphasizes the resemblances between the *ejido* and the Aztec *calpulli* based on the ancient *tierra de comunidad*. In the north of Mexico, however, recent research (as yet unpublished) by Lic. Moisés González Navarro appears to indicate that the *ejidos* differ considerably from those Caso describes; nor did they originate in quite the same way.

the north and the tropical areas. But the estate owners needed labour, and the best means of securing it was to take the land away from the villages so that the inhabitants would be forced to work on the large estates. Not only the traditional—and fairly localised —Indian 'communities' were absorbed in this way, but also the peasant enclaves between the large estates. In the central and southern areas this situation affected the long-established Indian communities, recognized as such during the colonial period but which, in the course of the nineteenth century, had lost any uniform cultural basis, had begun to speak Spanish, and had failed to retain their traditional institutions of mixed—native and Spanish colonial—origin. Above all they had often lost some of their old communal lands. Finally, there were also small secondary groups on independent strips of land, often gained at the expense of the Indians.

No precise study or figures are available to permit an evaluation, even on a local level, of, on the one hand, the gains made by the large estates and, on the other, the losses of the small communities, i.e. the actual situation on the eve of the 1910 revolution.

The evolution described here was particularly marked in a well-defined and relatively rich area—the province of Morelos near Mexico City. Here semi-independent groups of peasants still clung to small patches of ground, sometimes mere *tlacololes* or fertile hollows in the neighbouring mountains. They added to their resources by working as small craftsmen or hired labourers on the haciendas or in the city. The pressures exerted on them by the modern sugar plantations in the surrounding areas which wished to obtain cheap labour visibly served to increase their solidarity. In their efforts to avoid becoming mere peons and agricultural day-labourers, they appear to some extent to have regained their former communal spirit, which they had lost through contacts with the neighbouring capital and often through neglect of their native language. Thus it was that these peasant groups stood firmly by one of their fellows, Zapata, when he revolted in order to defend the modest agrarian programmes of Madero. This general movement can certainly be described as the 'last great Indian uprising', in the words of M. L. Chávez Orozco,[7] even

---

[7] Cf. F. Chevalier, 'Un facteur décisif de la révolution agraire au Mexique: le soulevement de Zapata' (1911–19), *Annales E.S.C. 1961*, pp. 66–82. There do not seem to have been divergences of opinion

though it is true that this area had lost much more of its native culture than other more traditionally Indian regions.

These villages, inhabited by many peons (far more numerous than the small groups who lived on the haciendas), and well served by the unflinching will of Zapata, whose understanding of the problems involved steadily grew clearer, finally imposed agrarian reform on the central government in the capital. This reform was achieved essentially because the villagers were determined to throw off the crushing burdens imposed upon them and to recover all that they had lost. Their most vivid and bitter memory was the loss within the last few decades of their communal fields and pasture lands, or *ejidos*, a word which soon came to refer to the recovered lands as a whole, especially the cultivated fields where the village groups were eventually established.

Unfortunately there is only very limited information about the first *ejidos*—in the Mexican, revolutionary sense of the word— which were created in the rural areas of Morelos, Puebla, Mexico, and Guerrero provinces by the Zapatista movement after 1912, and especially in 1915 and 1916.[8] This new form of organization was probably quite simply derived from the traditions of the old peasant communities of the colonial period: the allocation of individual patches of ground for cultivation, which were then declared inalienable to prevent their reabsorption by the haciendas, with the proviso that they must be cultivated or would otherwise be reallocated; the right of members of the group to cut wood, graze animals, and cultivate parts of the recovered common land; all this no doubt under the supervision of traditional, elected authorities. However, as the concept of private property had been firmly rooted for centuries—and since the main purpose of the peasants was to prevent expansion of the haciendas at their own

---

(unless imposed by force) among the rural populations of Morelos towards Zapata, in spite of the suggestions put forward by Oscar Lewis in his classical work on Tepoztlán (*Life in a Mexican Village*, Univ. of Illinois Press, 1951).

[8] Especially Ixcamilpán and Jolalpán (Puebla); Ticumán, Tlaltizapán, Anenecuilco (Mor.); Mixquiahuala (Hgo.). Cf. A. Díaz Soto y Gama, *La cuestión agraria en México* (Mexico, UNAM, 1959), pp. 6, 203, etc. Dr Díaz Sota y Gama, who was Zapata's legal adviser, has assured me that there were many similar cases. Cf. also Mendieta y Núñez, *Efectos sociales de la reforma agraria en tres comunidades ejidales* (Mexico City, UNAM, 1960), p. 146.

expense—private property was recognized as well as communal or village property.

At this time there was one additional innovation of real significance: the creation of the Rural Loan Bank of the province of Morelos, which functioned regularly in the years 1915–16 under the authority of the Zapatista government as a kind of agricultural friendly society and confined its membership to those individuals who were considered responsible and trustworthy.

The Zapatista laws of 26 October 1915 and 3 February and 5 July 1917 perfected the organization of the *ejido*, still on the basis of the communal system but with the addition of an 'indigenous' element which is reminiscent of the *calpulli* of the pre-Hispanic era (fairly similar to the clan), together with certain ideas taken from international socialism and the Christian socialism of Díaz Soto y Gama. But since Zapatista legislation was not officially recognized, these *ejidos* had, in fact, no legal sanction, and those in charge of agrarian policy simply ignored them. However, with the exception of a few details, they seem to have been recognized a short time later by a law passed by the government in the capital,[9] which could not easily have put the clock back and revoked the Zapatista solution so widely acclaimed by the whole of the rural population of the south. Lastly, in 1920, President Obregón sanctioned the use of the word *ejido* in its new sense of allocation of land (especially of cultivated land).[10]

As envisaged at this stage of the revolution, this Mexican *ejido* represented a rebirth of the traditional village community which was already losing its hold on individuals in the nineteenth century —more or less as it was at the end of the *ancien régime* in eastern France, or more recently in certain regions of the Iberian peninsula which have retained the old agrarian structure. It was not merely a kind of semi-collective agricultural system substituted for the large estates, while adopting certain elements of their structure. The concept of discipline and authority on which the organisation of the hacienda was primarily based was not taken over either by the officials responsible for the *ejidos* or by the representatives of

---

[9] All available official documents assign relatively late dates, subsequent to the death of Zapata, to the *ejidos* of Morelos. It would be necessary to examine the actual situation; legalization probably often came after actual creation of the *ejidos*.

[10] *Ley de ejidos* of 30 Dec. 1920, Art. 13: 'La tierra dotada a los pueblos se denominará ejido'. The word does not figure in the 1917 constitution.

the central government—except later on, and then only partially
in certain collective *ejidos*, or else as a result of state planning (or
even private planning) in agricultural sectors which benefited from
a reasonable level of capital investment.

In this connexion it is very significant that certain groups of
peones acasillados (i.e. living on the haciendas) were not authorized until 1934 to form new centres of population endowed with
ejidos; even then these groups of workers from the haciendas were
only recognized as new *ejidos* at their express request and when it
was not possible to distribute them among neighbouring *ejidos*
which were already in existence.[11] This measure was in line with
a very old tradition, since the viceroys had already authorized
certain groups of peons living within the limits of the haciendas to
form village communities with their own administration, but
without any land over and above the 'legal endowment' of approximately 101 hectares.   Nevertheless the estate owners were
apprehensive of this semi-autonomous status which their workers
could achieve, particularly in the north of Mexico.[12]

It is also significant that it was only with the agrarian code of
1934 that the local government of the *ejido* became really distinct
from that of the village, as a result of the formation of a *comisariado
ejidal* consisting of three members; today each unit is still organized
in this way.[13]

The *comunidad* or pueblo from which the *ejido* sprang arose from
a mixture of elements from the *calpulli* of ancient times and the
Spanish community village, as represented to a great extent by the
reducción and the mission village.   The pueblo was enlarged and
often divided into several *ejidos*, but it underwent no substantial
alteration.   Frequently it even received plots of *ejidal* land which
were too small to provide more than an additional source of food
or income for the inhabitants, who remained day-labourers on the
neighbouring haciendas.[14]   Although sometimes the villagers took

[11] Mexican Agrarian Code, dated 22 Mar. 1934, Arts. 43, 45, and 99
(President Abelardo Rodríguez)—confirmed and developed by Cárdenas.
[12] F. Chevalier, 'Survivances seigneuriales et présages de la réforme agraire
dans le nord du Mexique', *Revue historique*, July–Sept. 1959.
[13] Agrarian Code, Arts. 119–22.
[14] Cf. R. Fernández y Fernández, quoted by J. Silva Herzog, *El agrarismo
mexicano y la reforma agraria* (Mexico City, 1959), pp. 546–7.   Cf. too
Alfonso Caso, 'Renaissance économique des communautés indigènes
au Mexique', *Diogène* (Paris), 1963.

action against the oppressive hacienda system, as for instance when the followers of Zapata burnt down sugar mills, after regaining their rights and at least in part restoring the balance, they apparently did not wish to abolish an institution which was as traditional as the villages themselves and formed an essential part of their cultural horizon.

It is also remarkable that before the time of Cárdenas these ideas were implicitly accepted by most of the Mexican governments which, from Carranza to Calles, considered the aim of the agrarian revolution to be the establishment of individual holdings of small or average size as 'inalienable family property'—to use a term of the 1917 constitution (Art. 27, VII f)—without excluding *a priori* the existence of the haciendas. Acceptance of the concept of the *ejido* was essential under the pressure of popular and peasant opinion in the central and southern provinces which had been aroused by the Zapatista movement. In spite of its local character and apparent failure since the assassination of its leader, the Zapatista movement still 'cast a shadow'—a significant expression used even by its enemies—over government debates, assemblies, and decisions.

Without daring to admit it, most members of the government brought up in the liberal tradition considered the *ejido* as a kind of makeshift solution, a mere stage of development which brought no hope of economic progress, a compromise made necessary by circumstances and serving to convert to the system of peasant small-holdings those pueblos which were still so bound up with their community traditions that the 1917 constitution refers to them as corporations.[15] Thus in 1923 the administration deemed it sufficient to allocate a plot of 4 hectares to the *ejidatarios* as against 25 to the 'smallholders', the reason being that the *ejidatario* would be more or less satisfied and would be able to grow enough produce to feed his family, while the smallholder would grow produce for sale as well. Finally, the government was composed mainly of men from the north, that is to say from states where peasant communities were not so deeply rooted as in the states of Indian

---

[15] Art. 27, vi. The term *'corporaciones de población'* reappears in a decree of Calles dated 31 July 1925. The comments made above in connexion with Carranza and Calles do not affect the fact that certain ideas of socialist inspiration were included in the 1917 constitution under the influence of a left wing of the Zapatista movement, which had more radical tendencies.

tradition in the central and southern regions. Apart from the large haciendas, the members of the government were best acquainted with small commercial towns and cattle ranches.

Cárdenas: Decisive Stage in the Development of the Ejido

The agrarian measures of Cárdenas (1934–40) must be emphasized because, while apparently changing the character of this movement, they made the agrarian reform irreversible and final.

After a long period of government by men from the north, the new leader of Mexico came from Michoacán and grew up in an environment of peasants and smallholders; he was certainly more aware than his predecessors of the aspirations of the pueblos, with their ancient Indian traditions. Cárdenas came to look upon the *ejido* not as a kind of temporary measure imposed by circumstances and bound to be replaced one day by a different system, but as an institution well adapted to the needs of the country and destined to last for a long time. For, as he once wrote, the smallholding 'cannot in any circumstances be considered as the final form which the *ejidos* will take, since the *ejido* is a separate institution whose origin, organization, and economic function are all quite distinct'.[16]

Like Zapata a few years after the initiation of his movement (but far more clearly), Cárdenas was influenced by international socialism—a movement to which he claimed allegiance—and his ideas appeared to extend and renew the communal agrarian movement established by the Zapatists twenty years earlier. Above all, like Zapata, Cárdenas had the will to achieve his aims.

It has repeatedly been stated—although the figures which are quoted vary—that Cárdenas distributed much more land than all his predecessors taken together; that some of this land was the finest in the country; that the average amount allowed to each *ejidatario* more than doubled under his régime; that he drove out usury as a source of finance by founding the Banco Nacional, which gave a considerable new impetus to the rural credit schemes founded in 1926 by Calles. Observers take less trouble, however, to distinguish between unconfirmed allocations or occupations of land, and land for which definite deeds of ownership are held. As Moisés de la Peña points out, the work carried out in the past

---

[16] Quoted by Silva Herzog, p. 410.

twenty-five years in this field represents to some extent the regularization and confirmation of ownership of land already allocated or occupied.

Cárdenas's predecessors allocated a total of 8,738 million hectares on a provisional basis and 6,666 million with definite deeds of ownership, concerning 778,000 *ejidatarios*, while Cárdenas alone allocated 9,861 million, subject to confirmation, and 17,889 million hectares on a definitive basis, relating to no less than 810,000 *ejidatarios*. These figures are more impressive than those which are usually quoted, for everything points to the fact that definitive allocations made after 1940 (and especially after 1946) relate to part of the 9,861 million hectares handed over subject to confirmation under the Cárdenas régime.[17]

In 1936, for the first time, irrigated haciendas—the most productive and the richest—were transformed into 'collective *ejidos*', differing from the existing *ejidos* which had sprung from the old peasant *comunidad*, even though the new institution still retained certain features of the old, and was certainly not conceived along orthodox socialist lines. Finally, in 1937, all the peons of the haciendas were given authority freely to request permission to form *ejidos*.[18] At the end of Cárdenas's mandate, the *ejidos* owned more than half of the high yield irrigated land: 994,320 hectares, as against 905,770 in private ownership. This represented a real economic and social revolution.[19]

A further initiative of fundamental importance, though one which is not often quoted, was the organisation of the *Confederación Nacional Campesina*, or CNC, which was first established in 1935 as a peasant trade union and which, in 1938, was incorporated in the official government party (the *Partido de la Revolución Mexicana*, later to become the *Partido Revolucionario Institucional*, or PRI). This measure has generally been considered as a further means made available to the President and the party essentially to control the vast mass of peasant electors. While it is true that the CNC has always served this purpose (and still does so),

[17] De la Peña, pp. 895, 336. Figures published by the Departamento Agrario (figures below 1,000 omitted here).
[18] Modification of Art. 45 of the Agrarian Code by decree of 9 Aug. 1937.
[19] *Censo ejidal* of 1940 (according to this source the total area of *ejidal* land was 28,922,000 hectares in 1940). My thanks are due here to Jean Meyer, *agrégé d'histoire*, who was good enough to complete my figures from these sources.

especially during presidential elections, the converse is also true, and we believe that through this body the millions of *ejidatarios* really do play a certain part in directing the internal politics of Mexico—as was Cárdenas's aim when he associated them with the party. But by what methods, how, and to what extent this influence is exercised is a subject which requires further research.

After the introduction of this important reform, it would have taken a real political revolution for the *ejidatarios*, henceforth bound up with the system of government of the country, to lose all their influence. An upheaval of this kind was difficult to imagine at a time when a growing number of members of the majority class in the country were becoming aware that their interests clearly lay in preserving the results already achieved. From any standpoint these are considerable results, which basically represent the extension and development on a vast scale of a reform which, as has been seen, was deeply rooted in the very structure of rural society. It is therefore easy to understand why, twenty-five years after leaving office, Cárdenas still enjoys unrivalled prestige in the rural areas of Mexico.

New Agrarian Policy after 1940

In spite of the great efforts made between 1934 and 1940, there were still latifundia, although these were not as important as has often been maintained. Thus, on the basis of the 1950 census, it was thought that at this date there still existed officially 708 agricultural estates of over 800 hectares each, making a total of more than 3½ million hectares of cultivated land [20]—still an enormous proportion. But a study of the geographical conditions would show that these estates are in areas of very sparse population, mountainous, tropical, and poor; and the ground may be cultivated only in one year out of ten, or even less, using the system of itinerant cultivation. Moreover, it is on record that of the 19,928,211 hectares under cultivation shown in the census, 9,105,707 were fallow. Finally, it is possible that the figures quoted for large estates include public property and land belonging to native communities.

Even more important are the large cattle-raising, forest, or grazing estates. Of these the census showed 10,519 of over 1,000 hectares,

[20] In a work of great interest: Michel Gutelman, *L'ejido dans la réforme agraire au Mexique* (Paris, 1961, unpub. thesis), pp. 269, 293.

the total area concerned being 80,974,000 hectares. But Sr Moisés de la Peña—who has made some most illuminating comments on the statistics—points out that this total includes 7,393 communal and public estates amounting to 20 million hectares. It is nevertheless true that there still are, or were recently, several thousand immense private estates representing 60 million hectares—and no doubt this is a conservative figure! [21]

The areas in question consist of tropical bush and above all mountain regions and semi-desert plains, which are suitable only for cattle-raising on a very extensive scale. In fact it was Cárdenas himself who created the notion of *inafectabilidad ganadera*—i.e. inalienability of lands used for cattle-raising—subject to periodic revision—so as to prevent breaking up this kind of cattle-raising.

But with the construction of new highways and access routes, and under the effect of increasing population pressure, the value of some of these vast estates has increased and it is this type of land above all which has been the object of further allocations. These have been less numerous under President Cárdenas's successors but they increased again under President López Mateos (1958–64), who allocated 10,043,000 hectares between 1958 and 1962 alone. Of these, 4,453,000 hectares were handed over to the *ejidos* and 2,206,000 hectares to native communities.[22]

If there has been a change of direction since 1940 in the movement for agrarian reform, this has not affected the large estates of poor-quality soil, especially after the accession of President López Mateos to power. As far as the rich, irrigated lands with high yields are concerned, the situation is different. In this connexion the official statistics tend to be fairly discreet.

The policy of Cárdenas's successors in respect of these lands has been to act as though the basic, essential agrarian measures had already been taken, and to decide that the country must now above all increase production by means of agricultural and technical progress, to say nothing of industrialization. Concern with economic development rapidly overtook social preoccupations, especially under President Miguel Alemán (1946–54). The construction of irrigation dams where the soil was rich was intensified

[21] De la Peña, pp. 338–43.
[22] Departamento de Asuntos Agrarios y Colonización, *Memoria de labores . . . presentada por . . . Roberto Barrios* (1962). Tables showing land allocated in 1958–62 and 1961–2.

in order to grow produce for export. Foreign capital was attracted and, without any formal declaration to this effect, the tendency was to consider that the *ejido*, even of an improved type, could not adapt itself to modern commercial exploitation. Private property was once again in favour: not a 'family smallholding' of the type favoured by Calles (who in spite of his militant anti-clericalism adopted this concept from the Christian socialists), but a rich estate of ample size created in the newly irrigated areas. Such estates passed into the hands of individuals and friends of the government. President Alemán's first legislative measure, on 31 December 1946, was to increase from 100 to 300 hectares of irrigated land the maximum area of the 'smallholding', which retained this name (so as not to frighten the CNC!), when the crops grown were 'rich', i.e. coffee, cocoa, fruit, grapes, sugar-cane.

On the north-west coast and in various irrigated areas with a moderately hot or tropical climate, there developed a highly capitalized agriculture which found almost unlimited markets in the neighbouring United States. A wide variety of legal devices were used in order to exceed the upper limit of 300 hectares. A number of large estates or plantations were established which, while they did not extend like the old estates over tens of thousands of hectares, nevertheless produced higher financial yields.

This new type of property, run by modern methods with wage-earning staff, does not figure significantly in statistics, and information is difficult to obtain, since such estates are usually controlled by influential persons and powerful interests which prefer to remain in the background, as they are extremely sensitive to criticism from 'the old agrarian guard' and the younger elements of the CNC.

In addition to these highly capitalized estates there are others, generally smaller, but also consisting of good irrigated land, usually formed from parts of the old haciendas which have remained in the hands of their original owners. These have been obliged to go over to intensive, modern farming in order to obtain the maximum yield from limited areas. As the agronomist René Dumont points out in his *Terres vivantes*, this has been an unforeseen result of agrarian reform and the pressure of the *ejido* on private property. The area of irrigated land in private hands almost doubled between 1940 and 1950 (1,788,000 hectares as against 905,000), while the figures for the *ejidos* show an increase of only 23 per cent (1,221,000 hectares against 994,000). The census of 1960 reveals a relative improvement as regards the *ejidal* allocations (1,427,949 irrigated hectares in the *ejidos* as against 2,087,360 in private ownership).

The profits achieved by these various capitalized undertakings have been all the more marked since, because of inflation, real wages have lagged behind the purchasing power of the currency. According to calculations made by the economist López Rosado, the real value of the minimum agricultural wage diminished by 46 per cent between 1940 and 1950. Considered as a proportion of the gross national product, its share of general wages was reduced from 30·5 per cent in 1939 to 23 per cent in 1950, while at the same time profits increased from 26·1 to 42 per cent.[23]

These figures are perhaps open to question, but even if they are exaggerated it remains true that the real value of wages earned by agricultural labourers has fallen in many parts of Mexico, thus intensifying the seasonal movement of *braceros* (day-labourers) to the United States. The situation has been different in certain rich agricultural regions bordering on the United States, and it would seem that recently, in the country as a whole, real agricultural wages have regained a part of the lost ground.

This highly capitalized type of agriculture was so profitable that it even spread to certain sectors of rich irrigated land belonging to the new *ejidos* created by President Cárdenas, or less frequently by his successors. An excellent example—pointed out to the author by Claude Bataillon, on the basis of a very recent study made by the agronomist Fernández y Fernández [24]—is provided by the Yaqui valley in the north-west (state of Sonora). The situation here is as follows:

Ownership of Land in Yaqui Valley

Year	Owners of land (*ocupantes*)	Irrigated surface (ha.)	Average size (ha.)	Ejidatarios	% land in ejidos	Per ejidatario (ha.)	Privately-owned small-holdings (ha.)
1937	3,178	52,000	16	2,300	37	8	39
1952	4,933	120,000	24	2,700	30	13	38
1962	6,301	203,000	32	3,200	32	20	44

[23] D. López Rosado and V. J. Noyola, 'Los salarios reales en Mexico 1939–1950', *El Trimestre Económico*, 18 (1951), p. 206, quoted and discussed by Silva Herzog, p. 500.
[24] Agrarian Congress in Tepic, Mexico, 1964.

However these figures do not give a true picture of the situation, since estates in the hands of some families amount to 500 and even 1,000 hectares. On the other hand, a considerable number of *ejidatarios* invest the credits granted by the *Ejidal* Bank in only part of their land and lease out the remainder (40 per cent of the area of *ejidal* land is leased in this way). Again, certain more enterprising *ejidatarios* rent land to add it to their own allocation. Their holdings may then become profitable capitalist undertakings with access to private credit, as is often the case for viable *ejidos* as a whole.

In the Yaqui valley there exist side by side with these small *ejidatarios*, who obtain credit from the state and are protected against eviction by the *ejidal* law, farmers who operate average or large estates which are highly capitalized. From the high degree of technical development of this system, Fernández concludes that the government has no wish to destroy it even though it is semi-illegal. This region produces 40 per cent of all the wheat grown in Mexico and 8 per cent of the cotton, on a total of 60,000 hectares, where at least 6,000 day-labourers find work.

In the regions closer to the United States, which have generally been developed since the war, a large private company (Anderson & Clayton) advances the money necessary for growing cotton and purchases the crops both from the *ejidatarios* and from private owners. This is the case at Mexicali (Baja California) (which produces 20 per cent of the total Mexican cotton crop), where the 20-hectare *ejidos* receive as much irrigation water as the private estates. At Matamoros (Coahuila) the *ejidos* represent only 20 per cent of the cultivated land and private holdings predominate; many of these are owned by politicians who have been able to obtain land on credit from the government.

In most of the collective *ejidos* the plots of land have passed to individual owners (338,621 hectares of communally farmed *ejidos* against 9,990,625 hectares of individually farmed *ejidos* in 1960),[25] a system more suited to the wishes of the *ejidatarios* and which has been assisted by the granting of adequate credit facilities by the *Ejidal* Bank, especially under Presidents such as Miguel Alemán (1946–52). A parallel development was the reconstruction effected by private initiative and capital on the fringe on the *ejidal* system. In this way entrepreneurs who paid rent to the *ejidatarios* were able

[25] *IV Censos agrícola . . . 1960*, p. 561.

to reconstitute large agricultural units. However, this process can hardly be described as a restoration of the large estates, because the new undertakings are on a precarious and temporary basis and are subject to frequent changes.

The *Ejidal* Bank reserves its credit for irrigated, rich land, especially for land on which cotton is grown, and this appears to account for more than half of the sums advanced. From the economic point of view the spectacular development of agricultural production in Mexico is due above all to these undertakings with high capital investment—private properties and certain rich *ejidos*. Agricultural production appears to have more or less tripled over the past twenty-five years—a remarkable achievement in a mountainous and poor country. For example, cotton production increased from 65,495 tons in 1940 to 414,000 in 1959.

From the social point of view this kind of agricultural development is of direct concern to a limited number of people. In 1958 the census showed only 15,104 *ejidatarios* possessing over 10 hectares of irrigated land (6,191 of these owned over 20 hectares). Even if one assumes that some of the irrigated *ejidal* plots of between 5 and 10 hectares belong to the agricultural system with high capital investment, it still remains true that this system concerns only a fraction of the 16,670 *ejidatarios* in this sector.[26] As for the non-irrigated land which should be included with the above because of an exceptionally favourable climate, or because it is used for cattle-raising based on capital investment, this again only concerns a small number of *ejidos*. The number of *ejidatarios* directly interested in this type of development cannot be more than a few tens of thousands, or about 2–3 per cent of the total.

Finally, the number of private owners of over 10 hectares of irrigated land amounts to only 28,657,[27] many of whom are town-dwellers (known in Mexico as 'nylon farmers'). Even if the owners of irrigated farms not included in the census carried out by the Ministry of Hydraulic Resources are added, as well as all the estates of average or large size which are not irrigated but which include capital investment, the total would still be relatively modest.

The *ejidatarios* of the new type clearly carry some weight in government circles and perhaps also in the CNC, for the same

[26] Mexico, *Cincuenta años de Revolución*, i: *La economía* (1960), pp. 125, 366.
[27] Ibid. Total obtained by adding 'former smallholders' to 'colonists' (census 1950), 28,486 in 1960 (1960 Census p. 31).

economic reasons as the owners or farmers of rich, irrigated estates. The influence of the latter is all the more important as a number of them are politicians who are closely linked with the government, or friends of one or other of the past Presidents. Because of the prosperity of their estates, which produce crops for export and provide an essential source of dollars, a blind eye is turned to certain legal irregularities.

Further, from the social point of view, these partially mechanized estates cause relatively few problems, because they are situated primarily in low-lying areas or recently irrigated tropical areas, all sparsely populated and remote from the poor, overpopulated *ejidos* of the plateaux. Thus serious difficulties, tensions, and conflicts normally provoked by proximity are avoided.

The government has therefore succeeded in maintaining an equilibrium based on compromise, between the requirements of an agricultural development policy founded on free enterprise and the tendency, under certain social pressures, to maintain agrarian reform on the lines laid down by the Mexican revolution.

The Traditional Ejido and Peasant Smallholdings

In 1960 the number of *ejidos* in Mexico totalled 18,699, of which 5,088 were irrigated to a very unequal extent. The great majority of them still conform to the tradition of the *ejido* as a development of the village community, that is to say they are either divided into small non-irrigated plots, practising basically subsistence agriculture without credit facilities, or else with a little governmental credit cultivating minute parcels of irrigated land expropriated from neighbouring haciendas. As demographic pressures have increased, these *ejidos* have certainly continued to grow in number and size, above all at the expense of large-scale extensive farming; that is to say that they have swallowed up vast stretches of scrub and pasture, consisting of millions of hectares, even during the last presidency. There are fewer figures, however, for allocations of irrigated land, which were much the most important ones: according to the last census, they totalled 206,000 hectares between 1950 and 1960.

But the population continued to rise rapidly, latterly by nearly a million a year, to give a total of 40 million people. It is relevant to ask what proportion of this population depends on *ejidos*. But it is not easy to ascertain this with any precision, even though the 1960 census marked a great advance from a demographic point of

view. According to the 1940 *ejidal* census, there were 1,601,479
registered *ejidatarios,* although the total of different categories
only amounted to 1,222,859. The 1950 census figures were
1,378,320 and 1,552,926, doubtless according to whether or not
the beneficiaries of certain categories of unconfirmed allocations
of land were included, the lower figure representing only the
ejidatarios provided with title-deeds for their plots. According to
the very convincing calculations of the economist Edmundo
Flores, the peasants who had received plots by 1958 amounted
to 2,196,043.

But the 1960 census, which was far more precise than the earlier
ones, shows that, out of a total of 2,321,227 *ejidatarios,* 1,523,796
had holdings, 738,955 were landless, and 723,536 were 'associated
ejidatarios'. It even calculated the number of inhabitants in the
ejidatarios' families which, including those 'who recover more than
half their expenses by the produce of the *ejido*', totalled 12,320,824
persons. The census also shows how many people over fifteen years
old worked on the *ejidos* for a salary or daily wage, namely 605,160
(and conversely, how many *ejidatarios* worked elsewhere: 387,428).[28]

What is the significance of these figures, which one knows to be
so difficult to get in the vast Mexican countryside? On the *ejidos*
live not only the *ejidatarios* entitled to be the beneficiaries of a plot
but also a large number of persons more or less associated with
them because they have no other permanent job, i.e. grown-up
children, relatives, etc. who live in *ejidal* communities between their
seasonal or occasional employment as *braceros* in the United
States, daily-paid labourers, etc. Flores also considers that in 1961
there were at least a million men who had vainly asked for an *ejidal*
plot but had succeeded only in obtaining a document recognizing
their future rights (*certificado de derechos a salvo*).[29] Thus
certainly well over a third of the total population of 35 million in
1960 depended on *ejidos,* even if only partially. And one also has
to take into account the very small peasant proprietors and sharecroppers (*medieros*) who, as will be seen, closely resemble
ejidatarios and are often mistaken for them.

Poor *ejidos,* like the communities in which they originated, and
very often overpopulated *ejidos,* too: this is the undeniable situation

[28] IV *Censos agrícola . . . 1960,* pp. 557, 558, 560.
[29] J. L. Tamayo, *Geografía general de México,* 2nd ed., iv: *Geografía
económica* (Mexico, 1962), pp. 83 f., 92.

of the majority of them, which thus from a strictly economic point of view hardly attract either private or state capital.   But for political and social reasons the state, although inadequately, extends credit to the less underprivileged sectors: according to the 1960 census, 633,535,000 pesos (about £18 million) have been advanced to *ejidos* by national institutions while private banks have advanced 242,911,000 pesos to the more prosperous *ejidos* (though too much reliance cannot be placed on census figures).   However, unlike the highly capitalized *ejidos* and properties, these majority *ejidos*, while they have little economic value, have considerable social importance, and we believe that they still exert political influence.

Let us take a closer look at the economic and social situation of the great majority of the *ejidos*.   The causes of their economic stagnation are simple and almost self-evident.

In the first place they result from the fact that the *ejidos* were naturally created where the villages of their origin were situated, i.e. the old nuclei of population established for historical rather than for economic reasons, naturally with the exception of semi-desert zones which could not be cultivated before the introduction of modern irrigation.   True, this phenomenon is common to all peoples prior to the development of a modern economy, but its effects were far more serious in a country such as Mexico, which is essentially mountainous and cut up by the ravines of the high plateau, and which suffers from a completely dry season that is increasingly prolonged as one goes farther north.

The configuration of the country and the climate thus govern the economy of these *ejidos* to an extent that the hand of man has not greatly altered.   The great modern development projects have passed them by—both (as statistics have shown) the irrigation of vast areas by the construction of dams and the 'march to the sea', i.e. the attempts which have been made especially during the past twenty years to develop the hot coastal plains.   Official figures also show that between 1940 and 1950 the total arable land belonging to the *ejidos* increased by only 1,545,647 hectares, against 3,311,537 hectares for private farms.   Between 1950 and 1960 the increase was 1,538,381 for *ejidos* (against a grand total of 10,329,247 hectares in 1960) and 2,350,268 for private farms (grand total of 13,487,663 hectares in 1960).[30]

[30] *IV Censos agrícola . . . 1960*, p. 25.

True, considerable progress has been made, in education, electri-
fication, the opening up of communications, etc, but this has not
always raised the standard of living of the *ejidatarios* and peasants
straight away.   Tremendous advantages in communications net-
works have often been cancelled out by a rise in the cost of living,
the disappearance of local workshops, and fresh claims on the
purse.   Finally, the distributions of land which have been made,
especially for raising livestock, have often had limited results
because of a rapid population growth that has not always been
offset by the emigration to towns encouraged by 'industrialization',
however important that may be.

The *ejidatarios* were more fortunate than the inhabitants of the
old pueblos at the beginning of the century, who were squeezed by
the haciendas, in that they had individual holdings, but these were
very small.   According to the 1940 census, 87·4 per cent of
registered *ejidatarios* farmed holdings of under 10 hectares.   Even
10 hectares is a small holding considering the small proportion of
irrigated land and the fact that on land which is generally poor it
is difficult to cultivate the whole area every year.   Eventually the
situation apparently improved very gradually, the proportion dropping to 84·28 per cent in 1950 and 83·8 per cent in 1960.[31]   But
actual personal knowledge of the traditional *ejidos* leads one to
believe that since 1940 the number of people dependent for their
livelihood on these small individual plots increased and has certainly
not decreased, because for the last twenty-five years a number of
adults have been living on an *ejido*, either with their relatives, who
are registered *ejidatarios*, or as tenants of a fraction of a plot
(obviously contravening the *ejidal* law), constituting a partly floating
population which is attached to the *ejidal* community but has no
rights.

Many of the men who live with the *ejidatarios* who own land are
seasonal day-labourers in the United States and sometimes carry
on small trades or else work as manual labourers.   Though linked
with the pueblo, they are also to some extent itinerant.   A smaller
number rent the holdings of *ejidatarios* who are incapacitated and
these increase still further the numbers who depend, if only in part,
on the *ejidal* land.   Without being able to put forward any figures
other than the very general ones quoted earlier, it is pointed out

---

[31] Ibid. p. 562 (percentages calculated by the author).

that this new population appears to be roughly equivalent to the number of legal owners of *ejidal* land—which generally represents the total number of heads of families at the time at which the *ejido* was established.

This situation is in part similar to that in certain Indian communities in the mountain regions of Peru, where two types of inhabitant are to be found: the landowning *comuneros* or *vecinos*, who enjoy the benefit of land which cannot be passed to a new owner outside the community. They constitute a kind of upper class in relation to all those who have no land. The one essential difference is that in Peru the neighbouring haciendas are still intact, and the Indian communities are generally encircled by these large estates with which they often live in a state of permanent friction, especially as the memory of the loss of some of their land to the haciendas only a few decades ago is very much alive today. Whenever possible these communities encroach upon the haciendas, hoping to ease the problem of rapidly growing population and insufficient land.

The position of the Mexican *ejidos* is much more satisfactory. However small they may be, the *ejidal* plots are usually larger and less poor than the few miserable furrows owned by many communities high in the Andes. The neighbouring haciendas have been eliminated after a long period of rivalry which culminated in the revolution and the Zapatist uprising. The rich private properties which still exist today generally do not come into contact with the *ejidos*.

The peasants in the *ejidos* therefore have the impression that they have won the day: although they have little or no access to normal credit facilities, they are owners of land. The moneylenders are always ready to provide the needed cash advances. The very poor peasants depend on them for advances of maize in the sowing and harvest seasons, for hiring beasts of burden, for assistance after accidents, or simply for loans on the occasion of marriages or funerals. In many cases half or three-quarters of the crop serves to repay such loans. But the simpler illiterate peasants do not clearly understand the link between these evils and the absence or insufficiency of credit facilities. Possession of land appears to be an end in itself, and they find it difficult to look any further especially as the people who exploit them have often the same local origins as themselves.

However, certain *ejidatarios* sometimes do have access to government credit, especially in regions such as Morelos, where sugarcane is grown. In return the *ejidatarios* have to undertake to reserve at least one-third of their land for this crop. These *ejidos* enjoy more favourable conditions than any others.

Another economic difficulty associated with the traditional *ejido* is the stagnation (*situation congelée*) caused by an organization which in the words of the agronomist René Dumont 'impairs the mobility which is always necessary for economic progress'. The Mexican economist Manuel Girault expresses himself almost in the same terms. Similar statements were however made by enlightened observers of eighteenth-century France and by liberals in Mexico in the nineteenth century; the first denounced the serious difficulties created by the collective servitude of the old French peasant communities, while the second spoke out against the immobility arising from the archaic organization of the Indian *comunidades*. In the opinion of the old French economists and the Mexican reformers, these traditional structures prevented progressive individuals from increasing or improving their farms. These observers were not wrong, but since then experience has shown that in Mexico the slow evolution of the communities towards individualism could not be hastened without the risk of provoking their destruction, followed by the absorption of all their land by the neighbouring haciendas or the money-lenders and *mestizo* cattle breeders who are far more advanced than the simple peasants.

This is a further common factor linking the traditional *ejido* and the community from which it partially arose. Liberal experiments carried out in South America in the nineteenth and twentieth centuries (which are unfortunately very little known) indicate the necessity for great care if the *ejidos* are to avoid the fate of many communities both in Mexico and throughout the American continent, especially in the Andean countries.

At the present time the organization of the *ejidos* is not usually very rigid, and one cannot really speak of immobility. Persons with initiative certainly have the possibility of improving their lot in their own local area. This can be seen from an outstanding study made by T. Schwartz of an individual *ejido*,[32] which confirms the

---

[32] T. Schwartz, 'L'usage de la terre dans un village à éjido du Mexique', *Études rurales*, No. 10, 1963, pp. 37–49.

observations made by the writer. This case provides a general illustration of a number of the phenomena which have been described.

The *ejido* in question was founded in 1924–30 (although it may well have merely been a continuation of a Zapatista *ejido*). Credit is available in return for an undertaking to cultivate sugar-cane on one-third of the ground, which is not always the case on other *ejidos*. The following are the principal characteristics of the *ejido*:

127 hectares of irrigated land;
 54 *ejidatarios* holding title-deeds to their land, of whom:
     19 cultivate their own plot of land, and no more;
     11 cultivate more than their own plot;
      6 rent out the whole of their plot (1 woman, 5 invalids or alcoholics);
     18 rent out part of their plot (5 women, &c.).

Besides this a considerable number (no figures are available) of non-*ejidatarios* live on the *ejido* for at least part of the year. Among these, 21 help their parents to cultivate their plots or else have rented sections of plots. Thus the total number of persons actually cultivating land is 69 (for an area of 127 hectares with a few small surrounding plots). The other inhabitants, who are much more numerous, are usually agricultural labourers. The amount of land actually cultivated (not merely according to legal statistics) by each head of family is as follows:

At the upper extreme, very modest holdings averaging 4.08 hectares each.
19 *ejidatarios* on their own plots averaging 2·18 hectares each.
At the lower extreme, 21 peasants with very small holdings (14 of these not *ejidatarios*) averaging 1·4 hectares.

Among the first group, certain enterprising farmers grow rice, which brings in much higher profits but requires far more careful cultivation and a higher investment. At the other end of the scale a number of agricultural labourers are making desperate efforts to become smallholders (tenants), which is difficult because of the high rents (800 to 1,000 pesos per hectare, i.e. £25–30), caused by land scarcity. If they do succeed in renting land, this is sometimes thanks to savings which they have been able to make from their work as seasonal labourers in the United States.

In his detailed study of this *ejido*, Schwartz concludes that 'the best advantage is being taken of a difficult situation' due to over-population and the fragmentation of the land. He adds that this is a 'relatively balanced picture of land distribution' and estimates that if agriculture were mechanized, 15 per cent of the present labour force would suffer—the real solution would therefore be to employ these men elsewhere.

The author has often made similar observations in visits to other *ejidos*, where the situation is not so favourable. The majority of *ejidos* possess only non-irrigated land on which essential foodstuffs are cultivated, especially the traditional crop, maize. Above all, these *ejidos* do not have access to credit, and the result is greater dependence on moneylenders. These may be capitalists from outside the *ejido*, or local shopkeepers or farmers who are more enterprising or thrifty than the others. Here the danger of seizure of the plots, even of complete ruin and elimination of the *ejidatarios*, is greater than elsewhere. The situation is comparable to that in certain ancient Indian communities which, at the end of the nineteenth or the beginning of the twentieth century, were literally dispersed or destroyed by the penetration and incursions of mestizos who—since they were much more economically advanced than the Indians—rapidly took over all the land.

The regulations governing the mobility of landownership within the *ejido* therefore appear to be very sensible, at least as things stand at present. The situation is not sufficiently stationary to prevent certain illegal initiatives which the purists are perhaps too eager to call abuses, provided that they remain within limits. But if all the legal restraints were removed, it seems quite certain that both in the richest irrigated areas, which are of interest to large-scale capital investment, and in the poorer regions, which are deprived of credit and where usury thrives, land would often be taken over and the weakest peasants would be driven out. The law, even though it is not strictly applied, remains a threat when those whom it is intended to protect carry a certain weight in the politics of the government, as the CNC has done since Cárdenas.

Lastly, between the extremes of the *ejido* with a high level of capital investment and that which is completely without credit facilities, we find the beginnings of an *ejidal* peasant system, as in the example quoted in the province of Morelos. Here the *ejido* is no longer the traditional community and individualism has made slow and steady progress. The *ejido* as a reflection of popular feeling clearly springs from such a period of transition. One has the impression that the mental outlook of the *ejidatarios* continually evolves towards that of the smallholder rather than towards a form of socialism, as certain observers believe. At least this is the case if the *ejido* proceeds by its own inner impetus, in the absence of external intervention. The same phenomenon has been noted in the Bolivian agrarian reform, where an extraordinary fragmentation of the land occupied by the village groups has often taken place in spite of some effort to introduce at least the beginnings of a co-operative system.

This evolution of *ejidal* land towards smallholdings can clearly be seen in the province of Morelos. Here 30 or so *ejidatarios* (out of a total of 54 who own land) cultivate a few hectares each of irrigated land and have done so probably for thirty-five or forty years. Schwartz mentions in passing that these are 'conservative' people. The case is perhaps particularly clear when the *ejidatarios* grow several crops under more or less favourable conditions—in the provinces of Mexico and Morelos, for example. These men lead a stable life and have become deeply attached to their plots of land. For them the cultivation of the soil is a way of life more than a means of making a living.

What is the difference between this category of *ejidatarios* and the smallholders who have acquired their land since the revolution? Is it that the latter are entitled to sell or mortgage their land? The *ejidatarios* could also dispose of their land, but in fact both groups rarely use this facility, for they cannot really envisage any different means of earning their living. Again both groups feel close attachment to the agrarian revolution, or more precisely to the persons who symbolize it (with certain reservations for long-established groups of smallholders, for religious reasons). This explains the extraordinary and in fact unique popularity of men like Cárdenas or Zapata, although Zapata's popularity is more localized and more remote in time because it is now only old people who knew him personally.

To return to the precise example of Morelos: it is true that a certain number of *ejidatarios* have transferred (temporarily at least) all or part of their land as a sort of natural selection process sets in. But it is the stable smallholders who set the tone; among those who own no land the hope arises of acquiring a plot by obtaining a long lease; thus they become smallholders on a very precarious basis. Considerable efforts are made to achieve this aim, especially by means of saving earnings as day-labourers. But the savings are sometimes used unsuccessfully, because such high rents must be paid.

The *ejidatarios*, therefore, have much in common with small-holders, with whom they tend to be confused: there is the same attachment to the soil and usually the same stability when owner-ship of the plots is guaranteed. There is also sometimes the same tendency to excessive individualism, although this is partly a recent phenomenon. The long-established traditional authority which used to dominate the communities has almost disappeared. Each member tends to fall back on his own land and to isolate himself from his neighbours, unless a new type of discipline is created, i.e. mainly by government control in cases where the government is able to supply credit facilities and technicians.

Because of the population increase the government is faced with the problem of excessive subdivision of plots, a problem not fully reflected in the statistics. Until this can be remedied it would be best to increase the number of *ejidos*, as in the case studied by the writer at Santa María Nativitas (Mexico State). Here the governor has regrouped the minute portions of each plot of land sown with maize, beans, vegetables, and fodder into four or five areas of relatively large-scale cultivation which are worked by teams. He has also encouraged crafts (carpentry, welding, etc.) and facilities for small-scale cattle-raising to give the *ejidatarios* additional occupations and resources. But this experiment in reorganization, although on the whole successful, was fairly expensive and required the presence over a period of several years of an agronomist and subordinate officials—and experts of this kind are scarce in Mexico. Finally, tensions arose in the *ejido* because of the criticisms of those who saw 'communism' behind every effort at establishing a co-operative basis for work.

Similar problems are raised by very small holdings, which cannot be examined in any detail here. These are even less well docu-mented than the *ejidos*, for no one has even an approximate idea of how many were established before the revolution but which did not appear in statistics. While restricted to certain localities, smallholdings were nevertheless numerous, for example in the highlands of Jalisco State and adjacent areas, where they appear to

have provided the main body of men who took part in the *Cristero*
uprising—which was partly counter-revolutionary for religious
reasons.

However, the majority of smallholdings were in fact created by
the revolution. The 1950 census showed a total of 1,020,747 holdings of less than 5 hectares, covering 1,504,397 hectares, i.e. 82·54
per cent of the holdings in the country, occupying 13·51 per cent
of the cultivated area.[33] By 1960 they were 899,108 on 1,328,106
hectares. But are those figures reliable? For according to calculations made in 1964 by the CNC, there are at present about half
a million (498,399) properties of less than 1 hectare.[34]

Like the very small *ejidos*, these smallholdings can be maintained
only under certain conditions. This refers to such phenomena as
the seasonal emigration of *braceros*, which far exceeds the number
quoted in statistics—about 800,000 every year seems a likely figure.
The day-labourers, *ejidatarios*, and smallholders go to the United
States to earn money to supplement the lack of credit facilities,
thus enabling them to avoid falling into debt and to have less
recourse to usury, to acquire and maintain a plot of land, generally
part of the old communal land, or to rent part of an *ejidal* plot.

'Thanks to God and the Americans I have been able to acquire
my land', I was told in Tlacotepec (Mexico) by the owner of 3½
hectares of non-irrigated but relatively fertile soil, who still becomes
a *bracero* from time to time in order to maintain or better his
position. The proximity of the United States and its immense
capital reserves acts in this and also in other less direct ways as a
factor of social stabilization, perhaps precarious, but indispensable
to the lower strata of Mexican peasantry.

The situation of certain groups of smallholders in Colombia
seems even more precarious—in spite of the resources of coffee
cultivation—and one might well wonder whether the tensions which
have arisen in Colombia are not explicable in part by the absence
of regulating factors comparable to Mexico's seasonal migration
to the United States.

From the economic point of view, the position of the vast majority
of *ejidos* is still mediocre—as one might expect of an institution
which has remained closely linked to the traditional form of

---

[33] *III Censos agricola-ganadero* for 1950 (the percentages were calculated
by Gutelman, *L'ejido*, p. 269); *IV Censos . . . 1960*, pp. 16 and 25.
[34] *Prensa latina* (Prague), 799 (6 Jan. 1965), p. 7.

settlement in a very large country most of which is mountainous and very dry. The important progress which has none the less been made since the agrarian revolution has been partly cancelled by demographic growth—and also, to a lesser extent, by the general increase in needs, which is a universal phenomenon of our times. No satisfactory, rapid solution can be seen to this problem, without very large investment in industry and in the irrigation or improvement of land which would then be made available to the peasants. Peasant labour would then be more efficient and yields higher, if, as in the example of Santa María Nativitas, minute plots of land could be consolidated in order to make team working possible, craft and trade activities developed, and hybrid corn sown.

From the psychological, social, and political points of view, the situation appears to be different. This account has tended to show that, in the absence of energetic outside intervention, peasants in the *ejidos* often very closely resemble the individualistic smallholders who live for their land rather than by their land.

Even if they are very poor and have no source of credit other than sporadic income from work as *braceros*, the *ejidatarios* who have received their plots of land on a permanent basis (which is not always the case) have the impression that the land belongs to them, and for the moment they can see no essential aim other than to conserve this pseudo-property. The oppressive haciendas have disappeared for good, for those which still remain no longer have any decisive importance on the Mexican plateaux; for the most part the new irrigated estates are situated in other areas, thus giving little cause for friction, even though irrigated areas are sometimes occupied by *paracaidistas* ('parachutists'), or landless peasants.

After all everyone had their opportunity—this seems to be the opinion of the *ejidatarios*, who sometimes show grudging admiration for the clever men who knew how to help themselves first and keep the best part of the cake for themselves. There are, it is true, new masters, sometimes even minor despots, who are disliked and feared: the store-keeper who is also a moneylender, the local politician (*ejidal* commissioner, deputy, municipal president and so on) who may be a sort of *cacique* or local political boss. But they allow the peasants to live as best they can on their plots.

As for the government, it makes frequent declarations in favour of the peasants, emphasizing the results of the revolution and the distribution of land to the *ejidos*, promising water, roads, schools

—and often pointing to the fact that these promises are being kept. The peasants are still as poor as ever but they remain attached to the revolution which gave them what they desired most: a patch of ground. When their support is required, they give their vote to the party which adheres to these principles (except sometimes when the priest tells them to vote otherwise). They remember Cárdenas and they wait patiently for better days. As one of the great experts on rural Mexico, Moisés de la Peña, has said, 'They live in hope'.[35]

This attitude offers a clear contrast to that found elsewhere in the Andes region, where old social patterns still remain—especially that of land tenure. Sometimes the peasants, who have sunk to a degree of wretchedness below poverty, seem quite impassive, while at other times they display a disquiet and unease that scarcely conceals hostility and agressiveness. The situation is quite different from the comparatively relaxed atmosphere of the Mexican *ejidos* and even, it would seem, among Bolivian groups which have recently seized land.

As for the internal organization of the *ejidos*, this is certainly not as democratic as it appears on paper, since the general assemblies of each unit—which are supposed to be self-governing—are in fact often dominated by small *caciques*, by coalitions of private vested interests or *compadrazgos*. They are also restricted by a certain measure of governmental control (sometimes even neo-paternalism), which is tending to increase under the supervision of the Mexican Agrarian Department. This is rightly concerned with checking certain abuses and malpractices on the part of local officials, and with controlling the economy of the *ejidos* by granting credits and purchasing crops through official organizations.

Yet in spite of this some of the *ejidatarios* do meet periodically in order to discuss problems which are of vital interest to them; and they do reach decisions in cases which do not involve the personal interests of those with influence or they may at least be able to compel the influential members to solicit their votes or support— even if this is only a formality. Thus to a certain extent—and much more so than the ordinary smallholding—the *ejido* represents an apprenticeship in the administration of the communities' own affairs and a means of arousing the co-operative spirit. Sometimes, it is

[35] I have found confirmation of the preceding observations in De la Peña, pp. 330–6.

true, the meetings arouse little interest among the *ejidatarios*, and attendance is poor. Sometimes, however, they take the opportunity to express their complaints or wishes. Especially when the *ejido* is small or of moderate size the meetings tend to make up for the weakness of the municipalities, which have very little autonomy in spite of popular aspirations expressed many times in the last century (at least in the north) and even though the first liberal revolutionaries saw municipal life as an essential basis of democracy.

The *ejidos* play another role in politics through the CNC, and its incorporation in the PRI. Every three years the executive committees elected in each *ejido* delegate two of their members to select over 500 local committees throughout the country, which in turn appoint 32 provincial committees. Finally, the latter select from among their members the national executive committee of the CNC (14 members), which represent the *ejidos* in the official party and exerts an influence on its central executive committee—hence also on the appointment of the President and on government in general.[36]

According to a statistical table of trade union strength associated with the PRI drawn up by Scott, who also points out the semi-theoretical nature of these figures (since membership is obligatory), the CNC and associated unions have 2,650,000 members, 2,500,000 of whom are *ejidatarios*, out of a total general union membership of 6,621,000; a far higher membership than the Confederación de Trabajadores Mexicanos with its 1,500,000 members. All the other unions are much smaller, except for the National Confederation of Agricultural Smallholders, which has 850,000 members and is linked to the 'popular' sector of the PRI which was founded only after the time of Cárdenas. This union also, however, included under the designation of 'smallholders' highly-capitalized estate owners and large-scale farmers who have gained great influence in it, whereas the CNC appears to have remained closer to the *ejidatarios*, even to the extent of defending the interests of the *ejidos*, somewhat inflexibly, as Scott points out.[37]

But it is also evident that the government (under the direction of the President, who may well not be concerned primarily with an 'agrarian' policy) also intervenes in the choice of the members of

[36] William P. Tucker, *The Mexican Government Today* (Minneapolis, Minnesota UP, 1957), pp. 53–54.
[37] Scott, p. 171. Union membership, pp. 166–7.

the CNC, at least on the higher levels—the influences are therefore at least reciprocal. At the local level private interests are still powerful. Nevertheless it seems that through the CNC a more thoughtful and vocal fraction among the vast mass of peasant *ejidatarios* manages, at least to a certain extent, to associate the presidency with its own tendencies and aspirations, as Cárdenas wished, while the CNC itself constitutes as it were the left wing of the PRI.

It is difficult to estimate the extent of this influence, even though it is possible, for instance, to list the number of PRI deputies in the federal parliament, or the number of provincial governors who belong to the agrarian sector. But the effects are visible. In spite of evident pressures from urban sectors and powerful economic interests with which successive Presidents are bound to come into contact, it is significant that no President—even though their temperaments have varied widely—has ever taken any measure against the *ejido* as an institution, although some have clearly favoured other agricultural sectors. All have defended the *ejido* as if it were the very symbol of the revolution. All official statistics or statements have tried to show that the work which culminated under Cárdenas still continues.

His predecessor, in particular, expropriated in favour of the *ejido* many of the large estates which existed in remote or arid zones as 'non-mortgageable lands used for cattle-raising'. On the other hand it is not clear whether the proportion of newly irrigated land allocated to the *ejidos* is at all significant. This is an important question, on which available statistics give no reliable information. The future alone will reveal the direction in which Mexican agrarian policies are going. But it seems that protests arising under the pressure of increasing population and a slowly growing awareness on the part of younger and better educated elements in the CNC are reaching the presidency. Finally, the agrarian revolution which has taken place in Cuba is not without influence on certain sections of opinion, and certainly on government policies.

Since the time of Cárdenas, agrarian policies have been of constant importance to the Mexican government. Particularly in recent years it has tried to pacify the mass of *ejidatarios*, who have sometimes shown signs of discontent although always on the whole remaining attached to the memory of the agrarian revolution, which in fact represents the only real and tangible advantage gained by rural society for a very long time. However backward this society may be, it is still aware where its interests lie, and I have never heard a single *ejidatario* express any regret for the past.

But is it not true that *ejidal* policies, social peace, and political stability go hand in hand? Are (or were) they not—to a very great extent—all facets of a single historical phenomenon? It is impossible to draw a parallel between the peace and stability of Mexico and that assured in other countries by long periods of government by one man or family—always with greater or lesser support from the military or the police. Mexico is unique among the countries with a large population of Indian or *mestizo* origin, that is to say with a colonial heritage. It is very probable that political stability is linked with the absence of serious social tensions, and even with some possibilities of expression being available for the majority of the population, which is concerned above all with preserving results already achieved, even if these have now become more or less illusory from the economic point of view.

Of course, this stability is deeply connected with the important progress made in industry, the urban economy, and to some extent the agricultural economy, by better communications and trade partly facilitated by the immense reservoir of capital provided by the neighbouring United States. But one must not lose sight of the fact that the urban sectors (including several working-class sectors) who derive the greatest benefits from this situation are in fact privileged groups, and despite their growth, still remain a minority in a large country. What would happen to this political stability if the situation deteriorated in a rural society which is becoming more overpopulated, just when both urban and rural generations are now growing up for whom the work of Cárdenas is either unknown or obsolete? Would the most prosperous urban sectors and those people who are still satisfied by the results of the revolution be able to maintain complete control over the political situation?

Finally one might wonder whether industry and irrigation (which require enormous capital investment) combined with other factors (new activities, *braceros*, emigration) will by themselves suffice to prevent tensions by lightening the burden of over-population in many rural areas. Or will economic growth be sufficient to resolve the problems on a short-term basis? In any case it seems probable that, in the near future, the government will have to show imagination and make serious efforts to retain the social benefits of its great agrarian revolution.   Perhaps the country which created an original, political agrarian concept, will discover new solutions which are satisfactory from the social and political as well as the economic points of view.

Religion, the Church, and Social Change in Brazil[1]

EMANUEL DE KADT

IN discussions of the social and political problems of Latin America one nowadays often hears the question asked: Where does the Church stand on this matter? (The Church, in this context, of course means the Roman Catholic Church.) It is not necessarily a very enlightening question. Although in many countries of the continent 'the Church' continues to be a near-monolithic entity, in others conflicting tendencies and groups have become more and more distinct from each other. 'As it attempts to become a force for social and economic reforms, the Church finds that its own leaders, whether they be bishops, priests or laymen, are divided, often bitterly divided, in regard to the type of changes that should be introduced', writes Pike in the Introduction to an interesting collection of essays on the subject.[2] To talk about 'the Church' in countries such as Chile, Venezuela, and Brazil—and Churchmen themselves are particularly prone to do so—therefore merely befuddles the issues. In the following pages I shall always try to make it clear which part of the Church is under discussion—bishops, priests in parishes, other priests, religious lay leaders, or merely the faithful—and what differences exist among and between them.

The quotation from Pike takes for granted the role of the Church in matters of socio-political reform. But one may wonder to what extent an organization such as the Church is expected to act at all outside the 'purely religious' field. Churches are supposed to deal

---

[1] A number of friends and colleagues were kind enough to comment upon an earlier version of this essay. Of these, I am especially indebted to Marina Bandeira, whose intimate knowledge of the Brazilian Church scene has saved me from a number of inaccuracies in the latter part of this essay, and to Dr Thales de Azevedo, for his valuable information on the historical context of certain of the problems discussed.
[2] Fredrick B. Pike 'Introduction', in W. V. D'Antonio and F. B. Pike, eds., *Religion, Revolution and Reform* (London, 1964), p. 7.

in religious beliefs, not in socio-political ideologies, and the Church is, in the first place, a body religious. I shall, therefore, first have to devote some attention to the religious behaviour and needs of different groups in the population of Brazil, and the way Churchmen react to these. They must be taken into account for a proper understanding of the problems faced by Church groups turning towards possible intervention in secular matters.[3] After briefly discussing the traditional forms of Catholicism, one notable age-old response to change and disaster (Messianism), and the more widespread current adaptations by means of conversions to Protestantism or Spiritualism, the essay will move to the nature of Catholicism as it developed in the cities, and examine the extent of its adaptation to the needs of the new city masses, and their response. I shall then consider the progressive ideas in the Catholic Church which have recently become more important in Brazil, and the kinds of organizations involved in socio-political action inspired by these. Finally, the possibilities for success of these progressive groups will be evaluated in the light of fundamental patterns of thought and behaviour, analysed in the earlier part of the essay, which have been, and continue to be, prevalent in such widespread areas of life in Brazil.

Folk Catholicism

For most people Latin America is the Catholic continent *par excellence*. In Brazil, the census of 1950 reported that over 93 per cent of the population declared themselves to be Catholic. At first sight, therefore, Brazil seems a country in which 'the Church' ought to have a substantial influence on the people. The ensuing analysis will show that this view is mistaken. There are many complex reasons for this situation, but a simple and very important one is the sheer expanse of the territory and the low number of priests per inhabitant. If the vast but hardly populated regions in the North and Centre-West are disregarded (they distort the averages very much), the average size of the parishes for the rest

---

[3] It is remarkable that in the still quite limited sociological literature on religion and Church in Brazil the socio-religious situation and the intervention of Church groups in secular matters are not usually related to each other. There are a few exceptions (notably François Houtart and Émile Pin, *L'église à l'heure de l'Amérique latine* (Tournai, 1965)), but on the whole attention is focused exclusively on one aspect or on the other.

of Brazil is approximately 300 square miles. It is almost double in the North-East. The average number of inhabitants per priest is 16,600.[4] So in the rural areas of the country most people see a priest only at very long intervals, and the focus of religious activity is the home altar or the community chapel rather than the parish church. The amount of time most priests can spend worrying about the economic problems of their parishioners is quite limited.

But other factors have contributed, historically, to make the priest's relationship with the common people tenuous. In the sugar-growing areas of the North-East the plantation chaplains were, till far into the nineteenth century, more dependent upon the master of the plantation than upon their bishop. Gilberto Freyre describes them as 'priestly uncles' in the family.[5] They served slave-owners for whom religion was a convenient means of deflecting the slaves' attention from their workaday situation. It was, in the words of Roger Bastide, 'an "opium" capable of weakening terrestrial resistance, of emasculating the will to revolt of the oppressed'.[6] This was to be achieved on the one hand by inculcating a Providential Catholicism, emphasizing hope, charity, and recompense after death, and on the other hand by tolerating barely disguised African tribal rites, in which slaves could blow off steam and use up energies in perhaps 'demonic', but politically harmless, rituals.[7]

As will be seen, religion has indeed contributed to keeping the masses politically ineffective. But this came about in a way very different from that vaguely anticipated in the semi-deliberate policy of the colonial plantation owners. The religion which spread

---

4 Adapted from figures in Gustavo Pérez and others, *O problema sacerdotal no Brasil* (Brussels, FERES, 1965), p. 19. The most unfavourable ratios are generally found in the very large towns. The number of inhabitants per priest declines as the towns become smaller. The countryside, however, is as badly off as the great urban centres. The average numbers of inhabitants per priest for the whole of Brazil, for 1962, were as follows. Towns with a population over 500,000 : 17,400; towns with a population of 50,000–500,000 : 14,700; towns with a population of 10,000–50,000 : 12,100; rural zone : 16,400; overall average Brazil : 15,800 (from Alfonso Gregory, *A igreja no Brasil* (Brussels, FERES, 1965), which I was privileged to see at the proof stage).

5 See his *New World in the Tropics* (New York, 1963), p. 70 and his classical study of the plantation society, *The Masters and the Slaves* (New York, 1946), pp. 192–3.

6 Roger Bastide, *Les religions africaines du Brésil* (Paris 1960), p. 195.

7 See also an interesting article by Donald Warren Jr, 'The Negro and Religion in Brazil', *Race*, 6/3 (1965), p. 203.

through Brazil owed more to the vigorous folk beliefs and the rites of African slaves and the *caboclo* [8] descendants of Portuguese men and Indian women than to an other-worldly resigned Catholicism, emphasizing man's duties 'in his station' and 'poverty as the estate richest in the means of salvation'.[9] While priests and landowners stressed the latter aspect, and attempted to use religion as an instrument of social control, the vast majority of the population seemed quite untouched by it. In their own 'folk Catholicism' practised outside the churches, in home chapels, courtyards, or communal meetings, the Virgin and the saints were endowed with characteristics similar to those of ancestral African gods or Indian spirits. They were regarded 'not as providers of celestial grace, but as the protectors of life on earth'.[10]

Folk Catholicism continues to be the dominant form of religion in the major part of the country's rural areas. Handed down from generation to generation with only a minimal influence of the priests as official interpreters of Church doctrine,[11] it does not focus on man's sinfulness and the means to salvation from hell, nor on diffuse piousness, nor on the ethics of everyday life. It is a means of establishing control over nature—a supernatural way of overcoming adversities which man cannot cope with in a human, temporal manner.[12] It is wholly concerned with the satisfaction of man's 'natural' daily needs—health, a good harvest, a happy family or love life, subsistence—which it attempts to ensure by means of near-magical rites, thought to have intrinsic value and inherent efficacy. Prayer is experienced as the calling down of a special blessing. Priests, in so far as they enter the picture at all, are seen as men with miraculous powers. Their blessing protects in a way similar to that of the saints; they are needed mainly as miracle-workers. Most priests seem to be well adapted to this role. In part this results from the training till recently provided in most seminaries,

[8] A person of mixed white-Indian descent. Also used more generally to indicate a (poor) rural worker.
[9] Pike, in D'Antonio & Pike, p. 6.
[10] Bastide, p. 198.
[11] The most valuable discussion of the inter-relation of life situation and religious attitudes or behaviour is still found in Max Weber's essay 'Die Wirtschaftsethik der Weltreligionen', trans. in H. H. Gerth and C. W. Mills, *From Max Weber* (London, 1948), pp. 267–322.
[12] See Thales de Azevedo, 'Problemas metodológicos da sociologia do Catolicismo no Brasil', *Rev. Museu paulista*, 14 (1963), p. 368.

which cultivate an exalted priestly ideal, of angelic spirituality.[13] It leads priests to regard themselves as the repositories of spiritual goods, and to see their main task as that of dispensing these goods.[14]

The saints are especially powerful protectors and helpers. When the occasion warrants it, man assures himself of their benevolence by an appropriate gift or promise. He pursues his immediate interests by endless bargaining with his celestial protector—in a personal relationship whose main principle is that of *do ut des*. Of this relation Thales de Azevedo has written: 'As a matter of fact the most common and binding relationship, of the faithful to the Saints and God is through a *promessa*, consisting of a petition of *proteção*, or help, in a crisis, under the promise of compensation by the faithful . . .' In folk Catholicism the most important concepts are *promessa*, *proteção*, *pedido* (request), *milagre* (miracle) and *mostrar respeito* (to show respect).[15]

Now the character of the relationship between believer and saint is strikingly similar to the patron-dependant relations prevailing in traditional secular society between peasant or worker and his *patrão*. There, also, the *patrão* takes it upon himself to pursue, as a favour, the peasant's immediate interests in return for specific services and a general show of respect on the part of the peasant. There too the peasant will look forward to a secular miracle in the form of very special favours.[16] In short, the key concepts of folk Catholicism are very nearly identical to the key concepts operating in the traditional socio-political sphere.

It may be impossible to determine whether folk Catholicism preceded the development of these dependence relations or followed upon it. But it is certain that the religious and the secular rein-

---

13 This information comes from an anonymous document, written by an extremely well-informed Belgian priest in Brazil: *Notes sur la situation des prêtres belges au Brésil* (Campinas, 1960, mimeo.), p. 46. I shall henceforth refer to it as *Prêtres belges*.

14 Ibid. p. 7; also Pérez & others, p. 27.

15 de Azevedo, *Social Change in Brazil* (Univ. of Florida Press, 1963), p. 76.

16 I have discussed some of the problems of paternalism and clientelistic relations in modern Brazil in 'The Brazilian Impasse', *Encounter*, Sept. 1965. Some further references will also be found there. An extremely perceptive analysis of this problem, as seen in the day-to-day workings of Brazilian society, is to be found in Anthony Leeds, 'Brazilian Careers and Social Structure', *Amer. Anthropologist*, 66/6, pt. 1 (Dec. 1964). Cf. also Bertram Hutchinson's excellent 'The Patron-Dependant Relationship in Brazil', *Sociol. Ruralis*, 6/1 (1966), which came to my notice after this essay had gone to print.

forced each other once they were in existence. This reinforcement took place not only because the *patrão* became a substitute saint or vice versa. Folk Catholicism also strengthens the *status quo*, because believers try to manipulate their natural situation—including their economic and social relations—by supernatural (magical) means. They are for ever awaiting miraculous help. If it does not materialize all they do is to ask for it more insistently, perhaps promising an even greater sacrifice should their appeal be successful. Obviously this is neither the most rational nor the most effective way of achieving changes in the *status quo*. By channelling their efforts into continuous invocations of the supernatural the peasants in effect buttress the existing social, economic, and political relations.[17]

Messianic Movements

Under stable social conditions the people in the backlands will have come to expect a certain unavoidable dose of troubles. At the same time 'miraculous' deliveries from pain, hunger, or lovelessness do occur, in such an unchanging society, with sufficient regularity to underpin the whole structure of belief. But the conditions are precarious and stability is far from absolute. It is easily broken by temporary or permanent forces from the outside, which undermine the familiar patterns of life. Then the perceived ratio of 'success' of the old rituals may diminish to such an extent that a radical breakdown of the whole system occurs, unless under a new guise it can be given new vitality and lead again to 'success'.

A specifically religious transformation of folk Catholicism has occurred from time to time with the rise of so-called Messianic movements. Where they occur peasants gather around a natural leader who preaches against evil and often announces the coming of the kingdom of God on earth, exhorting his followers to be morally prepared for it. Such movements have been numerous

---

[17] 'Religious resolutions . . . are likely to compensate for feelings of deprivation rather than to eliminate its causes', writes Charles Y. Glock in a paper which tries to account for the rise and permanence of religious groups in terms of the basic idea that people in some way or other try to overcome deprivations which they experience. It is not a very tightly argued theory, and it explains too much—but the paper is interesting none the less. See 'The Role of Deprivation in the Origin and Evolution of Religious Groups', in Robert Lee and M. E. Marty, *Religion and Social Conflict* (New York, 1964).

in the drought-ridden areas of the North-East, where nature has made life hard, unpredictable, and often enough unlivable. They have also been found in areas where the existing system of agriculture has fallen into decay because of pressures from outside. They have been explained as irrational attempts to come to terms with hostile natural forces or as evidence of a desire to preserve or to return to cultural forms threatened by impersonal social or economic powers.[18] In some cases their character is, indeed, predominantly irrational, and they are not capable of producing any beneficial results for their adherents. But, as Maria Isaura Pereira de Queiroz has shown in a fascinating paper, they frequently fulfil a positive function in the process of adaptation to change.[19] The saintly leader demands of his followers a systematized, almost puritanical way of life. He arbitrates their differences and gives direction to the common efforts of the community, which usually isolates itself from the world. He sees as his task the integration of his followers in a moral community; often, more or less deliberately, he is also concerned to raise their standard of living and to adapt their productive methods to the surrounding open-market economy.[20]

The consequences of the appearance of a 'prophet' are therefore often beneficial. The stress laid on a life based on a consistently applied moral code and on hard and honest work could open the way to a radical departure from the hand-to-mouth supernaturalism of folk Catholicism. But in fact it is more likely that his appearance heralds a mere external transformation of its basic concepts. The 'theological content' of these movements consists usually of a reinterpretation of Catholic ideas. More significantly, however, the prophet is credited with the self-same quality of miracle-worker which is the most prominent characteristic of the saints in folk Catholicism. His followers seek him specifically for his supernatural powers, and his relation with them is thoroughly paternalistic. The beneficial consequences of his innovating

[18] Cf. Bastide, p. 217.
[19] 'Mouvements messianiques et développement économique au Brésil', *Arch. de sociol. des religions*, 16 (1963). She notes nineteen such movements since the beginning of the 18th century; the best known are those of Antonio Conselheiro at Canudos at the turn of the century, and of Padre Cicero at Juazeiro in the first three decades of this century. See also Pt. 2 of her *O Messianismo no Brasil e no mundo* (São Paulo, 1965)
[20] Ibid. pp. 118–21.

activities come to be interpreted as resulting from his miraculous qualities. In that way credibility is restored in a new form to the efficacy of invoking the aid of supernatural *patrões* for the achievement of natural effects.

Change and the Abandonment of Catholicism

In a way, then, the usually small bands around a Messianic leader are not 'saved' from the traditional, frustrating, and unpredictable *do ut des* relationship with the supernatural. These movements have only arisen in a few isolated rural areas, and most peasants affected by the changes which result from agricultural developments, industrialization, and—above all—their own migration to the towns have never come into contact with any of them. Yet their response is in some fundamental respects quite similar to that of the prophet-seekers. They experience acutely the loss of familiar relationships and search, in the changed or new environment, for substitutes. In place of the rural *patrão* appear the leaders of local political machines in the slums of the towns or of agricultural labour unions or peasant leagues in the countryside. The old religious patterns are discarded. But on the whole their place is not taken by a more sophisticated form of Catholicism: the urban churches, for example, have not shown any spectacular success in gaining the loyalties of the newcomers. More usually they turn to Umbanda,[21] Spiritualism, or Protestantism (especially the Pentecostal sects).

Thus many of the people who come to the modern part of Brazil from the traditional areas gravitate towards groups which re-create certain essential aspects of their past life patterns: a sense of community,[22] dependence relations, and a religion directed at the immediate solving of immediate problems. Research among converts to these religions consistently shows that the primary reason for seeking contact with the new creed is the search for

---

[21] A form of ritual which has developed out of the syncretism of original African cults and other elements, mainly Catholic, Indian, and Spiritualist.

[22] Emilio Willems, 'Protestantism and Culture Change in Brazil and Chile', in D'Antonio & Pike, p. 96. For the Spiritualists the point is made by C. Procopio de Camargo and Jean Labbens, 'Introducción sociológica' to Camargo, *Aspectos sociológicos del espiritismo en São Paulo* (Fribourg, FERES, 1961), p. 38.

solutions to 'personal problems'.[23]   Much trial and error goes into this search, particularly in the large towns where the profusion of associations and less formal groupings clamouring to cater to their needs can be quite overwhelming.   Willems suggests that 'a substantial percentage of the "uprooted" population in the large cities floats to and fro between political and religious radicalism, between Spiritualism and Pentacostalism, between the historical Protestant Churches and the suddenly emerging sects'.[24]

Yet it is significant that these different non-Catholic cults can be arranged with little ambiguity on a continuum with regard to their fundamental similarity to folk Catholicism.   Umbanda, with its frankly magical overtones, is in a sense closest—despite the fact that doctrinally it is about as far removed from Christianity as one can be.   It appears to be largely a lower-class phenomenon, particularly widespread among the inhabitants of the city slums.[25]   In the middle of the range we find certain forms of Spiritualism, and the Pentecostal sects.   These put great emphasis on trance-like states during which the faithful receive information respectively from disembodied spirits or from the Holy Ghost, which helps them to cope with their current problems.   These states also afford emotional compensation for the miseries of everyday life.[26]   Farthest removed are the Protestant Churches (of which the Baptists and the Presbyterians have been most successful in gaining new members, particularly, so it seems, in areas of recent agricultural colonization and in the industrial sectors of the country),[27] and the Spiritualists,

[23] Camargo, p. 78, and Willems, 'Protestantismus und Kulturwandel in Brasilien und Chile', *Kölner Zeitschr. f. Soziol. u. Sozialpsych.*, 15th yr (1963), p. 319.

[24] Willems (*Kölner Zeitschr.*, 1963), p. 316.

[25] Camargo & Labbens, p. 36.

[26] Willems (*Kölner Zeitschr.*, 1963), p. 312, reports that in 1958 the two largest Pentcostal associations together claimed more than half of the total number of Protestants in Brazil.   The membership of these two associations was estimated then to be 1·5 m.

[27] Accurate overall membership figures for the Protestant part of the population are hard to come by.   The census of 1950 reported 1·7 m. Protestants; the figures for 1960 are not yet available.   Growth between these dates has been great, but specific figures vary enormously.   The Evangelical Union claimed in 1958 2·7 m. members; but the Statistical Yearbook for Brazil (1963) mentions 2 m. at the beginning of 1962.   *Bilan du Monde* (Tournai, 1964), p. 394, gives the over-all percentage for 1961 of Protestants in the population as 6·1 per cent. This compares with 1·9 per cent for Argentina, 11·8 per cent for Chile, 2·6 per cent for Mexico, 0·7 per cent for Venezuela, and 3·8 per cent for the continent as a whole.

who are faithful followers of the teachings of Allan Kardec.[28]   The
latter two groups have made the most radical break with the
methods of folk Catholicism.   They emphasize, each in its own
way, the merits of a rationally organized life.   Personal favours
from the supernatural and miracles have been banished.   Merit
and evil are attributable primarily or exclusively to the over-all
way of life of the individual (in the case of Spiritualism also to his
life in previous incarnations), and man's efforts must be devoted
to the attainment of ethically consistent behaviour.[29]

I have suggested that the people who have been uprooted from
their traditional background seek a way of coping with the problems
of daily life which has a familiar ring.   If this is true, one would
expect that the proportion of adherents whose experience of social
change is very recent becomes smaller as one moves further away,
on the continuum, from folk Catholicism.   One might also expect
that with the passing of time, and successful adaptation to the
new social conditions, people would abandon the more 'primitive'
forms.   Religious mobility would then correlate with social
mobility—perhaps from one generation to the next.   Unfortunately
the large-scale studies of 'conversion histories' needed to test
these hypotheses do not yet exist.

The Church in the Cities

The truly remarkable growth of the non-Catholic part of the
population is filling Brazilian Catholic churchmen with increasing
alarm.   This is especially true for the Umbanda groups and for
the Pentecostal sects, with whom an ecumenical understanding
is quite out of the question.   Many of the more 'progressive'
Catholics are aware of the fact that conversions are occurring
primarily among the population groups caught in the processes of

[28] Their success among white-collar workers has been noted by Camargo
& Labbens, p. 34.   In the body of the study Camargo gives some very
intriguing data on the extent of adherence to this form of Spiritualism
among small-town professionals (pharmacists, dentists, and notaries) in
27 towns in the State of São Paulo: over 10 per cent were strongly
influenced by Spiritualism (cf. p. 142).

[29] In an interesting parallel to the much-discussed case of Europe, non-
Pentecostal Protestants exhibit a rate of economic success, and of upward
social mobility, substantially higher than the average (see Willems,
Kölner Zeitschr., 1963, p. 322); for a comparison in this respect with
Spiritualism see Camargo, pp. 147 f.

social change. This must be attributed both to the merely super-ficially Catholic character of the latter's beliefs, and to the failure of the Catholic Church to help them in absorbing the shock. As the horizons of the rural masses widen, many more are likely to sever the tenuous connexions they now have with the Church. A good part of these further losses would have to be attributed to the fact that most rural (and urban) priests who try to combat the practices and creeds of folk Catholicism (they are perhaps above all the non-Brazilian priests) [30] do so on the grounds of a doctrinal purity with whose main concepts the peasants and migrants remain totally out of touch.

The aspects of Catholicism stressed by these priests are found in their strongest form in the cities, especially among the well-to-do women. This form of Catholicism emphasizes devotional rites: frequent Communion, salutation of the Sacraments, pilgrimages, and external manifestations such as the wearing of medallions.[31] Directed at individual salvation alone, and totally unconcerned with the perfection of society as an expression of faith, it is mainly of Italian inspiration and was brought to Brazil on a massive scale when the religious houses of Europe established branches in the country after the separation of Church and state in 1889. The women's orders (which were particularly influenced by this move-ment) set up convents in the large cities, well within reach of the wealthy classes on whose resources they depended—and continue to depend. All engaged in activities imported straight from Europe, such as charitable social assistance and above all education.

The main legacy today is a network of secondary schools catering for the well-to-do, which provides a poor education that almost completely neglects the cultural background as well as the current

---

[30] In 1960 over 40 per cent of the priests in Brazil were from abroad (cf. Pérez and others, p. 16). They were particularly strong among the 7,200 regular priests (where they constituted 56 per cent of the total), with the largest contingents among them coming from Italy (16 per cent of all regular priests), Holland (12 per cent), Germany (12 per cent), and Spain (5 per cent). It is tempting to speculate that the Spanish and Italian priests are predominantly conservative, the Dutch, Belgian, German, and French priests predominantly progressive. There are, however, no data whatever that have a bearing on this hunch.

[31] *Prêtres belges*, pp. 26 ff, on which the account given here is largely based. See also Houtart & Pin, pp. 186 ff., who touch on many of the same questions when they discuss the form of religion they call 'the individualistic search for eternal salvation'.

problems specific to Brazil. This educational system developed out of the interplay of two main factors: the availability of men and women religious, willing and able to undertake the task of teaching the élite, and an understanding with the state—secular since 1889—regarding the teaching of religion in public primary schools. Such religious instruction was first tolerated in the constitution of 1934, and given a firmer recognition in 1946, after a great deal of high level pressure from the hierarchy. This left the Church free to concentrate its efforts on the secondary schools.[32] Those who pass through the Church schools are exclusively exposed to the pietistic outlook already mentioned, with its limited and limiting stress on certain specific sins (particularly sexual ones) and its virtually total disregard for the social teachings of the Church. They learn to believe that 'all is well with the Church'—an attitude often referred to as triumphalism—and, incidentally, that all is well with society.

Most of the male alumni of these schools seem to retain only their conservative social ideology. On the whole they become largely indifferent to religious matters, and mildly suspicious and perhaps a little contemptuous of priests.[33] The Church for them becomes part of the cultural and social environment, which it is expected to serve. A critique of society or culture with its basis in religion is unthinkable; those who engage in it none the less must be 'communists'.[34] But middle-class women reared in this tradition generally retain their devotional Catholicism. They are most active religiously, both as individuals and in organizations. A very substantial proportion of the urban clergy, and the vast majority of the male and female religious, are devoted to this form of Catholicism and give all their time and energy to keeping it alive. They, too, are largely suspicious of those Catholics, priests and laymen, who believe that the Church must take an open and

[32] Cf. R. J. Havighurst and J. Roberto Moreira, *Society and Education in Brazil* (Pittsburgh, 1965), pp. 142–4. In 1959 27 per cent of all secondary school students in the country were enrolled in Church schools (see Pérez & others, p. 114).
[33] de Azevedo, *Social Change*, p. 67.
[34] Will Herberg, in an interesting analysis of the 'new religiosity' in the United States, has called this kind of religion 'Civic religion': it 'validates culture and society, without in any sense bringing them under judgment'. Cf. *Protestant, Catholic, Jew* (New York, 1955), p. 279. For a similar appreciation of the Latin American scene see Houtart & Pin, p. 179.

explicit stand on the major social and political questions affecting the country, and they, too, will use the communist bogeyman in the attempt to stop reform.   'Against reformers no holds are barred. Anti-communism is an effective weapon: it also gives you a good conscience', write Houtart and Pin.[35]

This type of attitude has come much to the fore since shortly before the overthrow of the Goulart government in April 1964. In March of that year hundreds of thousands of people, mainly women, went into the streets of São Paulo, Rio de Janeiro, and Belo Horizonte to demonstrate for 'liberty and democracy', for the 'fundamental values' of Christianity, for the dignity of the family and the preservation of the Fatherland.   These 'Marches of the Family, with God, for Liberty' were manifestations of the virulently anti-communist and conservative lay sectors of the Church, supported by priests in middle and upper-class parishes, such as those who see the greatness of the Church expressed primarily in the greatness of its buildings, and who saw their ambitious construction programmes endangered by national unrest and 'subversion'.   The more active women leaders organized themselves into small cell-like units, pledged to militant lobbying and public action on behalf of 'democracy', and to full-scale exposure of the dangers from communism.[36]   Thus, for example, they organized a lecture tour in the major cities of the country for Juanita Castro, shortly after she had broken with her brother and had left Cuba.

The Foundations of Progressive Catholicism

In Europe Catholic social thought has been shaped for decades by the encyclical letter of Pope Leo XIII, *Rerum Novarum*, of 1891, and the elaboration by Pope Pius XI in *Quadragesimo Anno* of 1931. Most of the fundamental tenets of European Christian Democracy were formulated in these two encyclicals, particularly those which dealt with the manifold aspects of the relationship between the different social classes.   These documents, the authoritative statements of the Church's position, were related to current discussions among Catholic philosophers and sociologists; in turn, they influenced the further development of these discussions.

[35] Ibid. p. 104.
[36] See D. E. Mutchler, 'Roman Catholicism in Brazil', *Studies in Comparative International Development* (St Louis, Mo.), 1/8 (1965) for a valuable discussion of various political currents in the Church in Brazil today.

The initial impact of these encyclicals on Brazil was minimal. This is not really surprising, as they sought to pronounce on the conditions prevailing in Europe at the zenith of liberal capitalism. They were hardly relevant to the social structures of Latin America, and few people took any notice of them at all. In Brazil, moreover, the first two decades after the separation of Church and State in 1889 were given over to internal reconstruction, the next twenty years to attempts to purify and reinvigorate the far from orthodox beliefs and practices that pervaded Brazilian Catholicism.[37] But in recent years the 'social encyclicals' have been given greater weight by 'moderate reformers' in the Church—a notable representative in Brazil is Fernando Bastos de Avila, SJ.[38] However, the importance attached to 'solidarism' and the right to private property, and the strong denunciation of socialism and class conflict have tended to turn them, in the Brazilian context, into tools more appropriate to those with conservative interests than to basic reformers.[39]

The real sources of Catholic radicalism in Brazil have been the people who elaborated these principles contained in the official doctrines of the Church. They are philosophers such as Jacques Maritain, whose *Humanisme intégral* strongly influenced Alceu Amoroso Lima, since decades Brazil's foremost Catholic thinker, and for years the leader of the Church's lay apostolate, Catholic Action. More recently it has been Emmanuel Mounier, founder and lifetime editor of the influential French journal *L'Esprit*, whose book *Le Personnalisme* has become required reading for many members of Catholic Action's youth movements. They are also sociologists and economists, such as the late French Dominican,

[37] For a penetrating short account of the gradual de-Brazilianization of the Church see Roger Bastide, 'Religion and the Church in Brazil', in T. Lynn Smith and Alexander Marchant, eds, *Brazil; Portrait of Half a Continent* (New York, 1951), pp. 339–42.

[38] He is a prolific writer, but his main arguments can be found in *Neo-Capitalismo, socialismo, solidarismo* (Rio, 1963).

[39] William Bosworth has made an observation in his excellent study *Catholicism and Crisis in Modern France* (Princeton, UP, 1962), p. 46, which is well worth repeating here. Church social doctrine 'is usually vague and imprecise, with many shadings of meaning capable of varied interpretations'. I would remark nevertheless that the basic trend of ideas is quite clear for those willing to see. Of course those not willing to see can always find some statement or paragraph which can be used to defend their own deviating point of view.

L.J. Lebret, and his group *Économie et Humanisme*.[40]   Lately the all-embracing and difficult evolutionist thought of Teilhard de Chardin has begun to provide the ultimate philosophical foundations for the social and political beliefs of the élite among the progressive Catholic intellectuals.   From within Brazil itself a strong influence on the younger Catholic intellectuals is exercised by Henrique C. de Lima Vaz, SJ.   He has written commentaries on secular philosophies of history (Hegel, Marx, &c.) as well as on the encyclical letters of Pope John, commentaries which have supplied a whole armoury of arguments with which to justify attacks upon the *status quo*.[41]

The latest statements of the Church's social doctrine, Pope John's encyclicals *Mater et Magistra* (1961) and *Pacem in Terris* (1963), have had a truly phenomenal impact on the radically inclined Catholics of Brazil.   They have, for instance, eagerly accepted the idea of 'socialization', which comments on the necessity to provide increasingly for man's needs through social as opposed to individualistic initiatives.   They have highlighted Pope John's insistence on the dignity of labour and its primacy over capital, and on the need to define the 'common good' always in relation to the specific historical conditions.   They have praised his discussion of the rise of the working class and the question of colonialism in *Pacem in Terris*, and have noted that his were the first encyclicals to make explicit reference to the problems of underdevelopment.[42]

Those who adhere to these radical positions are few in number. There is only a small minority among Brazil's Catholic leaders whose Christianity and social ideology are not set in rigid and conservative moulds.   They do exist, however, and they are much more vocal and visible than their numbers would lead one to expect.

---

[40] For a brief but good discussion of the principles of social Catholicism in the French context see *Catholicism and Crisis in Modern France* pp. 309–20.   As Brazilian Catholicism has been greatly influenced by France, much of Bosworth's book is relevant.

[41] See his 'Consciência e realidade nacional', *SPES*, 14 (1962) and 'A grande mensagem de S.S. João XXIII', ibid. 18 (1963).

[42] See Vaz (*SPES*, 18, 1963).   A typical example of the use made of Pope John's encyclicals by the extreme Catholic Left is found in a small book by Paulo de Tarso, sometime Minister of Education of President Goulart, *Os Cristãos e a revolução social* (Rio, 1963).   For the encyclicals themselves, I have consulted the excellent 2-volume edition with commentaries and an Introduction by Alceu Amoroso Lima, *As Enciclicas Sociais de João XXIII* (Rio, 1963).

They are also influential. They occupy many important posts in lay movements and in the ecclesiastical apparatus itself, posts which have enabled them to push these organizations (at least on the level of declared policy) substantially in a radical direction.

The Hierarchy

The interest of Brazilian bishops in matters of a socio-political or economic nature is something relatively new. It is really only since the 1930s that the hierarchy involved itself on this secular plane at all. In the turbulent third decade of this century, when ideas blew in from Europe with ever-increasing urgency, many bishops openly declared themselves behind the *Integralistas*: perhaps one-third of the Episcopate early on supported this Brazilian version of fascism which promised order, stability, and patriotic integration. But later, at least in part as a result of the increasingly totalitarian nature of the European examples, the enthusiasm waned. Only one bishop unreservedly voiced his acclamation of Vargas's *Estado nôvo*. Since 1945 the emphasis has increasingly been on the need for social and economic reforms, on the need to raise the living standards and to change the working conditions of the rural masses—although traditional religious goals, such as Catholic education and the prevention of divorce legislation, have been far from abandoned. In the summer of 1960, for example, before the impending national elections, a 'caravan' of five bishops toured Brazil from North to South to enlighten public opinion about the burning issues of the day. These were (rather over-simplified): the holiness of the family—and the utter rejection of any candidate who even hinted at divorce legislation; the right of Catholic schools to integral financial support from the state; the dangers of excessive nationalism; the need for economic development; and the need for serious agrarian reform.[43]

The Brazilian bishops have been discussing their common problems in regular meetings since the foundation, late in 1952, of the National Conference of Bishops of Brazil (CNBB). In these discussions there has been a growing concern with the social and

---

[43] See the special issue of *SPES*, 7 (July–Sept. 1960), which was devoted to the elections. It also contained a Decalogue of the Brazilian Elector, a curious mixture of progressive and conservative do's and don'ts to be observed when picking a candidate.

economic conditions which, in such large parts of Brazil, preclude the full human development from which alone genuine religious options are possible.   When one reads the pastoral letters of 1962 and 1963 of the CNBB—whose secretary and moving power was, until the autumn of 1964, Archbishop Dom Helder Câmara, one of the most outspoken progressives of the Brazilian hierarchy—the Church as a whole seemed ready to assume the task of 'leading the revolution'.   In fact, of course, each bishop remained autonomous within his own diocese, and what actually did get done was much less uniform and far less radical.   Even in the dioceses of the more progressive bishops wholehearted support for their ideas among the clergy (and the faithful) is often lacking.   In a similar way progressive lay élites have not, on the whole, been able to mobilize a substantial rank and file.

Moreover, it is quite clear that the tone of the declarations was influenced, before April 1964, by the general currents of political radicalization in the country.   The majority of bishops, bewildered by the opposing extreme views, refrained from dissenting from opinions formulated by the radical vanguard.   Since the establishment of the civil-military government after the overthrow of President Goulart the majority has asserted itself more forcefully, and the pronouncements of the bishops on worldly matters have become muted.   The replacement of D. Helder Câmara as secretary of the CNBB late in 1964 was probably in part related to these developments.   Nevertheless, the overwhelming climate of change prevailing in the Vatican Council has strengthened the position of the progressive bishops in Brazil.   The five-year plan adopted by the CNBB during their stay in Rome late in 1965 is couched in theological rather than political language and is concerned primarily with pastoral matters, but it gives plenty of scope for radical action in the socio-economic field to those bishops who wish to accept its logical implications.

It must be said again, however, that as yet the radical enthusiasts are few in number.   Of the 230-odd bishops in the country perhaps 10–20 per cent can be counted among the outspoken progressives.[44]

---

[44] David Mutchler (*Studies in Comp. Int. Dev.*, 1/8, 1965), divides the hierarchy into ultra-conservatives, conservatives, moderates, and progressives.   He does not indicate the proportion in each category.   There are, however, some valuable biographical details on various leaders of each of these vague groups.

Most forward-looking, though still far from homogeneous as a group, are the bishops of the North-East, who meet regularly in regional conferences and have sponsored a number of development projects in the area with the help of the federal government. Since his appointment to the See of Recife, in April 1964, D. Helder Câmara (a churchman with a truly remarkable grasp of the realities of economics in underdeveloped areas) has been the spokesman of the most forceful over-all progressives in the group. Another important figure is D. Eugênio Sales, the Apostolic Administrator of the See of Salvador da Bahia. D. Eugênio was for many years Bishop of Natal. There he founded the 'Natal Movement', an intensive programme of social, economic, and 'moral' improvement, run by priests, religious, and laymen under his close personal supervision.[45] His preoccupation with socio-economic matters is also great, but—in contrast to D. Helder—he finds it difficult to allow the laymen working under his direction in the secular field really wide freedom of action.

Catholic Action and AP

The 'progressives' are significantly stronger among the priests who are not engaged in parish work or education than among those who are. Non-educational, non-parish tasks fulfilled by priests are staffing the different diocesan commissions and bureaux, and acting as advisers to various lay groups. Of these Catholic Action must be specially mentioned. This group was imported in 1935 from Europe, inspired perhaps especially by the French and Italian organizations, and has since grown the whole formal apparatus which has also developed in Europe. It has, however, not been really successful in striking roots in the country, whether in terms of coping with the apostolic problems peculiar to Brazil, or in terms of expanding its adult membership. After an early but superficial and short-lived success in attracting large numbers to its mass meetings and manifestations, Catholic Action fell back to the 'level of a general staff', a general staff without an army, endlessly discussing hypothetical methods of action.[46]

---

[45] For a description of the movement see Arthur McCormack, 'The Catholic Church in South America', *Wiseman R.*, 501 (1964), pp. 250–2.
[46] *Prêtres belges*, p. 34.

But the youth movements of Catholic Action have proved to be a truly dynamic force in the Catholic life in Brazil.[47]   For the first ten years of their existence, until about 1960, their activities were mainly, of a liturgical nature and centred on individual apostolic contacts.[48]   To the extent that they were trying at all to insert themselves into Brazil's secular reality, their endless discussions remained abstract, and they found no way of relating themselves actively to the problems of the country.   Then a 'conversion to reality' seems to have occurred almost simultaneously in all of them (the most important of these are the workers' youth movement, *Juventude Operária Católica*, JOC; the secondary school movement, *Juventude Estudantil Católica*,   JEC; and the university branch, *Juventude Universitária Católica*, JUC).   The working-class youth movement became more militant and the students at both levels started by urgently pursuing reforms in the educational system of the country.   In the universities the focus was at first on the need to reform curricula more relevant to the problems of France or the United States than to those of Brazil.   Attention then shifted to the vested interests in the structure of the universities which were blocking the proposed reforms of educational methods and content.   Soon the students' criticisms were directed full blast at the surrounding social structure, of which the university came to be regarded as ' a mere reflection '.[49]   The transition of JUC to its socially *engagé* position meant a great deal of very advanced interpreting of Church social doctrine, frequently leaving JUC on the same wavelength as secular left-wing groups.   Its increasingly socialist programme found little favour in the eyes of most bishops, and in 1962, during a major clash with the hierarchy, JUC was almost suppressed.

Around this time some of the most determined radicals in JUC left the movement, which they regarded as hampered by its links with the hierarchy.   Their convictions were too strong a brew for the bishops, who also objected to JUC's direct involvement in

[47] The paragraphs on the Catholic youth movements are largely based on personal interviews with Catholic youth leaders in Brazil in the middle of 1964 and late in 1965.
[48] See Vaz, 'La jeunesse chrétienne à l'heure des décisions', *Perspectives de Catholicité*, 22/4.
[49] Brazil does not know the institution of university autonomy, as it exists in other countries of Latin America, where students have traditionally had an overwhelming, even crippling, voice in university affairs (see above, pp. 119–56 *passim*, esp. pp. 133, 148, 154 ff.).

political action side by side with non-Christian Leftists. Together with other non-communist radicals, those who had left founded a new organization, *Ação Popular* (AP), which in its short-lived open existence was to play an important role on the Brazilian political scene.[50] It grew rapidly, bringing together students who had left JUC with others who had retained their membership, outspoken Christians with agnostics and atheists—but all of them people who subscribed to a humanistic personalist view of the world, and to a philosophy of history whose linchpin was the advent, crisis, and disappearance of capitalism. AP soon spread outside the universities, found adherents among urban workers and in the professions, and even sought to play a part in the organization of rural labourers. In the course of 1963 it was more and more drawn towards a Marxist line of thought and action. Though remaining organizationally separate from the communists, AP acted increasingly in common with them, finally entering into Popular Front arrangements. Its terminology became hardly distinguishable from that of the Marxists, and ideological distinctions got blurred in the frantic activity of late 1963 and early 1964. During these developments the line between the youth movements of Catholic Action and AP became more clearly drawn; nevertheless many members of JEC and JUC remained also active in *Ação Popular*— and that despite a virtually official prohibition by the Central Commission of the CNBB.[51]

This open hostility of the hierarchy drove some of these young people away from all organized religion. Others, no less fervently Christian for the disapproval of their activities by the Church, became distrustful of the overall authority of priests and bishops, so many of whom were deeply involved in the *status quo,* and turned for guidance back to the Scriptures. They went through a genuine 'crisis of protest', and their religious beliefs hovered for a time in the precarious borderland between Catholicism and

---

[50] See Vas (*Perspectives*, 22/4), p. 288, for a valuable short discussion of the origins and early positions of AP.

[51] Eduardo Payssé González, 'The Catholic Church and Religious Political Forces in Latin America', in the special issue of the *International Socialist J.* devoted to 'Catholics, the Church and Politics', 2/9 (June 1965), suggests that when the hierarchy actively tries to intervene with specific directions or prohibitions, 'the struggle between the hierarchy and the left tends to escalate'. His provocative article is well worth close study.

Protestantism.[52]   But it never came to schisms or apostasy: the coup d'état of April 1964 sealed off the political options available before, options which could have forced them to resolve the dilemma whether to leave the Church in order to stay with Christ. Many of these radical and outspoken Catholic youths suffered interrogation, persecution, and imprisonment.   Most of them, however, were brought by the coup d'état to look deeper into the spiritual sources of their social protest, and to re-examine the links between their political ideologies and their Catholic faith.   An awareness developed that there had been some rather naïve parroting of other people's simplistic ideas.   Many have also become convinced that Goulart and some of his collaborators did not hesitate to use demagogic expedients.   Political circumstances have forced them to fall back upon themselves, and they have become more cautious.   Nevertheless they have been among the most outspoken critics of the anti-democratic practices prevalent since April 1964.

The hierarchy may have cracked down on the most extreme groups among Catholic youth, but in general these movements were left with a great deal of freedom in the years preceding the coup d'état.   This was because, in the first place, most bishops were simply overwhelmed by the political and social happenings, leaving the hierarchy divided and unable to come down forcefully on one side or the other.   It had also something to do with the fear, quite widespread among Catholics, of being left behind in the overall trend towards reform.   As a result, even some of the less whole-heartedly progressive Catholic leaders were willing to let a section of the Church get thoroughly implicated in the wider radical movement.   They regretted, certainly more than the young people themselves, the ideological weakness of those jumping on the band-wagon.   These middle-of-the-road churchmen gave warning of the dangers of naïveté, but had few, if any, positive and concretely helpful suggestions.   They took up the teachings of the Popes on social and economic matters, expounded them, and talked or wrote about the things Brazil needed.   But their theorizing remained abstract and divorced from reality.   Minimal attention was paid to the obstacles which prevented the achievement of those worthy goals in Brazil, or to the ways of surmounting them.   Great stress

[52] See Fernando Bastos de Avila, 'A Enciclica "Ecclesiam Suam" e a consciência católica brasileira', *SPES*, 23 (1964), pp. 19 f.

was laid on the idea that all Catholics are children of the Church; with this went a genuine abhorrence of violence, even conflict. The emphasis of the moderates on the 'solidary', harmonious character of the ideal society (churchmen will be preachers, and concerned above all with the normative) [53] drove many of those primarily interested in the real Brazil straight into the arms of those people whose theory purported to explain in detail why society lacked both harmony and solidarity.

The Church and Reform in Rural Brazil

In addition to the youth movements of Catholic Action there have been some other Catholic or Church-inspired groups where more than lip-service was paid to the need to fight exploitation and socially caused misery or illiteracy. In the first place one should mention the efforts of the Church in the field of peasant organization. The *Ligas* of smallholders which have attempted by legal or direct action (e.g. the invasion of estates) to improve the position of the small peasants, have been largely outside the sphere of the Church.[54] The leadership of the Peasant Leagues, organizations which disappeared from the scene in April 1964, appears to have been divided and thoroughly confused ideologically, vacillating between Peking-oriented communism, Castroism, and a more independent, but still revolutionary line.[55]

From the beginning of the 1960s the Church has, however, taken a major part in the organization of rural labour unions in some areas.[56] A start was made in three states in the North-East:

[53] Robert Lee, in Lee & Marty, a book informed by the growing awareness among American social scientists (and Protestant theologians!) that conflict is a permanent, and even necessary, attribute of all societies, reminds us that the ideal is not necessarily the harmonious society. 'It is too easy and even perhaps dishonest to think that the church is the solvent of social conflict' (p. 7).

[54] Cf. B. Galjart, 'Class and Following in Rural Brazil', *Am. Latine*, 7/3 (1964).

[55] Anthony Leeds, 'Brazil and the Myth of Francisco Julião', in Joseph Maier and R. W. Weatherhead, eds, *Politics of Change in Latin America* (New York, 1964), does not even credit the Leagues with revolutionary aspirations. He suggests that the leadership was merely a new paternalistic élite manipulating the peasants for their own benefit. A similar view is taken by Galjart (n. 54).

[56] Brazilian law does not allow more than one occupational organization per locality for each category (e.g. rural worker). By organizing a local branch and getting it recognized by the Ministry of Labour (often a laborious process, with much in-fighting and wire-pulling) the Church could ensure that 'its own people' would lead the peasants. Only a

Pernambuco, Sergipe, and Río Grande do Norte. The early Church efforts were particularly strong in the sugar-growing region of Pernambuco, where the labour force can properly be called a landless rural proletariat. It is one of the few areas on which data are available, mainly in the form of a valuable report by Mary E. Wilkie.[57] In 1961 the Archbishop appointed four priests who were given the express task of creating Catholic *sindicatos* in rural areas. They proceeded to organize courses in Christian unionism for selected potential peasant leaders, set up local branches, and created a Federation which provided extensive legal services. By the end of 1963 this Federation—Catholic in fact but not in name—claimed a membership of 200,000. The priests planned to withdraw from active leadership, in order to prevent the organization from acquiring a clerical character, but late in 1965 two of them, Father Crespo and Father Melo, were still hovering in the background, intervening in their different ways on behalf of the peasants. Wilkie suggests that the lawyers employed by the Federation assumed effective control of it, casting themselves in the role of substitute *patrões*. They sought to ensure the application of the existing laws relevant to rural workers, which became much easier after the Rural Workers' Statute had been passed in March 1963. They taught the peasants to see themselves not as fundamentally different from the landowners, but as sharing a common humanity with them. They stressed that the peasants did have rights, which could be underlined by collective action. The Federation has tended towards a conciliatory policy, and has stressed *vis-à-vis* the landowners that respect for the workers' rights leads to social harmony and the avoidance of conflicts. This policy seems to have met with some success, so that 'the peasant is increasingly aware of his dignity and the employer treats him with more respect'.[58]

The Federation proclaimed itself explicitly non-political. Not only was it not affiliated to any political party (it could not do so, by law), but it also took no stand on wider political matters affecting the peasants. While they were helped in obtaining justice, the conception of justice was tied strictly to the existing legislation.

---

take-over of the leadership from within could upset the arrangement, but under the prevailing conditions this was a remote danger.
[57] *A Report on Rural Syndicates in Pernambuco* (Rio, CLAPESC, 1964, mimeo.), on which this paragraph is based.
[58] Ibid. p. 10.

There has, of course, always been tremendous scope for a more consistent application of the law in a country in which law and practice have seldom been particularly harmonized.[59] But perhaps the rather limited pugnacity, the lack of emphasis on the continuing iniquities of the whole system of land tenure and land distribution, and the concern for good relations with the employers and avoidance of 'class conflict' would have meant a gradual loss of peasant support as the latter became more politically conscious and more influenced by alternative ideologies and groups.

There were signs of such a development (brusquely ended by the coup of April 1964) in the second half of 1963, after the setting up by the government of a national commission for rural unionization.[60] This commission greatly simplified the rules and regulations regarding the foundation and operation of rural *sindicatos*. The result was a veritable 'syndical rush', and the *sindicatos* organized under direct episcopal supervision were faced with a great number of rival organizations with views generally more radical, and programmes more aggressive, than their own. On the one hand the Communist Party—well-connected in the Ministry of Labour and in the various official commissions— organized unions and federations on a massive scale. Many of these consisted of little more than a town-based directorate, without much spontaneous peasant participation, let alone genuine peasant leadership. On the other hand AP sent its militants into the countryside: they organized rural labour into *sindicatos* which professed the peculiar AP ideology and acted with the characteristic AP aggressiveness. Although, as we have seen above, AP was not a specifically Catholic organization, many of its activists found the inspiration for their ideas and action in Catholic sources. In the final months of the Goulart period the marginally Catholic AP drifted farther and farther away from the original Church-directed *sindicatos*; a major rift occurred in December 1963, during the elections for the directorate of the newly founded Brazilian Confederation of Rural Labour (CONTAG), when the Federations directed by AP entered into an understanding with the Federations led by the Communist Party rather than with those of a less radical

[59] Jacques Lambert, *Amérique latine* (Paris, 1963), emphasizes this problem throughout his analysis. See particularly pt 2, ch. 2.
[60] This paragraph is based on information from unpublished documents of various Catholic and secular organizations involved in *Sindicalismo* during this period.

character led by the Church. Finally, one must mention as adding to the ferment in the field of *sindicalismo* the Catholic *Movimento de Educação de Base* (MEB, see below). It was never officially involved in the setting up and running of *sindicatos* and tried to limit itself to educational and advisory activities. But its impact was not negligible, and its position (in fact, if not in name) in many respects was closer to the radicalism of AP than to the cautiousness of those more directly connected with the hierarchy.

The second effort of the Church in the rural areas has been directed at raising the educational level of the peasants. The rate of illiteracy in Brazil runs to over 50 per cent, and in many of the more backward areas of the country, such as the North-East, three-quarters of the population cannot read or write.[61]   In 1961 a major project for basic education, mainly by means of radio schools, was accepted by the federal government at the suggestion of a sub-committee of the National Conference of Bishops. The MEB was organized, presided over by a council made up of bishops, financed by the federal government and run, from national headquarters down to the local radio schools, entirely by laymen.[62] Many of these came to MEB after an active career in one of the youth movements of Catholic Action. Early in 1964 this organization, with 470 full-time officials, provided daily broadcast lessons to some 180,000 peasants, by means of 25 radio stations scattered over the less developed part of Brazil.[63]

But MEB was badly battered in the wake of the April coup d'état. It drew the wrath of all the outspoken anti-reformers in the country;

---

[61] At the time of the census in 1950 the overall illiteracy rate for Brazil was 52 per cent of those aged 10 and over. For some of the North-Eastern states the figures were: Alagoas 76 per cent, Piauí 74 per cent, Ceara 69 per cent, Pernambuco 68 per cent. It is widely assumed that these rates did not change significantly between 1950 and 1960. It is worth noting, incidentally, that illiterates do not have the vote. A literacy campaign thus helps open the door to political participation.

[62] Compare this situation with that in Colombia, where the much publicized *Acción Cultural Popular* (Radio Sutatenza) is controlled entirely by priests. See Camilo Torres and Berta Corredor, *Las escuelas radiofónicas de Sutatenza—Colombia* (Fribourg & Bogotá, 1961).

[63] As reported by Marina Bandeira in John J. Considine M.M., ed., *The Church in the New Latin America* (Notre Dame, Ind., 1964), p. 81. A large proportion of those reached are young people. Provisional figures from the 1960 census, published in mimeographed form, assert a spectacular improvement—but they are regarded as near-valueless by all experts I have consulted.

it was called communist and almost formally charged (during the military inquiries of 1964) with being subversive. Some of its officials were put in jail, and many others could not continue their work with MEB. By the end of 1964 the movement had lost approximately one-third of its personnel. Even before the April events it had got into deep water with the then Governor of Guanabara, Carlos Lacerda, whose political police had confiscated copies of a primer about to be distributed in the North-East, called *Viver é Lutar* (To Live Means to Struggle).

As the nature of youth movements makes them susceptible to discontinuities in orientation and weakens their organizational power, MEB is probably the most coherent expression of the progressive tendencies in the Church. It is not the only adult organizational stronghold of progressive Catholicism—the majority of Dominican monasteries and the Archdiocese of Recife are others —but, because of its size and the financial resources put at its disposal by the federal government, it is the largest and most effective. Those responsible for the movement see and use MEB as an organization which 'aims at helping a human being to open his own eyes, to look for and understand his own problems, using his own initiative . . . with consciousness'. They feel that MEB 'has the mission of helping men to interpret the social situation that is conditioning their life and destiny', and to show them that 'apathy is harmful and isolation is a deadly selfishness'.[64]

For Brazilians opposed to changes in the *status quo* such talk and such behaviour are truly subversive. And they may well be right, for MEB represents those forces which might really help to bring about a gradual but fundamental change in the social and political structure of rural Brazil. Officially directed by the hierarchy, its day-to-day command is in the hands of laymen, who do not see MEB as a clerical organization, and who have never been reluctant to press their views. MEB strives for social harmony, but this ideal does not inhibit its work. Nobody in the organization denies or fails to see the circumstances which make talk of 'solidarism' at present more than a little utopian. Finally, it is remarkably free from the paternalistic and patron-client

---

[64] Considine, p. 77. Excellent papers on some of the general problems encountered in mass communications programmes aimed at development can be found in Lucian W. Pye, ed., *Communications and Political Development* (Princeton UP, 1963). See especially chs 7, 8, 13 & 14.

relationships from which most other organizations in Brazil continue to suffer. But it is far from certain at the time of writing that it will be allowed and enabled to continue its work, dependent as it is on the financial support of a by now far from friendly government.[65]

Conclusions

It seems to me that the effectiveness of the reform-minded element in the Catholic Church will, in the end, depend predominantly upon the extent to which it can help to overcome not only opposition to reforms, but these deep-seated tendencies in Brazil to look to a *patrão* (landowner, political boss, priest, or the federal government) for the solution of all problems. Changes in structure and in mentality are needed. The latter are, of course, the most difficult to achieve, not least because such an overwhelming proportion of those who must help develop grassroots leadership are themselves incapable of thinking and acting in any way but as *patrão*-substitutes. In a discussion of the general issue of cultural change in Brazil, Wagley distinguished between 'traditional' and 'new' 'culture brokers'. The former—local *patrão*, priest, or politician—act as forces for continuity, although they do link the local community to the changing outside world. The latter are the bearers of new values. Wagley believes, however, that these teachers, agronomists, public health officials, or new priests have difficulties in acting as 'culture brokers', because they do not understand the community and its old values.[66] In certain respects this is, of course, quite true. But in another sense the problem seems to me almost diametrically opposite from what Wagley suggests: most of the 'new brokers' fit only too well into the accepted socio-political ways of doing things and cannot serve as catalysts for a fundamental change of outlook.[67]

Such a change in outlook is achieved by the converts to non-Pentecostal Protestantism and the purer forms of Spiritualism:

[65] I am at present engaged in a study of MEB as an example of Church-directed efforts in the field of reform.

[66] Charles Wagley, 'The Peasant', in John J. Johnson ed., *Continuity and Change in Latin America* (Stanford UP, 1964), p. 45.

[67] A short but interesting discussion of the need for a change in mentality is found in Wilbert E. Moore, 'The Strategy of Fostering Performance and Responsibility', in Egbert de Vries and J. Medina Echevarría, *Social Aspects of Economic Development in Latin America* (Paris, UNESCO, 1963).

the emphasis on a sober and ordered life, the almost complete rejection of spiritual or theological authority or hierarchy, and the stress on self-reliance is apparently seen by many as the efficient cause of a substantial improvement in their social and economic position. But significantly, despite social-assistance institutions run on a large scale by these groups, such social mobility is of an individualistic nature. Spiritualism, with its teachings regarding reincarnation and the understanding of man's situation at any time as a result of his personal merits or failings in this or previous lives, leaves, in fact, no room at all for social evil. Protestantism is less explicit on this point, but has made very little of the social roots of misery.[68]

Catholic attention, in so far as it is directed at social change at all, is focused much more on the evils of the social structure, on landowners unwilling to comply with the law, or a state unable to provide education for the children of its citizens. Catholics hold up their own ideals of society, look forward to a 'solidaristic', harmonious social order, and condemn, with greater or lesser vigour, those whose behaviour does not conform to the ideal. The Church promotes rural syndicates or urban trade unions, and the betterment of the position of workers or peasants results from a nibbling away at the power of entrepreneurs or landlords. So the improvements are obtained collectively rather than individually.[69] But in the course of that fight for a better life the underprivileged often do not learn to think for themselves, decide on their own needs, and assume responsibility for their own actions. When they remain so dependent on the goodwill and help of outside leaders, there is little for them to do but to fall back into apathy once political circumstances force these leaders to disappear from the scene. Developments since April 1964 bear this out.

[68] In July 1962 a commission of the Protestant Churches organized a conference in Recife under the title 'Christ and the Revolutionary Process in Brazil'. They too suddenly seemed to climb on the bandwagon, and many fiery speeches and radical proposals were heard at that time. It seems, however, to have been a flash in the pan, very much disapproved of by top leadership and rank and file alike. See *Cristo e o processo revolucionário brasileiro* (Rio, n.d.).

[69] It is interesting to note how in a projected study of the impact of religious groups on the socio-political structure in the North-East the emphasis for the Catholic groups is on changes in the local power structure, but for the Protestant groups on the emergence of a new type of personality. ISS-FERES study, proposal by Candido Procopio de Camargo (mimeo, 1965).

It is, obviously, very hard for groups within a body such as the Catholic Church, which has been fundamentally paternalist, hierarchical, and authority-oriented for centuries, to take the lead in the kind of social and psychological changes necessary in Brazil. But the *Aggiornamento* initiated by Pope John XXIII, the new self-confidence gained by the 'progressive' bishops during the sessions of the Vatican Council, and the increasing impact of putting the decisions of the Council into effect are beginning to make their mark. The Catholic Church has started to break age-old patterns, which had been aggravated in Brazil by peculiar historical circumstances. At present the influence of those wishing to preserve the *status quo* (perhaps with minor modifications) is still overwhelming, and among the reformist elements paternalism predominates. But there are significant and possibly powerful sections dedicated to different ideals—in which secular reforms go hand in hand with religious innovation and a consequent change in mentality. Should they come to dominate the scene, the Church could still play a fundamental role in the transformation of Brazilian society. There is little doubt, however, that the general political climate in the country will have much influence on the ability of these reformist elements to make themselves heard and followed.

European Immigrants in Argentine Industry and Politics

OSCAR CORNBLIT

POLITICALLY speaking, the apparent passiveness of the industrialists is one of the most conspicuous aspects of the contemporary struggle for power in Argentina. It therefore seems appropriate to review the formative stages of industrial entrepreneurship and its dependence on the massive European migrations of the decades following 1880. This will be done in the light of the main hypotheses: first, that by the end of the first world war there were industrial entrepreneur groups in some parts of the country—chiefly in the Buenos Aires and Rosario areas—sufficiently mature to try to influence the central government's economic policy; secondly, that the tenuous influence they actually exerted resulted from their lack of contact with the political élite, especially with the Radical Party, which remained in power between 1916 and 1930; and, lastly, that this failure of communication occurred because the system of selection of the political élite discriminated against the immigrants, who promoted the great majority of the industrial undertakings.

Many studies which take into consideration the negative political impact of the numerous migrants who entered Argentine society during the period 1880–1930 attribute this chiefly to the low level of political integration of the foreigners. But this is only one of the variables, and here the attempt will be made to discover the role which the host society plays in the complex problem of assimilation.

The Expansion of the 1880s and the Settlement of Immigrants

The date 1880 symbolizes Argentina's decisive entry into the world market as a major producer and exporter of agricultural products. This was not an easy development. The wealth and fertility of the *pampas* had of course been there all the time, but a number of political and technological adjustments were necessary before they could be effectively exploited. Many of these obstacles were eliminated during the administration of President Roca (1880–6), which is generally regarded as the period when the Argentine hinterland was tamed and brought into production. The successful completion of the Desert War of 1879 and the final elimination of the Indian threat opened these lands to colonization by native and foreign settlers. As the marginal productivity of the soil was so greatly superior to any alternative form of investment, the impact on the national economy of this sudden incorporation of unused resources was stupendous, and it continued to offer great investment opportunities until about the period of the first world war.

The opening up of the interior was greatly facilitated by the dramatic extension of the railway network, which within two decades increased from less than 1,000 km. in 1871, to 12,000. The main purpose of the new lines was to collect the primary produce from the interior and bring it to the ports for shipment to European markets. A parallel development was the encouragement of immigration to solve the shortage of labour. In the four years between 1885 and 1889 more than 700,000 immigrants entered the country and the flow continued almost without interruption until the 1920s (see Table 1).

TABLE 1

Percentage of Foreigners, 1869–1930

Year	No. of foreigners	% of population	% of native-born Argentines
1869	210,300	12·1	13·8
1895	1,004,500	25·4	34·0
1914	2,358,000	29·9	42·7
1920	2,155,400	24·0	31·6
1930	2,834,300	23·5	30·8

Source: Gino Germani, *Estructura social de la Argentina* (Buenos Aires, 1954), p. 81. The figures for 1869, 1895, and 1914 are based on the respective censuses; those for 1920 and 1930 on estimates. Argentina, of course, is not the only Latin American country to have received such a large group of immigrants. In 1900 Montevideo

Source, cont.

> had as many foreigners per 100 inhabitants as Buenos Aires between 1895 and 1914, while the proportion of foreigners in the total population of Uruguay in 1860 (35 per cent) was higher than that found in Argentina.

The Argentine ruling groups of 1880 accepted the intake of these immigrants but only within strictly defined limits. For them change, initiating accelerated economic development employing the middle- and lower-class masses, foreign and native, was to be started by an enlightened minority (such as themselves), the masses to have a minimal say in the necessary economic and political decisions. The mission of the immigrants was to act as a technical catalyst, especially in the fields of agriculture and animal husbandry. To a limited extent this was in fact what happened, as thousands of foreigners settled in the provinces of Córdoba, Entre Ríos, and Santa Fé, developing the technical expertise which made possible the development of the country's wheat-growing potential. At a slightly later date the province of Buenos Aires also became a wheat-growing centre through the activity of immigrants, but this time as tenant farmers and not as small proprietors.

But the expectations of the ruling groups were only half realized. The immigrants spread not only in the rural areas, but also in the cities, which certainly held greater attractions for them. In fact the majority preferred the cities, as the figures of the 1914 census clearly show (Table 2).

TABLE 2

Percentage of Foreigners: Urban and Rural Areas, 1914

National origin	Urban centres		Rural areas	Total
	No.	%		
Argentina	2,915,093	52·74	2,612,192	5,527,285
Italy	637,205	68·53	292,658	929,863
Spain	613,032	78·36	216,669	829,701
Russia	53,638	57·28	39,996	93,634
France	54,580	68·66	24,911	79,491
Germany & Austria-Hungary	36,774	56·46	28,344	65,118
Brazil	19,370	53·15	17,072	36,442

Source: III° censo general de la nación, 1914.

Of the 2,300,000 foreigners settled in the country before 1914 almost 70 per cent lived in the urban areas. This was in sharp contrast with the figures for the native population, which was at that time more or less evenly divided between rural and urban zones. It is also interesting to note the rural-urban preference according to national origin, the two most important groups numerically, the Spaniards and Italians, showing a marked preference for the urban environment. If one takes the federal capital as a reference point, the difference between immigrants and native-born is even more striking. Only 14 per cent of the native-born Argentines lived in the city of Buenos Aires as compared with 33 per cent of those born abroad. Clearly the great port had retained the recent arrivals, transforming itself in the process into a vast cosmopolitan agglomerate where one out of every two inhabitants had been born on the other side of the Atlantic. Table 3 shows the distribution of immigrants over the period 1869–1947.

TABLE 3

Percentage of Foreigners: Buenos Aires and Other Regions,
1869–1947

Year	Buenos Aires	Córdoba & riverside provinces	Rest of the country
1869	48	42	10
1895	39	52	9
1914	41	49	10
1947	44	42	14

Source: Germani, *Política y sociedad en una época de transición* (Buenos Aires, 1962), p. 186.

For eighty consecutive years Buenos Aires has maintained this dominant position. It was in this urban strip and its numerous suburbs that the important social and cultural transformations in the life of the immigrants took place. It was there too that literature, music, social habits, and cultural mores were most radically changed under the impact of so many immigrants. Among the new elements appearing on the social scene, the hardest to assimilate in the long run were the skilled industrial workers and entrepreneurs. Traditional occupations such as those of merchants and shopkeepers soon reappeared in the new environment but others especially those involving craftsmanship tended gradually to disappear.

Occupational opportunities are evidently important in determining where immigrants settle. Of course, these opportunities are not only found but are also created, and in this the mental equipment of each generation of migrants is the determining factor. Among rural zones, Santa Fé seems to have been the most attractive to the foreigners, probably because it was easier to buy land there. The immigrants in the Santa Fé region have tended to begin with cereal farming and later on to move into animal husbandry. In the province of Buenos Aires, on the other hand, cattle-raising is more important and the native-born predominate. In this region the immigrants are generally tenant farmers and seldom manage to become landowners, as is shown by the small proportion of foreigners owning land in 1914 (see Table 4).

TABLE 4

Ownership of Land by Foreigners, 1914

Occupational & economic categories	% of foreigners
Proprietors of real estate of all kinds	10
Proprietors of cattle estates	22
Tenants of cattle estates	34
Administrators, directors, managers, proprietors, & tenants of estates:	
(a) predominantly used for rearing cattle	44
(b) predominantly used for growing cereals	57

Source: Germani, *Política y sociedad*, p. 193.

The attraction of Santa Fé for foreigners engaged in primary production activities is also clearly reflected in the figures available for 1895 and 1914. The remarkable increase in the province of Mendoza is related to the rapid development of the wine industry.

TABLE 5

Percentage of Total Population Engaged in Primary, Secondary, and Tertiary Economic Activities

(a) *Primary*

Provinces	Argentine-born		Foreigners		Total	
	1895	1914	1895	1914	1895	1914
Federal capital	0·5	0·4	1·5	0·5	2·0	0·9
Buenos Aires	21·7	14·5	23·9	18·6	45·6	33·1
Santa Fé	15·1	14·3	25·6	21·1	40·7	35·4
Entre Ríos	24·9	29·7	19·6	12·2	44·5	41·9
Córdoba	30·3	26·1	8·0	15·4	38·3	41·5
Mendoza	27·3	18·2	9·1	18·2	36·4	36·4
Catamarca	48·6	44·7	0·6	0·9	49·2	45·6
Total for Argentina:	23·7	16·0	13·2	12·0	36·9	28·0

(b) *Secondary*

Federal capital	7·6	10·8	32·6	29·9	40·2	40·7
Buenos Aires	11·3	15·4	13·9	20·9	25·2	36·3
Santa Fé	11·2	14·5	14·6	19·0	25·8	33·6
Entre Ríos	14·5	20·6	6·8	6·3	21·3	26·9
Córdoba	28·5	22·9	3·1	8·4	31·6	31·3
Mendoza	21·0	16·8	5·1	14·6	26·1	31·4
Catamarca	31·5	31·6	0·8	1·3	31·8	32·6
Total for Argentina:	18·8	18·9	11·6	16·6	30·4	35·5

(c) *Tertiary*

Federal capital	18·0	22·2	39·7	36·3	57·7	58·5
Buenos Aires	15·0	15·0	14·3	15·4	29·3	30·4
Santa Fé	14·8	14·9	16·8	16·3	31·6	31·2
Entre Ríos	23·7	22·2	10·5	8·4	34·2	31·2
Córdoba	25·4	18·5	4·7	8·8	30·1	27·3
Mendoza	31·2	18·5	6·2	13·7	32·4	32·2
Catamarca	17·6	19·9	1·0	1·9	18·6	21·8

Sources: II° & III° censo general, 1895 & 1914.

The differential participation of Argentines and immigrants in secondary economic activities is most marked in the federal capital. In 1895 there were almost four and a half times as many foreigners than native-born Argentines engaged in manufacturing industry. Twenty years later the situation had not changed very much: three times as many foreigners as Argentines were still engaged in secondary activities. New industries are, of course, included under this classification, and the dominant position of the foreign-owned and foreign-managed industrial concerns is an additional indication of the degree of concentration of this type of activity in the urban centre of Buenos Aires even at these early dates. It is possible to generalize and state that wherever modern commercial and industrial activities were found in Argentina, there, too, foreigners were to be found, as proprietors or in management. Conversely, relatively fewer seem to have been attracted by the civil service, lesser industrial crafts, domestic service, or, unexpectedly, the professions:

TABLE 6

Percentage of Foreigners Engaged in the Main Secondary and Tertiary Economic Activities

Occupational categories	1895	1914
Proprietors of industrial firms	81	66
Proprietors of commercial establishments	74	74
Commercial employees & workers	57	55
Industrial employees & workers	60	50
Professions	53	45
Industrial & domestic crafts	18	27
Civil servants	30	18
Domestic servants	25	38

Source: Germani, *Política y sociedad*, p. 195.

Within the industrial sector the foreigners tended to be associated with the more modern establishments while the native-born were mostly found in industries in which traditional techniques and forms of organization predominated. This was clearly the case in the garment industry, which, in a country like Argentina, is closely linked to domestic crafts. On the other hand, the chemical and metallurgical industries, which need to be based on up-to-date techniques, were mostly staffed by foreigners (see Table 7).

TABLE 7

	Argentine-born		Foreigners		Total	
	1895	1914	1895	1914	1895	1914
Garment industry	11·8	10·3	6·9	5·7	18·7	16·0
Building & construction	2·2	3·9	7·3	7·7	9·5	11·6
Chemical & metallurgical industries	0·5	1·5	2·7	3·2	3·2	4·7

Source: Gustavo Beyhaut and others, *Inmigración y desarrollo económico* (Buenos Aires, 1961), p. 31.

The growth of Argentine industry is clearly discernible from 1895 on. The 1914 war reinforced the growth of the new sectors giving them a natural protection for about five years. The fact is that from the early years of the present century the import coefficient shows a distinct tendency which can be reasonably explained by the steady growth of an import-substitution industry.

TABLE 8

Period	GNP	Total imports	Import coefficient in relation to GNP
	(in millions of pesos of 1950)		
1905–9	15,890	4,544	28·6
1915–19	19,131	3,345	17·5
1925–9	33,184	8,214	24·8
1930–4	33,863	4,985	14·7
1940–4	45,908	2,956	6·4

Source: ECLA, *Análisis y proyecciones del desarrollo económico*, V: *El desarrollo económico argentino* (Mexico City, 1959), pt. 1, p. 26.

The share of industrial production in GNP increased from 13·8 per cent in 1900 to 17·7 per cent in 1925–9, and 23·4 per cent in 1955. But agricultural production, accounting for 33·3 per cent of GNP in 1900, decreased to 27·7 per cent in 1925–9 and 17·3 per cent in 1955.

It is fair to suppose, on the basis of these figures, that by the end of the 1914 war the share of industrial production showed a further advance on the 14 per cent of 1900. As has been noted, there are no precise statistics for the period between 1914 and 1935, but a number of informed guesses can be taken as reasonably accurate. For instance, according to Ricardo Ortiz, who based his figures on Alejandro E. Bunge's calculations, capital invested in industry increased by 22·5 per cent during 1914–18, while the industrial labour force increased by 25 per cent and the value of industrial production by 50 per cent.[1] As for the geographical distribution of industrial production, it is evident that from the beginning this was highly concentrated in the riverside and Buenos Aires regions. In 1914 70 per cent of all industrial establishments, 79·7 per cent of total industrial production, 72·1 per cent of all industrial capital, and 76·5 per cent of the industrial labour force were situated in the province of Buenos Aires and the riverside or 'litoral' region. The increase in the industrial labour force during the period 1895–1935 was also significant, though not as sustained, as the following figures indicate.

TABLE 9

Numbers of People Employed in Industry, 1895, 1914, and 1935

	1895	1914	Increase %	1935	Increase %
Federal capital	72,761	149,289	105·2	244,231	63·6
Buenos Aires	31,286	98,937	216·2	128,276	29·6
Santa Fé	18,195	42,726	134·8	50,531	18·2
Entre Ríos	10,689	18,004	68·4	12,667	− 29·6
Corrientes	3,040	4,673	53·7	3,854	− 17·5
Córdoba	7,187	20,243	181·6	23,600	16·6
Mendoza	4,290	14,598	240·2	11,525	−210.0
Total for Argentina:	175,682	410,201	133·5	526,594	283·0

Source: Censo general, 1895 & 1914; Censo industrial, 1935.

Some authors have pointed out that an important part of what is normally classed as industrial production in Argentina is in fact closer to agricultural production. If what is being measured is the degree of change from a traditional towards a modern style of

---

[1] Ricardo Ortiz, *Historia económica de la Argentina* (Buenos Aires, 1955). See also *Informe de la Confederación Argentina del Comercio, de la Industria y de la Producción* (Buenos Aires, 1921).

economic behaviour, then it is a mistake to associate all manufacturing production with the so-called process of secularization or modernization. It is, of course, extremely difficult to estimate the relative significance of all the subsections into which industrial production is generally divided, but for the purposes of the traditional-modern dichotomy, Roberto Cortés Conde has made a detailed study of the industries listed in the census of 1914 and has prepared a new classification. According to this, only 13·6 per cent of the industrial capital classified as such in the census really corresponds with 'basically manufacturing industries'; 54·8 per cent corresponds with 'basically extractive industries'; 23·4 per cent represents public services; and 8·2 per cent cannot be considered as manufactures at all.[2] It is obvious that the most dynamic entrepreneurial and industrial group is associated with the 'basically manufacturing industries', accounting for 13·6 per cent of the total, but it would be a mistake completely to disregard the importance of the other groups.

The problem of the relative degree of modernity of different industrial sectors should not be ignored, especially as this factor has been given some importance as an explanation of the apparent weakness of the industrial groups of that period. However, this is not as relevant as it would appear at first sight. Two industrial sectors of differing modernity can have similar interests which impel them to co-operate in exerting political pressure to obtain mutually beneficial ends.[3] Tariff protection, for instance, has traditionally been a common goal both for sugar producers and metallurgical industries.

The struggle for tariff protection affords a very good indication of the relative political power exercised by different economic groupings. As a protectionist commercial policy is evidently one of the most effective means of ensuring the ascendency and continuing growth of an industrial group, the absence of such a policy in

---

[2] Roberto Cortés Conde, *Corrientes inmigratorias y surgimiento de industrias en Argentina, 1870–1914* (Buenos Aires, 1964).

[3] From a theoretical point of view it appears that the model 'traditional society/modern society' is not a very useful one although it may have some virtues as a yardstick. In reducing the process of social change to a linear movement between two rigidly complementary poles it simplifies what is highly complex and rules out the multi-dimensional movements which in fact take place in the process of development. See Oscar Cornblit, *Modelos, medición y teoría en ciencias sociales*, monograph of the Instituto de Sociología, Universidad de Buenos Aires.

Argentina before 1930 is eloquent proof of the lack of political weight of the local industrial groups. This is even more striking when compared with the success of the northern sugar-mill owners in obtaining favoured commercial treatment and protection.

During the first world war the obvious difficulties in obtaining manufactured imports resulted in the proliferation of industrial establishments. But when the war was over, no attempt was made by the government of President Yrigoyen and the Radical Party to protect these newly-formed industries. On the other hand, the production and milling of sugar, both of which had traditionally been controlled by powerful vested interests in the northern part of the country, received substantial encouragement from the government. In fact, no other industrial activity has received such favoured treatment and no group has used these advantages so effectively to perpetuate the dominance of a small landowning caste. The government protected local sugar production over a long period of time, only to have the doubtful satisfaction of paying much more for it than if free imports had been allowed, and of reinforcing the economic position of a tiny sector of the population enjoying political power out of all proportion to its importance in the economic life of the nation.[4] A possible explanation of this might lie in the degree of concentration of capital in these two

TABLE 10

National Origin of Owners of Industrial Establishments, 1935

	Province of Buenos Aires	*Federal capital*	*Total for Argentina*
Argentine*	6,486	7,331	23,405
Italian	2,998	3,911	11,309
Spanish	2,606	3,857	9,687
Russian	123	651	1,024
Polish	71	752	959
German	142	254	615
French	112	249	571
Uruguayan	105	263	510
Other	822	1,635	4,237

* Including naturalized Argentines.
Source: Censo industrial,1935.

[4] Ortiz, ii. 137.

activities, but this would be misleading. The fundamental problem was political and it reflected the inability of the existing political parties to incorporate and represent the interests of the new industrial groupings. This is particularly important in view of the fact that industrial growth in Argentina was principally due to the activity of foreigners. In 1895 over 90 per cent of the owners of the industrial establishments of Buenos Aires were foreigners. In 1935 the proportion was still well over 60 per cent.

The apparent political passivity of the industrial groups of this period must be examined in the light of the national origin of the new entrepreneurs and their failure to secure adequate political representation for their interests.

The Political Situation

Although the incorporation of immigrants in political parties and activities is often directly related to the success with which they become assimilated into the host society, the two processes are in fact mutually independent. In Argentina, for example, it can generally be said that the process of assimilation—excluding political participation—was as successful as that of similar groups in other countries. The immigrants were able to settle and carry on economic activities without difficulty. Only in the province of Buenos Aires were they unable to acquire property rights over any significant amount of land, but this was because of the system of land tenure, which also excluded Argentine nationals who did not belong to the ruling landholding groups. The participation of the immigrants in political activities, on the other hand, was insignificant. The number of immigrants who became naturalized Argentines reflects this.

TABLE 11

Naturalized Immigrants

	1895		1914	
	Total	*% of foreign population*	*Total*	*% of foreign population*
Argentina	1,638	0·16	33,203	1·4
Federal capital	715	0·2	18,450	2·37
Province of Buenos Aires	277	0·09	6,973	0·99

Source: Censo general, 1895 & 1914.

Considering that naturalization is an essential prerequisite for even the most elementary political acts, such as voting, these figures show an almost total lack of interest in politics on the part of the immigrants. This is also reflected in contemporary political writings. For example, Domingo Faustino Sarmiento, in several articles published during the decade of 1880, called on the economically successful foreign community to take a greater interest in the political life of the nation.[5] Juan B. Justo, the socialist leader, also described their indifference as an important anomaly in the life of the country:

what matters to the citizens of this country is that the government should be constantly and effectively controlled by the people. This will not be possible if the half million foreigners who live among us, and who take the lead in production, stand aside and take no part in the political life of Argentina. As long as the foreigners allow this country to be under governments like the one we have now, they must not complain if they have to pay forced loans imposed on them through the issue of paper money, or if they are subjected to other forms of exploitation. The conversion most urgently needed in this country is not that of gold for paper or paper for gold but that of the inhabitants of this land, born in Europe, into human beings with all the rights inherent in members of a civilized society: the conversion of foreign subjects into citizens.[6]

Those who, like Sarmiento, advocated a restricted participation of the immigrants in politics as well as those who, like Justo, would have thrown open opportunities for their political and social integration, were agreed that their political apathy was a grave problem. This was something peculiar to Argentine political history. Numerous studies of the parallel situation in the United States, for instance, show that foreign immigrants participated actively in the political life of their adopted land, either as voters or as holders of power at various levels of importance.

Bradley and Zald stress the importance of immigrant political participation in Chicago.[7] Dahl, in his classic essay on the methods of political participation in New Haven, emphasized 'ethnic politics'. He said that

[5] *Condición del extranjero en América* (Buenos Aires, 1928).

[6] *Internacionalismo y patria* (Buenos Aires, 1933).

[7] D. S. Bradley and M. N. Zald, 'From Commercial Elite to Political Administrator; the Recruitment of the Mayors of Chicago', *Amer. J. Sociology*, 21/2 (Sept. 1965).

since political leaders hoped to expand their own influence with the votes of ethnic groups, they helped the immigrant overcome his initial political powerlessness by engaging him in politics. Whatever else the ethnics lacked, they had numbers. Hence politicians took the initiative: they made it easy for immigrants to become citizens, encouraged ethnics to register, put them on the party rolls, and aided them in meeting the innumerable specific problems resulting from their poverty, strangeness and lowly position. To obtain and hold the votes, the political leaders rewarded them with city jobs. They also appealed to their desire for ethnic prestige and self-respect by running members of the ethnic group as candidates for elective offices.

Immigrants were never important in Argentine politics to a degree even remotely comparable to this. To understand the opportunities open to them it is necessary to describe the political structure of Argentina into which, for better or worse, they became integrated. This refers to the period of the beginning of the first world war, for it was then that Argentina, as a result of industrial development, reached a peak of economic power.

There were four political groups with a certain degree of stability: the *Unión Cívica Radical*, the Progressive Democrats (or Southern League), the Conservatives, and the Socialists.

During a political struggle lasting over twenty years the *Unión Cívica Radical* had secured the solid backing of the masses. Its principal adversaries had been the followers of Roca. The Union's basic aim was to establish electoral freedom. It believed that there was no possibility of negotiating with the régime in power and that the only way of restoring pure republicanism over the entire country was by revolution. This method failed (an unsuccessful Radical revolution broke out in 1905) but in the end it achieved the ratification of the Sáenz Peña Law in 1912, which laid down that the vote should be secret, universal, and compulsory. From this point, the framework of political participation was considerably broadened, the percentage of the adult male population with the franchise increasing from 20 per cent in 1910 to more than 60 per cent in 1916.

During their long political struggle the Radicals did not define any government programme apart from the one reforming the electoral laws. Yrigoyen himself, in his argument with Pedro C. Molina over protectionism, emphasized the virtue of this lack of a

---

[8] R. A. Dahl, *Who Governs?* (Yale UP, 1964), p. 34.

political programme. Molina opposed protectionism and demanded a definite plan of action.

> During the last four years . . . we have debated the most serious and fundamental issues of government, among them the foreign policy we ought to adopt, armaments, the naturalization of foreigners, the representation of minority groups, the improvement of our monetary system, whether the doctrine of freedom or protectionism is to dictate our financial system and our treaties with foreign nations, etc. But can you tell me what the Party's opinion has been on each one of these momentous issues?

And further on:

> It has been demonstrated . . . that this party . . . has reneged on the Republic in the field of economic freedom (which is but one of the many facets of the principles of freedom), as well as the ideology and teachings of the founders of the Radical Party.

In his reply Yrigoyen contended vaguely:

> This movement [Radicalism] was formed for common and general ends, but its objectives have acquired a considerable degree of definition. Not only are all social attitudes compatible within it, but together they stamp it with its true significance.

And further on:

> It is essential to regain the constitutional character, the basis of all legitimate authority, which has been perverted to such an extent that leaders act for their own exclusive ends.
> It is indispensable, therefore, to re-establish the electoral system, to be operated legally on democratic principles and under which peace and public order will endure.[9]

In the literature of the time, the question of the Radical programme repeatedly appears from differing viewpoints.

The party's flexible attitude to government measures, implied in the position taken by Yrigoyen, presupposes that it was sensitive to the interests of all the social groups which it represented. From this point of view, one aspect of Radicalism reflected the aspirations of some sections of the upper class, many of whom were linked to

[9] Hipólito Yrigoyen, *Pueblo y gobierno* (1956), ii. 124, 131, 139.

traditional oligarchic families. These sections tended to be part of the 'anti-personalistic' faction of Radicalism and counted among them names as well-known socially as Alvear, Saguier, Pereyra Iraola, Gallardo, Herrera Vegas, Molina Mihura, Cantilo, Paz Posse, Pueyrredón, Le Breton, Castellanos, Laurencena, etc.

These formed a group on the highest rungs of the social and economic ladder (better placed in this sense than the Conservative élite) a group which was characteristically engaged in traditional activities such as fruit and cattle farming.[10] At the same time, the Radicals were a party of the masses, as electoral results demonstrated: in 1928, out of a total of approximately 1,300,000 votes they obtained almost 840,000. The people who backed Yrigoyen were basically middle- and lower-class natives, most of whom were 'old stock' or second-generation immigrants. This traditional indigenous mass had earlier supported Juan Manuel de Rosas in the province of Buenos Aires, and after the Battle of Caseros had upheld the *autonomismo* of Alsina against the nationalism of Mitre. Leandro N. Além, founder of the *Unión Cívica Radical*, was a member of the Alsina party, exerting his influence in the poor quarters of the city's outskirts. It is important to note that class support for Radicalism varied considerably from region to region, and that the situation described applied mainly to the provinces of Santa Fé, Entre Ríos, Buenos Aires, and the federal capital.[11] Throughout the period when it was in power Radicalism was always sensitive to the desire of the masses for an egalitarian, distributive economic policy.

Meanwhile, at the beginning of the new century, the Conservative political groups, which had united as a result of President Roca's victory in the *Partido Autonomista Nacional*, began to lose strength. Heirs to the progressiveness of the 1880s (equivalent to the

10 Ezequiel Gallo and Silva Sigal, *La formación de los partidos políticos contemporáneos: la Unión Civica Radical, 1890–1916*, pp. 163 ff.
11 In some publications of the period attempts were made to describe the class composition of Radicalism. These descriptions are necessarily impressionistic but within certain limits they agree with each other. (See for example C. Sánchez Viamonte, *El último caudillo* (Córdoba, 1930), p. 59, in which 'Yrigoyenism' is considered to be a phenomenon typical of the urban periphery and a synthesis of the two migrating currents, one originating from the hinterland, the other coming from abroad.) This interpretation of the social composition of the Radical movement is supported by some statistical studies which I shall mention later. Other descriptions are to be found in Gabriel del Mazo, *El radicalismo* (Buenos Aires, 1957).

'expansionism' of today) their leading groups were cosmopolitan, 'Europeanizing', open to the modern influences of the Old World, and had an aristocratic concept of public power. They based their political decisions on agreements between the dominating groups and an almost non-existent popular opinion. Rivarola defined it in the following manner.

The Conservative Party is subject to a double drawback: first, that it is not a party; second, that it is not conservative. It is the name which was adopted in the provinces by the old officials of the *Partido Autonomista Nacional* after the failure of the organization as the National Union. It is the party which resists the progress of the Radical Party, but it does not even have the standing of a national committee which it had during its period of national officialdom.

It is not conservative. On the contrary, it has been progressive, reforming, centralist, aristocratic. It never believed in universal suffrage. It never had faith in a republican form of government. In its opinion, the masses were not ready for the vote. Yet omnipotent as it was for thirty years it never thought of qualifying suffrage and it accepted all the great ideals of political freedom which have been written down in books. It proclaimed the sanctity of elections with universal suffrage, the impartiality of the government . . . 'the free-play of institutions' and many other things in which it not only did not believe absolutely but which it considered harmful to internal peace and material progress.[12]

With the approach of the 1916 elections this political attitude tried to find expression through a coalition of various provincial parties, among them the powerful Conservative Party of the province of Buenos Aires.[13]

Within the coalition of Conservative parties, which took the official name of the *Partido Democrata Progresista*, the *Liga del Sur* (Southern League) was included, a party of great local significance in Santa Fé and in which Lisandro de la Torre figured prominently. The strongest groups were in Rosario, the most important city of the hinterland. Much of the political action was directed to increasing the political importance of the southern part

[12] Rodolfo Rivarola, 'Crónicas y documentos', *R. argentina de ciencias políticas*, 8 (Mar. 1914), p. 95.
[13] There is a vast amount of literature on the period. The following may be consulted: Roberto Etchepareborda, 'Aspectos políticos de la crisis de 1930', *R. de historia*, 3 (Jan.–Mar. 1958); Academia National de la Historia, *Historia de las presidencias* (Buenos Aires, 1963); Rodolfo Puiggrós, *Historia crítica de los partidos políticos argentinos* (Buenos Aires, 1956).

of the province of Santa Fé, to the detriment of the northern part. The new economic groups created by immigrants had settled in the south, whereas the north was the bastion of the old traditional economies. Rivarola describes the League in the following manner.

The League originated in Rosario and set itself up as the party representing local interests. Its programme consisted of the reform of the communal régime in order to decentralize it and free it from the executive power; reform of the composition of the Senate which gave the north an advantage over the south; the drawing up of a new census to maintain a proper ratio of representation to minority groups; the granting of the political vote to foreigners who fulfilled the necessary property-owning and residential qualifications. Under the Southern League programme, constitutional and legislative reforms tended to free the south of the province from the preponderance of the north, which benefited more from governmental help, partly owing to the positioning of the capital.[14]

Finally, there was the *Partido Socialista*. This was a party based essentially on the federal capital, and it was there that it obtained approximately 80 per cent of its votes. It was formed in 1894 from a number of socialist groups, practically all of which consisted of foreigners; for over a year the *Centro Socialista Obrero* was the only Spanish-speaking socialist group in the city of Buenos Aires.[15] It made its first electoral appearance in 1896, when it obtained 1 per cent of the votes cast in the federal capital. As a result of the Sáenz Peña Law, it considerably increased its support and several times obtained a majority in the capital's elections.

The *Partido Socialista* was closely linked to ideologies brought from central European countries. It was initially called the *Partido Socialista Obrero Internacional* (Socialist Workers' International Party), and its main political concern was the interests of the working masses. The minimum programme established during its first meeting and maintained throughout the first decades of the century included a maximum 8-hour working day, equal pay for men and women, abolition of indirect taxation on imported goods, increase in the value of paper money, official recognition of labour associations, secular and compulsory education, separation of Church and state, dissolution of the professional army, extension of

[14] Rodolfo Rivarola, 'El Presidente Sáenz Peña y la moralidad política argentina', *R. argentina de ciencias políticas*, 8 (1914), pp. 21, 22.
[15] Jacinto Oddone, *Historia del socialismo argentino* (Buenos Aires, 1934), i. 200.

citizenship rights to foreigners with a year's residence in the country. A large part of the labour legislation was introduced by the Socialist Deputies, who vigorously competed with the Radicals for the support of the lower classes.

At the same time, they were opposed in the trades unions by the anarchists and syndicalists (the latter following the doctrines of Sorel and Labriola), who displaced them from a good many trade union positions. From the time of the Russian revolution they also had to contend with the communist schism.

Such is the general outline of the political system into which immigrants could hope to be integrated. The physical transfer of this enormous mass of individuals had taken place under conditions which did not vary much from those obtaining in other countries. For each displaced person it meant giving up a set of social, group, and family roles which had been established in their native country. From a psychological point of view, the sudden limitations imposed on social activity have deep repercussions which tend to disorganize the personality. Although sometimes entire villages decided to emigrate, the vicissitudes of adapting to new conditions rapidly destroyed the old basic relationships brought from Europe, replacing them with new ones based on the opportunities afforded by the new country. Very often this substitution was not successful and gave rise to fringe and illegal activities (crime, mafias, etc).

But wherever conditions were found to be favourable, the immigrant groups established numerous links with the various institutions of the host society. In this a special part was played by individuals who, for various social or personal reasons, tended to become leaders of the first groups of recently arrived immigrants. Most of these leaders came from the same places as the new arrivals and were often immigrants themselves. Such were priests (whose function has been described by Eisenstadt *à propos* of immigration into Israel),[16] or well-educated men, or men with a special political background. Leaders might also be local people, civil servants, or political officials of varying importance. Even consuls or other officials from the country of origin could assume this role. This type of leader crystallized the psychological aspirations of the

[16] S. N. Eisenstadt, 'Communication processes among immigrants in Israel', *Public Opinion*, Spring 1952, p. 42, and 'The Place of Elites and Primary Groups in the Absorption of New Immigrants in Israel', *Amer. J. Sociology*, 67/3 (Nov. 1951), p. 22.

immigrants and in many senses determined the way in which they were assimilated.

Bearing this in mind, it would be well to analyse the possibilities open to the various immigrant groups. The two parties with the best opportunities of attracting and leading them were the *Partido Socialista* and the *Liga del Sur* (later to be called the *Partido Demócrata Progresista*). Originally formed from a nucleus of foreign groups, these parties clearly understood that their electoral potential depended on the foreign vote. One of the main platforms of both was naturalization.[17] This was not a feature of the Radical or Conservative programmes. (See for example the draft programme drawn up by Isaias R. Amado for the Radicals.)[18]

In the case of the *Partido Socialista* the original groups of foreigners which had formed its nucleus had basically consisted of German, French, and Italian socialist refugees who had been involved in revolutionary movements which emerged in Europe during the second half of the nineteenth century. Wherever there was a sizeable number of immigrants that included such people, they became the natural leaders of the many mutual and protective societies that were formed. This was not only because of their education and dynamism, but also because local ruling groups who might have contested their influence offered no opposition. The reasons for this are peculiar to Argentina. In the United States, which also received exiled revolutionaries, a similar growth of socialist groups took place towards the end of the nineteenth and the beginning of the twentieth centuries. They too consisted mainly, or to some extent almost exclusively, of foreigners.[19] But the growth of a socialist leadership was impeded by the active competition of the local political leaders belonging to the two traditional North American political parties: Republicans and Democrats. These quickly regained their lost ground and from 1912 the percentage of socialist votes began to decrease until this party was virtually eliminated from the North American political scene.[20]

The famous 'party machines' of the principal North American cities, of which the most celebrated was Tammany Hall, were

---

[17] Enrique Thedy, 'Indole y proposito de la Liga del Sur', *R. argentina de ciencias políticas*, 1 (1910), p. 90.

[18] I. R. Amado, 'Programa de partido', ibid. 12 (1916), pp. 102–10.

[19] H. Wayne Morgan, ed., *American Socialism, 1900/1960* (New York, 1964), p. 13.

[20] Ibid. p. 65.

denounced as dens of corruption by every shade of political opinion and built up a veritable industry out of buying votes. Nevertheless they fulfilled a very important role for the immigrants, which could not have been easily replaced. Commenting on the situation, Handlin says:

Many observers viewed with anger the deterioration in American political life in the years after the Civil War. Not a few of them were inclined to blame it all upon the immigrant citizens in the growing cities. Their antagonism was particularly directed at the urban political machines which seemed to function with the support of immigrants. Certainly the new voters had new attitudes toward the state. But perhaps the state itself was changing and less responsive than it once had been to the needs of its citizens; and it may be that the machine was the means through which the immigrants sought services no one else performed.[21]

Numerous reports on the functioning of these political machines permit us to follow the special role played by the political élite, in relation to immigrants recently placed in a new environment.[22]

References made to the naturalization of immigrants in Argentine socialist literature are unequivocal;[23] for example the following explicit statement made by Justo:

If foreigners of like interests were to join with the native people who shared their interests and took part in politics, there would be no linguistic, educational, or traditional differences capable of weakening such a great movement. It would result in the creation of organized parties which, by controlling the litoral would dominate Congress and the government of the country.[24]

The case of the *Liga del Sur* has already been mentioned. Gallo and Sigal have confirmed the indications from other sources by analysing voting figures by zones.[25] Table 12, which divides Santa Fé into South, Central, and North zones, shows the percentage of foreigners voting.

In the same way that the *Partido Socialista* concentrated on the city of Buenos Aires, the *Liga del Sur* concentrated almost exclusively on the southern zone of the province of Santa Fé.

---

[21] Oscar Handlin, *Immigration as a Factor in American History* (New York, 1963), p. 95.

[22] Ibid. p. 101.

[24] Justo, p. 207.

[23] Oddone, ii. 185.

[25] Gallo & Sigal, p. 158.

TABLE 12

Percentage of Foreigners Voting in 1916 Elections

Region	Foreigners	Unión Cívica Radical	Liga del Sur	Partido Demócrata Progresista
South	39·7	30·3	43·4	26·3
Central	29·2	62·0	9·6	28·7
North	14·9	57·0	—	40·4

Source: Gallo & Sigal, p. 158.

For the Radicals and Conservatives the incorporation and representation of the foreigners was a problem which proved difficult to surmount, particularly during the first three decades of the century. So far as the Conservative groups were concerned the question of the integration of immigrants *en masse* was not even considered, as this would have entailed a profound revision of their aristocratic concept of politics. The fundamental problem was not that the immigrants were foreign, but that their numbers were large and they belonged to the lower end of the social scale. The party's cosmopolitan and internationalist ideology had approved the opening-up of the country to the influx from abroad. It did not object to the inclusion of foreigners in leading positions as long as they were people who had climbed far enough up the social and economic ladder. In fact, in cases where they accepted the mechanism of electoral decisions, the Conservatives were quicker than the Radicals to use electoral procedures of the type described in the United States.[26]

The *Unión Cívica Radical* had a more complex character. It is evident that in the federal capital, as in the province of Santa Fé, there was no effective link with the immigrants. There are various arguments on which these assertions are based:

(a) The negative linear correlation between the percentage of the Radical vote and the percentage of foreigners for the province

---

[26] Joaquín Carrillo, 'Crónicas y documentos', *R. argentina de ciencias políticas*, 6 (1913), p. 200; and A. N. Peralta, 'El pueblo quiere principios', ibid. p. 137.

of Santa Fé, calculated by Gallo and Sigal to have an index of
−0·44. Analogous estimates based on the figures for the 1928
election in the federal capital had an equally negative correlation
index, although of a lower level of significance. ($\rho = -0·328$ N=
20).

(*b*) Contemporary reports revealed a radical xenophobia when
faced with the immigrant masses. Ricardo Caballero, who had
been a Radical Party national Senator and leader for the province
of Santa Fé, constantly attacked the foreigners' greed and supposed
lack of interest in the country. The following paragraph taken
from his book on Yrigoyen, selected from a variety of similar
sayings, eloquently characterizes his attitude.

This group (the *Liga del Sur*) comprises the plutocracy of Rosario,
who are of international origin, and the Italian settlers, whom it attracts
with the promise of control over the province's political destiny.
According to the members of the Southern League, creole incompetence should be relegated beyond the borders of the Salado river. The
Unión Cívica Radical had to fight resolutely against both the sinister
forces of hatred for the native-born and the social disorder stirred up
by the *Liga del Sur*.[27]

In Buenos Aires too there were anti-foreign manifestations.
For example, as a result of the Socialist victory in the federal
capital elections for national Deputies held on 22 May 1914, the
Unión Cívica Radical levelled the accusation that the result was a
'conspiracy hatched in the Ministry of the Interior against the
most glorious human rights' and that 'the victory had been obtained
with the help of immigrants without roots in the country'.[28]
Accusations of a similar nature are mentioned in Peralta's book.[29]
Lauro Lagos, Radical leader for the federal capital and the province
of Buenos Aires, includes the following paragraph among his
'Radical thoughts'.

Are we waiting for the European races now being added to our
own to join with us into a single entity and so produce a national
superman? To begin only then to speak of an Argentine generation?
What hymns of progress, of wealth, of culture and civilisation have
not been intoned on the basis of this refrain, in order to subdue the

[27] Ricardo Caballero, *Irigoyen* (Buenos Aires, 1951), p. 78.
[28] M. Ángel Carcano, *Enfoque histórico sobre la presidencia de Roque
Sáenz Peña* (Buenos Aires, 1965), p. 175.
[29] Peralta, in *R. argentina de ciencias políticas*, 6 (1913), p. 137.

energy of our native spirit, with its innate initiative, abounding in generosity, strength, and nobility! Does this mean that as yet there are no Argentines? That Argentines must come from abroad? How disillusioning! [30]

In the opinion of this writer, this lack of communication and the antagonism shown to the foreigner by the Radicals of the litoral can be explained by two factors which, due to the special conditions of the region, mutually strengthened each other. In the first place there were the bonds between Radicalism and the middle and lower classes—traditionalist, xenophobic, and nationalist—who joined the Radicals because of the *autonomismo* of Alsina and Além or through the provincial caudillos of Santa Fé and Entre Ríos.[31]

To these must be added the traditional upper-class families, influential during the Rosas government and marginally so after the Battle of Caseros. Some authors have pointed out the similarity between one of the key words of the Yrigoyen vocabulary, 'Reparation', and Juan Manuel de Rosas's slogan 'Restoration', a similarity which would evoke old memories in the social groups of that class.[32] Also, given the cosmopolitan and modernizing ideology of the Conservatives, heirs to the expansionism of the 1880s, the Radicals tended to adopt a body of political thought which in all its visible social aspects was opposed to the régime they were fighting. In the presence of such a sizeable immigrant community along the litoral, the phobia against foreigners was easily rationalized and transformed into an anti-cosmopolitan and anti-conservative policy.

From another viewpoint, the effective cultural assimilation of the foreigners' children allowed the new generations born of immigrant parents to participate in this process without guilt. In Argentine society, only those born abroad were considered foreigners. The immigrants' children and grandchildren rapidly became integrated into a new culture which they themselves had partly helped to create. In Santa Fé it is possible to see the marked difference between the old settlements in the centre of the province, where Radicalism predominated, and the southern zone, of more recent immigrant settlement, where the Progressive Democrats prevailed.

[30] *Doctrina y acción radical* (1930).
[31] Del Mazo, p. 14, and Caballero, p. 44.
[32] Viamonte, p. 81.

The case of the industrial entrepreneur groups can be analysed in the light of these antecedents. They settled mainly in the Greater Buenos Aires area, although some groups established themselves in Rosario. There are three conclusions to be drawn from the data we have examined. For those who settled in the federal capital, none of the existing parties offered political opportunities. For the Radicals, the problem was rooted in their disassociation from everything that was foreign. The Conservatives based most of their political support on agricultural interests and this made it impossible for them to have any appeal for such different, and at times even contradictory, economic interests. In this sense, as we have already pointed out, the powerful groups with agricultural and cattle-raising interests that formed part of the *Unión Cívica Radical* had a similar effect.[33] In the same way socialism, with its extreme distributive policies and its exclusive preoccupation with the problems of short-term consumption, offered little attraction to the well-defined interests of the rising industrial groups.

The lack of an efficient connexion between immigrant industrial groups and the Radicals was dramatically illustrated by the lowering of excise duties at the end of the 1914 war. By the end of 1918 Argentina's industrial development was already considerable, and throughout these years, the *Boletín* of the *Unión Industrial* strongly —and unsuccessfully—advocated a protectionist policy. It is interesting to note that the economic ideology expressed in those publications was in direct opposition to the then prevailing ideology of the country's intellectuals and the economic concepts of the Socialist, Radical, and Conservative political leaders. The Progressive Democrats of Santa Fé were the only exception. The generally accepted ideology was that of English political economy, which stressed the international division of labour based on comparative costs. The *Unión Industrial* tried to elaborate a different policy, and in the November 1918 issue of its *Boletín* protective duties were defended as necessary for industrial growth and the theory of free trade as a universal doctrine was attacked. The *Boletín* emphasized that this last was a theory which suited countries at an advanced stage of industrial development and that it had developed in England at a time when that country's unique position

[33] Amado (*R. argentina de ciencias políticas*, 12 (1916), pp. 102–10).

would be very much favoured by such a doctrine.[34]   When, just after the first world war, Congress debated the Radical proposal to lower excise duties, the violence of the arguments in defence of protectionism increased visibly.   From another standpoint, the argument presented by the Budget Commission of the Chamber of Deputies, presided over by Victor Molina (Radical), is liberalism at its most pure.   Molina said:

> The protectionist system . . . enriches a few with the money of the masses; this totally illegitimate system does not take into consideration this indisputable fact: that we are all consumers, few are producers; and it is natural that in favouring the producers at the expense of the consumers a perpetual and flagrant injustice is perpetuated against the rights of the community.[35]

The lowering of excise duties was finally passed by a crushing majority and with the decisive backing of the other parties, particularly the Socialists, who were so much in favour of free trade that they adopted it as party policy.[36]   They contended that customs tariffs were an indirect tax on consumers and as such conspired against the worker's living standards.   The arguments presented by the Socialist leader differed not at all from those of the Radical leader.   Juan B. Justo said:

> The protectionist paradoxes are an attenuated form of mercantilism.   This foolishness cannot be taken seriously.   New interests have now been created which reinforce the interests of those entrepreneurs who are in difficulties or have their profits lowered as a result of international competition.   Inept entrepreneurs, entrepreneurs anxious for monopoly control, entrepreneurs hungry for profits to be wrested from their own countrymen; these are the people who invariably hoist the flag of protectionism seeking to impose it as the national standard. Protectionism is an enormous lie, which can temporarily unite the interests of entrepreneurs and workers in certain branches of production, but this will always be at the expense of the people of the country as a whole.[37]

---

[34] R. A. Ramm Doman, 'Orientaciones en política aduanera', *Bol. Unión Industrial,* 33/559 (15 Nov. 1918), p. 3.
[35] V. M. Molina, 'Discurso en la Cámara de Diputados como Presidente de la Comisión de Presupuesto', *Diário de Sesiones, 1918–19,* v (31 Jan. 1919), p. 535.
[36] Ibid. p. 51.
[37] Justo, 'La falacia proteccionista', *La Vanguardia,* 8 May 1916, also printed in *Internacionalismo y patria.*

The popular character of Radicalism and its failure to link up with the interests of the industrial groups—due to lack of communication which has been described—led it to compete with socialism and to adopt an essentially liberal and redistributive type of policy.[38]

The economic policy of the Radicals in power was based on the export of primary products while the state was heavily dependent on the income from excise duties. It is to be presumed that the admission of imports produces a decrease in urban employment, which is compensated for by an increase in civil service jobs. The government's budget rose by 80 per cent between 1918 and 1923, and besides this there was an increase in the proportion of consumer expenditure to investment. The simultaneous international rise in prices for agricultural products allowed this policy to be pursued for a few more years. An alternative programme based on the encouragement of industrial production by means of protectionism and selective credit evidently could have been attempted, based on another formulation of interests. In this sense it would be well to emphasize that the *Partido Socialista's* position was not the only one possible for a party of its type. Australia provides a striking example of the opposite alternative. Here the Labour Party was already decidedly protectionist in 1890, and within the framework of its political policy established solid alliances with the emerging industrial groups. It is interesting to point out that the Australian example is particularly attractive in view of the importance to that country of the export of primary products. Between 1890 and 1910 the production of manufactures did not exceed 12 per cent of the gross product while agriculture accounted for approximately 25 per cent, exclusive of mineral production, or 33 per cent inclusive.[39] This would indicate a position of economic power for each branch of production similar to that of Argentina; and it affords an opportunity to study other aspects of the social situation which were more important in determining the aspirations of the industrial sectors.[40]

Finally, it may be concluded that there was no political party representing the interests of industrial entrepreneurs during the

[38] For a defence of the more popular character of Radicalism as against socialism, see M. A. Carranza, *Ideales y carácter* (Buenos Aires, 1924), p. 119.
[39] N. G. Butlin, *Australian Domestic Product, Investment and Foreign Borrowing* (Cambridge UP, 1962), p. 12.
[40] Colin Clark, *Australian Hopes and Fears* (Philadelphia, 1963).

early decades of this century. Neither the *Partido Socialista*, nor the Conservatives nor the Radicals, each one for the reasons demonstrated, was capable of representing those interests. The only party which could conceivably have played such a role was the *Partido Demócrata Progresista*, but as this had only regional importance in Santa Fé, its influence did not extend to the rest of the country.

Middle-Class Politics and the Cuban Revolution

HUGH THOMAS

IN the United States the fashionable view of the Cuban revolution
has been for some years that it is merely the latest example of a
'revolution betrayed' (initially a phrase of Trotsky's), that the
revolution began as a middle-class protest against the acknowledged
iniquities of Batista and was later diverted from safe social-
democratic ways by Castro; and that to justify totalitarian
socialism, the revolutionary leaders blackened the picture of what
Cuba was like before 1959, and described the country in terms
almost suggesting that it was as poor as Bolivia and as unjust as
ancient Egypt, whereas (so the fashionable view has it) Cuba was
in reality among the better-off countries of Latin America, with
a standard of living higher than Chile and a larger middle class
than Venezuela. These theories (to which I have myself partially
subscribed in the past) should be re-examined, both for their own
sake, and for the light they shed on North American judgements
about the hemisphere, e.g. in the United States White Paper on Cuba
issued in April 1961 and written by Arthur Schlesinger, or Draper's
Castroism, Theory and Practice (1965).

Cuba fits uneasily beside other Latin American countries in conventional tables of well-being or misery. It is a sugar island—the
largest and richest of the great Sugar Sea inaccurately known as the
Caribbean. More, Cuba has been for most of the last 130 years
the world's largest sugar producer. Further, as a natural consequence—for sugar implies Negro slaves—only Brazil among 'Latin
American' countries has anything like the same proportion of people
of African descent. At the same time, the indigenous Indian population of Cuba has vanished, though no doubt many who regard
themselves as of pure Castilian blood have Indian forebears. Still,
there is in Cuba no overt mixture of Spanish and indigenous

cultures; only a mixture of two immigrant cultures, one of which was slave till eighty years ago.[1]

Since she lives by selling sugar, Cuba's economy has always been at the mercy of the large sugar-consuming countries: if there are rumours of wars, sugar prices go up, Cubans are happy, it is a time of *puerca gorda*. War, not peace, brings back plenty. Of course, Venezuela depends on oil, Guatemala on bananas, Costa Rica on coffee, and so on, but the sugar market differs from these, for it is broader than any of them, broader even than the farrago of bribes and restrictions known as the oil market: for as incomes begin to go up in underdeveloped countries (from Western Europe in the seventeenth century to Africa in the twentieth) sugar is the first craving, simply because of its capacity to vary the usual appallingly dull diet of poor people.[2]

Thus, as a society Cuba might really be considered quite apart from Latin America, and together with the other sugar-dominated Caribbean islands, such as Martinique or Jamaica, its historical predecessors in the splendid task of sweetening the tea and coffee of the advanced peoples in the north. Of course, Cuba is not so black as those islands, though successive censuses may have underestimated the number of black or mulatto people there.[3] Even so, the Negro contribution to Cuba has been of the first importance, above all in the arts.

More, the sugar industry in Cuba made the country unlike any other in 'Latin America' in social formation. In the eighteenth century the aristocratic landowners, descendants of original grantees of the *siglo de oro* (who elsewhere south of the Rio Grande still control vast tracts of land), began to turn over their estates to sugar plantations. By 1860, when Cuba was producing 30 per cent of the world's sugar and in consequence was the richest colony in the world, there were 1,365 sugar mills in Cuba, mostly in the western end of the island, some already owned by companies rather

---

1 Slavery was finally abolished in Cuba in 1886, and was still at its height in the 1860s.
2 Cf. A. Vitón and F. Pignalosa, *Trends and Forces of World Sugar Consumption* (Rome, FAO, 1961), pp. 7–16.
3 The criterion used by the census-takers up till and including 1943 was to ask the doubtful cases if they regarded themselves as black or white; in 1953, the census enumerators made up their own minds. The number of coloured census enumerators, incidentally, is not available. The pictures in the 1953 census show all the enumerators as apparently 'white', as people of Spanish origin are still entertainingly known.

than individuals, perhaps thirty already owned by North Americans.[4] Already, the old landowners were falling behind. The largest sugar mills, with up-to-date machinery (Derosne or Rillieux vacuum boilers), were mostly owned by self-made merchants who had come quite recently from Spain. The sugar crisis of the 1880s, as well as the Ten-Year War,[5] brought further ruin to the old landowners. Only large mills able to afford private railways and to survive with small profit margins were economically viable against the competition of European beet. Germany overtook Cuba as the largest sugar producer in the 1880s (till 1914). In the decade before the final war of independence (i.e. between 1885 and 1895) most of the old planters either sold out to companies (increasingly North American) or ceased to grind sugar, though continuing to grow cane: they carried their cane by rail to be processed in new, million-dollar mills which acted as their agents, ultimately their masters. The present-day organization of the sugar industry was established before Cuba became independent. By 1900 there were between 160 and 200 big mills which all grew some cane, but got the rest from planters of varying wealth and capacity. The mills were owned in a few cases by individuals but more typically by public companies with equity shareholders, many North American.

A collapse of prices in 1920 caused the take-over of almost all the smaller, private mills by North American banks. After the depression Cubans bought out a number of sugar mills previously owned by North Americans. Still, in 1960 about 36 per cent of the sugar production of the country was controlled by United States-owned mills, mostly in the east of the country, opened up to development by the railway built by Van Horne in 1902. Over half of Cuba's cultivable land was devoted to cane,[6] either directly raised by the mill or by the planters without mills (*colonos*). Some *colonos* were well-off, among them Castro's father, a Spanish

---

[4] These figures come from Carlos Rebello, *Estados relativos a la producción azucarera de la isla de Cuba* (Havana, 1860). The US figure is a guess, based on the number of mills owned by persons having apparently Anglo-Saxon names. Some of these were English, and others were held by already cubanized people of Anglo-Saxon stock. About fifty mills in Oriente were owned by French ex-immigrants, from Haiti, or their descendants.

[5] Of Liberation, 1868–78, ended by the compromise peace of Zanjón.

[6] Agricultural census, 1946. Unfortunately no later figures exist, and it is possible that by 1960 the situation may have slightly changed.

immigrant, in the United Fruit Company zone of Mayarí. Others were farmers of aristocratic origin. But, because of the industrial structure of sugar, Cuba had, throughout the twentieth century, no traditional upper class in the sense of a single socially-exclusive group which controlled the bulk of the land. There were latifundia certainly; but these were the latifundia of stockholders, not individuals. There might still be Pedrosos, Montalvos, Calvos, or other names which had dominated politics and sugar 150 years ago; but such people would be probably carrying out jobs, and living on incomes, not rents. Elsewhere in Latin America rich businessmen became landowners; in Cuba rich landowners became businessmen. This is not to say that there were no rich in Cuba; indeed, it is probable (though it is not a statement that can be proved statistically)[7] that there were more Cuban millionaires (in dollars) per head of population than in any other country of Latin America. But these were in general people living off stock or who had made themselves rich by one sugar gamble or another. Where they were people with land they would be as likely to be self-made men, like Angel Castro, as descendants of original grantees by the Spanish Crown. The absence of an upper class in the old sense of the term not only altered the nature of the other classes, but also helped prevent the development of regionalism. There were cattle farmers in Camagüey, but that was a province only opened up since the railway. And even cattle farms were as likely to be companies as privately owned.

The foremost student of Cuban class structure, Professor Lowry Nelson (in his deservedly famous *Rural Cuba*)[8] put it differently. He said that he was 'not at all certain that a middle class exists in Cuba, but there can be no doubt about the upper and lower classes'. He may be right, but so am I: the essential characteristic of Cuba was that by the mid-twentieth century there were really only two classes, upper (or middle) and lower. Movement was not impossible between these classes.[9] Infinite possibilities for acquiring wealth existed in the early part of the century, and to a lesser extent in the years immediately after 1945. Such possibilities

---

[7] No reliable figures exist in relation to distribution of incomes in Cuba before 1958.

[8] Univ. of Minnesota, 1950, p. 139.

[9] Cf. Dr. Adams's essay (pp. 15–42 above), which I read after writing this sentence, though I do not agree with much that he says. His comment on Cuba is *simpliste*.

further sapped traditional class divisions. Birth probably meant less in Cuba than in any other country of Latin America. The mere fact that in 1953 only 42 per cent of the population lived from agriculture is less surprising than the fact that this was a slightly higher percentage than in 1943, and registered only a small change since 1899 when 48 per cent of the population lived on the land.

The Cuban middle class thus cannot be regarded as so solid a bastion of bourgeois liberties as might appear from its numerical size as reflected in the last census before the revolution of 1959. Such figures should anyway be related to their historical precedents. Now it has become clear that Cuba was a country of riches, not of poverty. But the riches were centred with lavish disproportion on Havana. This disproportion increased rather than slackened during the history of the Republic.[10] The table below shows that the population outside Havana went up three times between 1899 and 1943; during that time the number of doctors outside Havana increased by scarcely a third, dentists just doubled, nurses, incredibly, were actually fewer per head in 1943 than in 1899; teachers did far better on paper, though it was doubtful whether the real increase was anything so striking. There were, as is clear, substantial increases in the number of doctors and nurses between 1943 and 1953, though, in the absence of any definite figures, it would seem unlikely that the number of these per head of population outside Havana really attained the levels obtaining in 1899. And 1899 was not precisely a golden year.

The Cuban Bourgeoisie: Selected Professions

(a) Cuba

Year	Total Population	Doctors	Dentists	Nurses	Chemists	Teachers
1899	1,500,000	1,223	354	523	n.a.	2,708
1907	2,000,000	1,243	390	822	n.a.	5,964
1919	2,960,000	1,771	314	972	1,424	7,033
1931	3,960,000	n.a.	n.a.	n.a.	n.a.	n.a.
1943	4,800,000	2,589	1,018	921	662	19,758(a)
1953	5,800,000	6,201	1,934	1,763	1,866	36,815(a)

[10] Not least of the difficulties in reaching a proper consideration of Cuba is that the censuses became less and less complete. Thus the 1953 census, unlike its predecessors, gave no breakdown of professions by province, nor by colour.

(b) Cuba Outside Havana

Year	Total Population	Doctors	Dentists	Nurses	Chemists	Teachers
1899	1,337,000	727	181	301	n.a.	1,884
1907	1,751,000	729	226	423	n.a.	4,845
1919	2,525,000	1,087	217	545	953	5,293
1931*	—	—	—	—	—	—
1943	3,543,000(b)	969(b)	414(b)	270(b)	253(b)	11,592(a) (b)
1953	4,291,000(b)	n.a.	n.a.	n.a.	n.a.	n.a.

* All figures unreliable, due to depression and dictatorship.

Notes

(a) These figures should be regarded with even greater scepticism than usual when looking at figures from underdeveloped or semi-developed regions. By the 1940 constitution the security of teachers' tenure (and income) was guaranteed for life, so that there is no knowledge who was teaching and who had retired. In 1945 Lowry Nelson was told by the Ministry of Education that, despite the census figures, the number of working teachers probably only reached 7,000. Between 1944 and 1948 the Ministry of Education was the headquarters of corruption and thievery; teachers' jobs were sold by the hundred. Though the next Minister of Education, Sánchez Arango, tried to clean up the profession, there can be little doubt that the number of teachers actually working in 1953 was well below 30,000 and may even have been below 20,000.

(b) Havana province; previous figures relate to the city. This discrepancy adds even greater weight to the gloomy conclusions.

Source: Censuses 1899–1953.

Cuba had just finished a three-and-a-half-year war of an intensity unparalleled in the Americas.[11]

Such statistics go some way to explaining the reality behind the 'high standard of living' in Cuba before the revolution directed by

[11] The birth rate in Cuba between 1890 and 1894 was always over 13 per 1,000; in 1898 it had fallen to 5·7 per 1,000. Hence a permanent gap in the Cuban age-pyramid of persons born 1896–8. In 1959–60 there was an abnormally small number of people aged about 60—a politically critical gap, for that is the age when in most countries people are ready to retire from professions though they continue to be active in politics. On this reckoning, the collapse of 'liberal' Cuba is to be attributed to the Spanish Captain-General Weyler—a theory which has more to it than meets the eye.

Castro. Some play has been made with numbers of radio and television sets, cars, and telephones. Cuba, we are told,[12] had more telephones in use per head than any Latin American country except Argentina or Uruguay, far more television sets than anywhere else in the Americas south of the United States, more cars than any country except Venezuela.[13] These undeniably interesting facts, however, tell less about the actual standard of living in Cuba than the ease with which the Cuban market could be penetrated by North American salesmanship. Of course the size of the market was not negligible, and the very fact that Cuba had more television sets per head than Italy [14] indicates clearly that the political problems were of a more sophisticated nature than, say, those of Haiti. But such statistics do not mean that the country had got beyond the stage where a sense of outrage led people to dream of violent and radical changes. Indeed, unless such manufactured goods are fairly distributed, their number may actually exacerbate divisions in a country. Lavish wealth may boost a nation's per capita income; but if it is concentrated in few hands, it obviously causes more tensions in society than if it did not exist. France was richer in 1788 than in 1648.

A similar conclusion can be derived from the discussion of Cuba's national income in the years before 1959,[15] anyway vitiated by doubts about the accuracy of statistics.[16] But suppose we accept the highest estimate of per capita income for 1958: $521. What does this tell us about Cuban society? No more than the remark that the average Englishman drank in 1964 one-tenth of a bottle of champagne, since 5.5 million bottles were consumed in that

---

[12] Cf. H. T. Oshima, *A New Estimate of the National Income and Product of Cuba in 1953* (Stanford, Food Research Inst. Studies, reprint of Nov. 1961 issue, pp. 213–27).

[13] In Draper, *Castroism*, p. 100; cf. *Cambridge Opinion*, p. 32: Cuba, table 2, 3, p. 34.

[14] 56 per 1,000 in Cuba, 43 per 1,000 in Italy. I have no doubt that the number of guns per capita was even more remarkable—another example of US good salesmanship combined with a natural proclivity of Cubans to have a weapon. By the 1940s the machete had given way to the revolver as the typical symbol of the independent man.

[15] Cf. Oshima, *New Estimate of National Income*.

[16] Thus Oshima gives the per capita income of Cuba in 1958 as $521; the Banco Nacional Cubana has $407; the US *Monthly Bulletin of Statistics* has $356; the UN *Statistical Yearbook* (by calculation) $348. Admittedly Oshima is the only one to have worked sceptically on previously accepted figures.

year.[17] Even so, and again accepting the figure of $521 as accurate, it would certainly seem explosive that a country such as Cuba should have a per capita income five times smaller than her major trading partner.[18] It may also be worth remembering that the last time the United States had an average income of about $521 was in 1934, at a time when the author of *Red Star over Cuba*, not to speak of other worthy antagonists of the Cuban revolution, were members of the Communist Party of the United States.[19] After all, no one thinks Latin America has been saved from revolution because the average income in 1966 reached $450. There is the further point that, if, indeed, Cuba's per capita income was over $500, surely she could have done better than to allow about half her population to go without schooling? With a national income below $200 a head, the absence of schools might be comprehensible, but not one above $500. The truth is that it is not really possible to prove by statistics that such and such a country is ripe, or not ripe, for revolution; and the figures for Cuba, such as they are, are rather more instructive than they are sometimes made to seem.

In fact political causes, not economic; honest leadership or the lack of it; social aspirations or their frustration; dictate the course of revolutionary happenings, in Cuba as elsewhere; just as political reasons too prevent advanced countries from doing the only serious thing they can do to assist the underdeveloped world—restraining competition with the products which are their only standby. The point is instructive. Cuba and the Caribbean grow sugar very well. Capital thus naturally is concentrated in the sugar industry. But production is limited and possibilities of expansion are almost halted by beet-sugar development in the temperate countries of the north. This castigation applies slightly less to Russia, for before 1960 she had no access to, or responsibility for, cane-growing zones; since then, there has been nothing to choose between the United States and Russia in this regard: the beet production of

---

[17] *The Times*, 10 Nov. 1965.

[18] The US probably had a per capita income of $2,500 in 1957 (cf. *Historical Statistics of the USA*, p. 139).

[19] Mr Nathaniel Weyl, who claimed to be in the Ware cell in Washington. Mr Theodore Draper was busy on the *Daily Worker* and writing, as Theodore Repard (Draper spelt backwards) and with Harry Gannes, enthusiastic justifications of the Spanish Republic. (Cf. *Spain in Revolt*, Left Book Club, 1936.) I wonder what SNAG is 'up to now'.

both has expanded. But beet farmers are everywhere a political power. They probably are in Russia as well as in the Middle West.

What basis then is there for the theory that the revolution led by Castro was essentially a middle-class protest against Batista's illegal and unjust government? Remember that Lowry Nelson, the most learned of North American students of Cuba in the past, even doubted whether there was such a thing. That same authority also appropriately pointed out that Cuba in 1945 had, in fact, been in almost continual political turmoil for approximately a century.[20] This apparently sweeping statement is, if anything, an understatement. A slave society lasted till the 1880s. From about 1790 till 1860 Cuba had had a black majority, with frequent slave revolts. The planters' need to rely on a Spanish army to crush these was the main reason why Cuba remained a Spanish colony till 1898. After the slave revolts came the wars of independence. North American occupation lasted from 1899 until 1902 and was resumed, on Cuban request, between 1906 and 1909. In the next forty years all hopes for a just and well-ordered society foundered. If responsibility is sought—an invidious proceeding at best—guiltiest of all was no doubt Dr Grau San Martín, leader of the students in 1933, who finally came to power in 1944, to betray with graft and favouritism the best hope of a 'middle-class revolution'. In 1952 Batista's second coup undoubtedly put paid to the chances of the most progressive members of Grau's party who, having broken away under the name of *Ortodoxos*, hoped to save something from the wreck. Appealing though the Ortodoxos were personally, it is difficult to feel that they could have had much success in reviving, or better, founding Cuban political public life on a firm basis. The problem of Cuba went beyond their programme of abolishing corruption, important though that was. Where were the institutions, even in 1952, to sustain a solid constitutional system? Institutionalized corruption stretching back over centuries, institutionalized gangsterism stretching back twenty years, how to cope with these by good intentions? Their best leader, Chibás, had committed suicide histrionically even before Batista's coup. This was not the way to build the good society. In Cuba there was never really any normality to go back to after Batista was expelled; there had really been semi-crisis ever since the early nineteenth century; under a façade of wealth, Cuba had as her only traditions tensions,

[20] *Rural Cuba*, p. 140.

violence, and, above all, rebellion. It is customary in Europe or
North America to regard the coups and revolutionaries of Latin
America as belonging to operetta. 'Look who's back', exclaimed
Time magazine in March 1952, the only occasion when a Cuban
made the cover, and there was Batista: 'he got past democracy's
sentries'. This failure to appreciate the often tragic, always
neurotic consequences of coups is one of the Anglo-Saxon's chief
weaknesses in looking at Latin America.

Maybe had the elections of 1952 been held, the *Ortodoxos*
would have won. But their divisions and jealousies after the coup
do not show them in a good light. They were agreed on the illegal-
ity of Batista's rule but the challenge of his dictatorship did not
unite them; it divided them further. By 1959 the movement
consisted of four warring groups, one of whose leaders (Márquez
Sterling) was already in exile, and would have been arrested had
he come back to Havana, because of his participation in Batista's
fraudulent elections in November 1958.

These divisions, as early as 1953, led several members of the
Ortodoxo youth movement to join the communist youth, *Juventud
Socialista*. By reason of their age and their relative freedom from
family ties, members of the youth movement were naturally more
disposed towards revolutionary action than their elders. Among
the members of the *Ortodoxo* party proper was Fidel Castro. He
had been a candidate in the elections, never held, of 1952. In
1952–3 he was attempting to persuade the *Ortodoxo* leadership to
take a bolder, more united, and more violent path. His brother
Raúl, five critical years younger than him, turned more leftwards.
After a visit to Eastern Europe with a student delegation, he
solicited entry to the communist youth movement in June 1953.[21]

Fidel Castro carried on in his attempt to maintain *Ortodoxo*
politics. However by early 1953 he had formed the nucleus of a
personal political following, based chiefly (and entirely through
the accident of acquaintanceship) on the branch of the *Ortodoxo*
youth established in the small town of Artemisa, forty miles west
of Havana on the road to Pinar del Río. In the middle of 1953 he
resolved to launch his followers on an attack against the Moncada
barracks at Santiago de Cuba in the country. Who were these

---

[21] So he told the French writer, Robert Merle. See *Moncada*, p. 121;
also his own article in *Fundamentos*, June–July 1961, in which he states
that many young *Ortodoxos* were taking this line, though not mentioning
himself.

followers? Herbert Matthews, Castro's first apologist in the United States, explains that in the attack on Moncada Castro's followers were 'nearly all university students'.[22] This is far from the truth. The only organized group of students who took part in the assault on Moncada were five who withdrew at the last minute. One Moncadaista only appears to have been a student (Ramiro Valdés, in 1965 Minister of the Interior, who, like so many others, came from Artemisa); Raúl Castro who, despite his recent link with the communist youth, decided to join in without apparently telling the communist youth leadership, had just left the university. Of the other 165 men, only seven (apart from Castro himself) appear to have had any higher education,[23] and probably most had had no secondary education. Certainly a majority of Castro's followers were at this time lower class in origin, however that phrase is understood.

This question becomes of importance since it has already become history that Castro was chiefly sustained in the early days by the middle class. I have attempted a professional breakdown of the men of Moncada in the light of such information as I have:

Accountants: Montané, Santamaría, Tápanes (assistant).
Agricultural workers: Collazo, Elizalde, Guerrero (R) Rodríguez (Tomás), Rojo (M), Menéndez (R).
Bakers: Hernández (O).
Builders: Almeida, Mestre (A)—bricklayer.
Bus workers: Galan (R).
Business Men: Guitart (worked in father's export-import business).
Butchers: Betancourt.
Carpenters: Hernández (E).
Cartographers: Miret.
Chimney Sweeps: Dalmau.
Dentists: Aguilera.
Doctors: Muñoz.
Employees: Camera (shoe factory), Corcho (A.—milk worker), Costa (Jaime—turner's apprentice), Costa (José—liquor factory), González (E.—shoe factory), López ('Nico'—Mariano factory), Quintela (textile worker), López (José Luis), Santa Coloma (refrigeration company), Tasende (Nela milk company), Trigo (P.—textile worker), Almeijiras (Juan Manuel).

[22] H. L. Matthews, *The Cuban Story* (New York, 1961), p. 144.
[23] These were the doctor (Muñoz); Santamaría, Tápanes, and Montané (accountants); Miret (a cartographer and graduate of Havana engineering school); and the Martínez Arrarás brothers who led the attack at the Bayamo barracks.

Farmers: Tizol (chicken farmer).
Lawyers: Castro (F).
Lorry drivers: Mitchell, Valdés (delivered ice).
Mechanics: Badia.
Nurses: Fernández (military nurse).
Photographers: Chenard.
Pharmaceutical laboratory assistants: Alcalde.
Plumbers: López (Darío).
Printers: Ponce (owned small press Artemisa).
Sailors: Llanes (sailor at Havana Biltmore Yacht Club).
Shop assistants: Díaz (Julio—ironmonger's), García (Calixto—chemist's), Lazo (M.—confectioner's), Redondo, Trigo (Julio—chemist's), Díaz Cartaya, Peñalver (battery repairer), Rosell (in father's haberdashery).
Students: Castro (R), Valdés (Ramiro). (Four Havana university students dropped out on the morning.)
Tanner: Ramón.
Taxi-driver: Santana.
Watchmaker: Rodríguez (Eduardo).

In truth Castro was surrounded by a group intellectually his inferiors, who regarded him as *Jefe* and had little serious worry about ideas.[24] Much the same is true of the list of men who went on the famous yacht *Granma*. Apparently nineteen of those who took part in the attack on Moncada landed at Belic. Maybe a slightly higher percentage had had a higher, or at least a secondary, education. Nineteen of the eighty-two remained with Castro at the beginning of his guerrilla struggle in the Sierra;[25] most were again not of middle-class origin; the proletarian backgrounds of Almeida, Julio Díaz, Redondo, and Calixto García have been suggested; of the rest of the new men, Faustino Pérez was a medical student and Guevara a qualified doctor; but Universo Sánchez was a farm labourer, Ameijiras (E) a chauffeur, Cienfuegos an employee in a commercial business in Havana. Very soon too a number of

[24] Though incomplete, I have no doubt that the others who took part in the attack on the Moncada came from a similar background. 71 of the Moncada men were killed, 68 after the end of fighting. The list is similar to the men who, according to Prof. Rudé, formed 'the crowd' in the French Revolution.

[25] Not twelve, the figure which has entered folklore. Cf. Guevara's account in *Geografía de Cuba*, p. 575, where he speaks of first 'some seventeen' men and a few lines later of the 'Quincena'. The names of 16 men who survived were given by one of them, Faustino Pérez, to René Ray, for his *Libertad y revolución* (Havana, 1959, p. 28). 24 were killed out of the 82 in the first battle, the rest either were captured or escaped to the plains.

peasants had joined. The peasants (i.e. those of the Sierra Maestra) were, in fact, the critical factor in getting the different groups of wanderers together. It may be true that the core of this group was, as Theodore Draper says, middle class, though only if by 'core' is meant leadership.[26]   At the same time, though the peasants, charcoal-burners, and rural workers whom Castro and his comrades met in the Sierra certainly deepened their knowledge, it is doubtful if they had much effect on the programmes of the revolutionaries.

More important, these early followers of Castro were the people who generally held to him thereafter as bodyguards, special assistants, chief confidants, men of all work and for all seasons. Not that all did so. One or two of the Moncada or *Granma* men are in exile. One of the 19 (or 12, as it is now known) was shot as a traitor (Moran). Nevertheless, early on in his revolutionary career Castro became surrounded by a number of close followers, mostly of a less educated background than himself, mostly with no political views (except a general social conscience and resentment deriving from memories of childhood misery or absence of education), devoted to him as a leader rather than as an ideologue, who would have thoughtlessly followed him over any precipice, and indeed did over the icy one of communism. Nevertheless, the same people might in different circumstances have followed Castro into, say, *Auténtico* or *Ortodoxo* leadership; the difference being that those who defected would probably (though not certainly) have been different.

Of the social origin of these devoted followers there should then be no mystery. The career of Almeida appears typical. Eldest of ten children, he left school at the third grade. He spent the rest of his childhood delivering water to houses without running water. Afterwards he became a haberdasher and in the early 1950s a builder's labourer. He made spare money as a song writer and guitarist.

One day I made the acquaintance of Armando Mestre, a pupil at the Escuela Normal of Havana. . . . He lived near me, and we found each other sympathetic. We went out together, we talked. He asked me if I studied, and I said 'no'. . . . Then he said he would try and help me, to return to school. . . . I said that . . . I had first to gain my living, because I was of a large family and I had to help my parents.

[26] T. Draper, *Castro's Revolution* (New York, 1962), p. 11.

Through Mestre (later both at Moncada and on the *Granma*; he was killed at Alegría del Pio), Almeida was brought into contact with young men at the university. He met Castro (then himself no longer a student) on 10 March 1952, the day of Batista's coup. Castro said 'that the youth had to unite, that it was the only living force, that he counted on elements who had no compromise with the past'.[27] Thus was reborn the politically explosive myth of 'the unencumbered past'. From these followers, Castro learned his innocence; from him they took their political direction.

One point in Almeida's career was, however, untypical. He (like Mestre) was a mulatto. Perhaps a dozen of the Moncada men were Negroes or mulattoes, but the majority were not,[28] and it was rare to find even as many as a dozen Negroes taking part in revolutionary political activity. Batista's soldiers frequently expressed astonishment that there could be any Negroes among the revolutionaries they arrested. Some Negroes even owed their liberty after Moncada to the presumption that they could not be among the revolutionaries.[29]

The Negro or mulatto population numbered just under one-third of the total in Cuba; an exact figure is hard to give, for reasons suggested earlier.[30] This proportion had remained roughly the same since the beginning of the Republic,[31] though between 1931 and 1943 the figures suggest a drop, due to repatriation of the Jamaican or other West Indian workers who had come to Cuba in the era of *puerca gorda*. The drop during the early years of the Republic was caused by the Spanish immigration that followed

[27] Almeida's account of himself in Carlos Franqui, *Le livre des douze*, pp. 13–15.
[28] The following certainly were: Almeida, García (Calixto), Díaz Cartaya, Mitchell, Peñalver, Valdés (Humberto), Pez, Mestre, Sarmiento.
[29] Cf. Merle, *Moncada*, p. 151.
[30] See above, p. 250.
[31]   *Negro Population of Cuba*

Year	Total	% of total pop.	In Havana province
1899	505,443	32·1	108,328
1907	608,967	29·1	122,860
1919	784,811	27·2	135,842
1931	1,079,106	27·2	199,393
1943	1,225,271	25·6	263,907
1953	1,568,416	27·2	345,305

independence in 1902. Only nine municipalities had a predominantly Negro population. Negroes did less well than whites in entry into prestigious middle-class professions (though their advance since 1900 has been enormous: in 1943 one-fifth of Cuba's doctors were coloured, in 1907 one-hundredth only). On the other hand among the more important crafts Negroes were well represented, being, for instance, in an actual majority among coopers, builders, dressmakers, launderers, shoemakers, woodcutters, and tailors. At this level, it is indeed hard to think that any preference was given to whites as opposed to Negroes. Negro and white illiteracy seems to have been much the same; though the area with the highest illiteracy rate in Oriente, near the Niquerto sugar mill, was also the place with a high white majority. In 1943 (the latest year for which statistics have been found) just under one-third of the army were Negro, or slightly more than the national proportion.[32]

Was it therefore true that there was no colour prejudice in Cuba? The answer seems fairly given by Castro in January 1959 when he explained that there was 'some racial discrimination in Cuba, but much less than in the United States'.[33] He might have gone on to say that in so far as it did exist, it was a chiefly middle-class phenomenon; that in some respects it was imitative, the Cuban middle class being extremely conscious of North American behaviour in this matter; that in clubs or hotels of Havana and elsewhere frequented by the famous ABC community [34] prejudice was found as another example of the way that rich Cubans were in a sense already exiles long before Castro's revolution; having made your pile, you moved on to Europe or the United States; as early as the 1890s, after all, Cubans of this class had houses in Park Avenue and were renting Chenonceaux.[35]

That racial antagonism in Cuba in the past may have been overstated by the revolution is suggested by the fact that Castro did not allude to the subject in any of his speeches before the

---

[32] 4,039 Negroes or mulattoes to 14,637 white; in the police the figures were 947 to 5,491.

[33] *Revolución*, 23 Jan. 1959.

[34] American, British, Canadian.

[35] The Terry family, cf. Ely, *Cuando reinaba su Majestad el Azúcar*, pp. 385 f. Terry left over $20 m. in 1887, not bad for a Cuban, when it is recalled that his contemporary, William Backhouse Astor, the richest man of his day, left only twice as much (*Dictionary of American Biography*).

revolution. *To Read History Will Absolve Me* [36] would suggest that Castro was talking of a wholly white nation. But if there was less prejudice than in some other countries, that did not mean that the Negro population of Cuba were fully integrated into society. They were coping, like all the Caribbean Africans, with the heritage of slavery—above all the destruction of the family, the substitution for (in some cases) many generations of the Master for the Father (except in his strictly biological function).[37] The Cuban Negroes were still in some respects demanding true emancipation. One or two old men in Cuba in 1959 could have been brought from Africa as children.[38] Their lack of adjustment may have been made easier by the fact that African ceremonies and religions blended sometimes effectively with Catholic festivals, though it happened that in Cuba there would be Negro festivals in the streets of, say, Santiago, where most white people not only did not know what festival it was, but what god was being fêted. Their task may have been more difficult than in the English West Indian islands where the white population was relatively insignificant. It is possible that since colour is so much a question of physical attributes and noticeability, the predominantly sallow-skinned persons of Spanish extraction blend more easily, at least with mulattoes, than do Anglo-Saxons.[39] Afro-Cuban versions of African ritual not only survived but possibly expanded during the Depression, and lower-class whites sometimes took part.

If the racial issue was not discussed by Castro during his revolutionary struggle, what was? Was his programme middle class or revolutionary, bourgeois or totalitarian? He himself later described himself as a Marxist *de la première heure*,[40] and Guevara,

[36] The pamphlet reconstructed from Castro's speech in his own defence after the Moncada barracks.

[37] I am indebted to Dr Sherlock of the University of the West Indies for this point.

[38] Cf. my article, 'The Atlantic Slave Trade', *Observer*, 17 Oct. 1965, where I state that the last authenticated case of slaves arriving in Cuba (or anywhere else in the Americas) was in 1865. But the odds are that some slaves arrived later, even in 1872.

[39] This is not the place to enquire into the racial origins of Spaniards. But since, contrary to popular suspicion, most Spanish colonists of the early period came from Andalucía rather than Castile, there is probably a certain amount of Moorish blood in at least the Caribbean. Also the first Spaniard to grow sugar-cane in the Caribbean, like the first man to carry syphilis back to Europe, was Jewish.

[40] Speech of 1–2 Dec. 1961, *Obra revolucionaria*, no. 46 of 1961).

with his customary honesty, spoke with some scorn of the bourgeois politicians with whom he and Castro had to deal in the Sierra : 'No estábamos satisfechos con el compromiso pero era necesario; era progresista en aquel momento.' [41] Such comments cannot be over-looked, but their importance can be overestimated. To regard Castro as always a communist leader, Guevara always a revolutionary bacillus, is to take a rather schematic view. The conspiracy theory of history is usually suspect. Castro was first a leader—the word Caudillo is best reserved for chieftains of the Right—and only secondly an ideologue. For most of the time between 1953 and 1958 he was no doubt preoccupied with a desire for power in the end,[42] but above all to survive. Like the revolutionary leaders in France in the 1790s, once embarked on political action beyond the limits set by existing institutions, Castro was caught up in a whirlwind in which death seemed often a great deal nearer than power, and, in order to survive at all (not simply politically), he extended his hands in almost every direction. Land for the peasants? Of course. Nationalization of utilities? Probably, or a few years later, probably not. Restoration of the constitution of 1940? Of course, in its entirety. Elections? Within eighteen months of victory. Relations with the United States? Castro naturally wished to achieve the best possible relations with the United States. The different programmes suggested by Castro between 1953 and 1959 show inconsistency, but also at this distance of time, and taken together, a superficiality, suggesting that the deception practised on Castro's different groups of co-fighters against Batista was of a rather ordinary political nature, not that of high tragedy. Who would not behave in this way if their programme was as yet unformed and if the thugs of the enemy were at their heels? Castro offered alliance with all who offered to ally with him, and, apart from one fit of irritation, at the time of the Miami Pact of December 1957, accepted their programmes, sometimes (as in the case of Felipe Pazos) accepting their ideas as his own.

Castro's supporters grew in number during early 1957. He was himself with a small group of followers in the Sierra Maestra—only twenty or so in February, 150 in March. He had various groups of devoted supporters in Santiago, Havana, and some other

[41] *Pasajes de la guerra revolucionaria* (Havana, 1963), p. 103.
[42] Though he did specifically deny even this.

cities. But still he was only one among a large number of groups opposing the régime of Batista. What drove the opposition forces to coalesce behind Castro was the increasing realization that a policy of violence was the only means of getting Batista out, combined with the failure of various groups (the *Directorio* of students faltered after their leaders died in the March assault on the palace).

The need for violent tactics automatically discredited middle-aged politicians who were reluctant personally to follow this dangerous path. Castro held out in the hills, a symbol of indestructibility more than, for a long time, a conquering chief. In the cities a Civic Resistance was formed on the model of the movement against Machado in the 1920s and 1930s. The part played by this movement—led by a young Baptist schoolmaster (Pais) and a lawyer (Buch) in Santiago, and by another lawyer and an architect (Hart and Ray) in Havana—was very great indeed. As a movement which worried away, day in, day out, at the régime by placing bombs, staging demonstrations, showing flags, it really waged guerrilla war more than did Castro. But Castro remained the leader of these urban *guerrilleros*, though few of them knew him, and almost none knew him well: Ray, the leader of the Civic Resistance throughout 1958, met Castro twice before Batista's flight on 1 January 1954. There were, however, a number of actions in the Sierra Maestra, enough to tie down the Batista army, and Raúl Castro began to build up a position in the Sierra Cristal and near Guantánamo. The defeat of Batista's main (and only) major offensive against Castro in mid-1958 was masterly. Even so, Castro remained the distant political leader, as much as he did the warrior. The liberal men of goodwill only moved towards him about nine months before the communists did.[43] Castro's views continued to fluctuate. 'He won power with one ideology and held it with another': Mr Draper's sharp phrase exaggerates, even flatters. To call Castro's pre-1959 speeches, manifestos, and articles an 'ideology' is overdoing it. Javier Pazos, who worked in both the Civic Resistance in Havana and then in the Sierra, commented in 1962 that the Castro whom he had known in the Sierra was 'definitely not a Marxist' and 'not even particularly progressive'.[44]

---

[43] I am assuming the communists began to move to Castro in early 1958 (as Draper argues) and the formalization of the alliance between Castro and the progressive wing of the *Ortodoxos* was when Chibás and Felipe Pazos went to sign the Manifesto of the Sierra Maestra in July 1957.

[44] Javier Pazos, *New Republic*. Nov. 1962.

If one looks at the consistent points in Castro's programmes rather than their contrasts, the single question of national independence was the only one which always occurred. What was this? It could best be defined as the full enactment of the dreams of the 'liberators' of 1895, Maceo, Martí, and (to a lesser extent) Máximo Gómez and Céspedes. Revolutions are driven by pictures of the past more than of the future. It was only after some months of actual power that it became apparent to Castro that Martí's world was primarily poetic and afforded little guidance to a government of Cuba sixty-five years after his death. Cuba had changed. Máximo Gómez, the only formidable warrior to survive the wars of revolution, and the most realistic of the Cuban politicians of the 1890s, offered less appealing morals than Martí.[45] But the dream of pure freedom is in the case of a sugar island certain to be an illusion. Sugar has to be sold to someone. Relations, more or less intimate, are inevitable with customers. Hence, of course, the revolution's desperate but abortive attempt to escape from sugar—an intensification of the demands for diversification which had characterized Cuba since the 1920s.

The other demand which consistently occurred in Castro's programmes before 1959 was one for agrarian reform. But would it be division of the large estates among the landless ones—the old call of Iberian anarchism? Would it be collectivization of land? Or merely the division of the uncultivated areas held by large landowners? Agrarian reform, like irrigation in Spain, has for long been looked on as the panacea for all ills in Latin America. Considered as a blueprint which can be applied throughout the sub-continent, it is illusory. Cattle farms have to be handled differently from rice fields. Is the aim of agrarian reform *tout court* to create a 'bold peasantry their country's pride' which, when once destroyed (in England) can never be supplied? The question, 'what sort of reform?', was raised acutely by sugar production. There was, for instance, a strong case in Cuba for nationalizing

---

[45] After three years of war between Spain and the Cubans, and after Spain had already set up an autonomous government, the USA prepared in April 1898 to join in on the Cuban side. The Spanish captain-general wrote to Gómez and asked that the two should bury the hatchet in a common struggle against the USA. Gómez wrote back: 'up to now I have had only feelings of admiration for the USA. I do not see the danger of extermination at their hands to which you refer. If it should come, history will judge.' History has refrained, however.

the sugar mills. By 1958 they were only 161 in number. They no longer competed with one another. For the past thirty years they had begun their harvest only after a signal from the President of Cuba. Subject already to state intervention, controls, and quotas, nationalization would in one sense merely have formalized existing conditions. But was agrarian reform necessary in the sugar industry? Had not the number of *colonos*—the farmers who produced cane to be processed by the mill—increased by over 50 per cent between 1950 and 1958 and more than doubled since 1936? [46] Further, though it was true that many large *colonos* and mills themselves held land which they did not cultivate, this was a traditional and (without massive fertilization of land already in use) a justifiable usage. Cane can only be replanted on the same soil about six or seven times without fertilizer, giving cane fields an effective life of only about fifty years. So most mills were in the habit of buying more land than they were going to need, and in Cuba land was far cheaper than elsewhere in the Caribbean. Of course, the answer was to invest in research, fertilization, new forms of cane. The same might be said of the world sugar-cane industry, not simply Cuba. No comparable crop is so improvidently tended. If an agrarian reform were aimed at increasing social equality, it might have dismissed the manufacturing side as a matter for the reorganization of industry, not of agriculture. Perhaps the land might have been perpetually nationalized, existing *colonos* being regarded as tenants. But no pragmatic proposals were put forward for the sugar industry before 1959, except for a proposal in Castro's Moncada speech for a higher percentage of the sugar profits for the *colonos*.

At dawn on 1 January 1959 Batista fled. He attempted to leave government in the hands of the Supreme Court Judge, Carlos Manuel Piedra. The accident of his Christian name enabled Castro in his first speech in Santiago to point to the ominous precedent of the government of Carlos Manuel de Céspedes, brought in (with

---

[46] Cane *colonia* 1899: 15,521 (Census of 1899).
    1936: 28,486 (*Anuario azucarero*, 1937).
    1950: 40,000 (World Bank Report on Cuba estimate).
    1958: 68,152 (*Anuario azucarero*, 1959).
A great deal of this increase derived from the division of what remained essentially single holdings into several held by nominees, to avoid certain provisions of the 1937 sugar law. But not all. The average *colonia* produced about half as much sugar in the 1950s as in the 1920s (over-all production being much the same).

the support of American Ambassador Sumner Welles) to form a 'middle-class government' after the flight of Machado in 1933, only to be overthrown by Batista and the students a month later. The other judges of the Supreme Court refused to swear Piedra in. In a vacuum Castro, who had found a provisional president in Judge Urrutia, concluded a local deal with Batista's commander in Santiago, Colonel Rego, and proclaimed a provisional government Political prisoners were released. Colonel Barquín, a plotter against Batista in 1956, took over command in Havana, himself handing over to Castro's men (Guevara and Cienfuegos) twenty-four hours later. Urrutia immediately formed a government, Castro became commander-in-chief. The former arrived in Havana on 5 January, the latter on the 8th.

Government was now quite evidently chiefly in the hands of men (and women) whom it would be realistic, even in Cuban terms, to name middle class (President Urrutia, Premier Miró, Foreign Minister Agramonte, Finance Minister López Fresquet). But it became clear that the vast majority of the Cubans regarded Castro, despite his lack of political responsibility, as the saviour of the nation. No orator like Castro had been seen in the Americas since William Jennings Bryan, at least. Further, from the very beginning he controlled the police and the armed forces. Camilo Cienfuegos, in command at Havana, suggested initially that the army of the future might incorporate both the 'rebel army' and the elements within Batista's army which were not compromised by torture or murder; but though some officers did join the new force for a while, few of the rank and file apparently did so. Castro was thus never faced with the prospect of a strong and reactionary army such as disposed of Bosch and Arbenz in the Dominican Republic and Guatemala. The old Cuban army had been seriously discredited by the defeat of its major offensive in the previous summer. The last shreds of its prestige hardly outlasted the month of January, for every day brought new revelations and pictures of the bodies of those killed in prison, together with torture equipment.[47] During these weeks the rebel army, on the other hand, was establishing itself more or less as the executive of the country—for mayors,

---

[47] The Cuban army had also been damaged by its excessive politicking throughout its existence, particularly after the sergeants' revolt of 1933, which destroyed a whole generation of officers and brought in a new group subservient to Batista.

clerks, local leaders everywhere were in flight, compromised by collaboration with the old régime. The rebel army supervised both the rounding up of suspected 'war criminals' and presided at the courts which (usually fairly) tried them. The army was, it went almost without saying, loyal to Castro. Nevertheless even at this early stage the communists (who had played less of a part in the struggle against Batista than Prío's *Auténticos*) [48] began to extend their hand over some sections of the army. Despite inactivity on the national level, the party organization in the province of Las Villas had assisted Guevara and Cienfuegos when they had reached there from the Sierra Maestra in October 1958; and indeed the commander of La Punta in Havana in January 1959 was one of the Las Villas communists (Armando Acosta).[49] The extent of communist infiltration into part of the army is illustrated by the fact that even Marcos Armando Rodríguez, the 'Traitor of Humboldt 7', had got a job as an instructor at the La Cabaña fortress by early February 1959,[50] though he had only joined the communists definitively in the autumn of 1958, and though he was already under suspicion of having betrayed their comrades by the men of the *Directorio* (whose star, it must be admitted, was low in these weeks). Communist activity before January 1959 in respect of Castro had been the reverse of decisive. They had contacts with Castro certainly but also with other political groups. Castro welcomed them into rough alliance some time in late 1958, when they joined his followers in a united union front. His relations with them were correct but distant. A leading communist (Carlos Rafael Rodríguez) was attached to his headquarters but he was not the communist leader. The Communist Party, as usual, was ready for anything.

The margin of freedom for the middle-class members of the new provisional revolutionary government was (in the light of the extraordinary personal appeal of Castro and of Castro's control of the army, whatever its political complexion) rather smaller than was imagined. They had responsibility but little power. Yet even so, their behaviour (well known as it is in outline) is of interest.

[48] The famous attack on the palace in March 1957 had been led by men connected with Prío (Mora, Gutiérrez Menoya) and with Prío's guns.

[49] Cf. *Hoy*, 16 July 1965. Acosta is now secretary general of the Cuban Communist Party in Oriente.

[50] *Hoy*, Mar. 1964. He had betrayed some members of the *Directorio* in 1957 to Batista's police, apparently for personal reasons. He was tried for this offence and executed in early 1964.

After all, they held important portfolios, they were internationally well known, and they had excellent records as men, if not as co-ordinators of national movements: the Foreign Minister had been the disappointed *Ortodoxo* candidate in the abortive elections of 1952.

The weakness of the *Ortodoxos* and people who thought like them had been revealed in 1952. They were unable to unite. This made their task harder in 1959, but even so they surrendered many points in 1959 without even arguing about them. During January 1959 it was agreed that elections should be delayed for eighteen months; that until then government should be by decree; that sections of the 1940 constitution might be retroactively revised; there was even a decree abolishing political parties; military courts with powers of immediate punishment (including death) were set up to try 'war criminals'. In February 1959 came a new fundamental law of the Republic which vested legislation in the provisional government. All these radical, even autocratic, measures were enacted before Castro even became Prime Minister.

These things are explicable by the sentiment prevailing at the time. At that time many who later left Cuba were keen to subject their wills to a 'leader and guide'. Experience of past frustration led good liberals to acquiesce in authoritarian measures. Above all, there could be no betrayal of the revolution from the Right, as occurred in 1933–4; perhaps, as Trotsky said of Spain (in 1931), the revolution would have to pass from the bourgeois to the socialist phase to avoid defeat.[51] Purges and trials were necessary to clean up Cuba. To cleanse the nation was more important than to restore old institutions. Free elections? There was little public enthusiasm for them. The *Auténtico* leader, Varona, was the man who demanded elections, not the *Ortodoxos*. Batista's two elections, the last only two months before he fled, had further discredited a process which had only worked successfully three or four times since independence.[52] The 1940 constitution, model

[51] Isaac Deutscher, *The Prophet Outcast, Trotsky* (London, 1963), p. 160.
[52] 1901: under US occupation, opposition boycotted election.
    1905: election frauds, leading ultimately to war and new occupation.
    1908: honest elections, liberals won.
    1912: doubtful elections.
    1916: crooked elections, new civil war.
    1920: crooked elections.
    1924: crooked elections leading to Machado-dictatorship.

though it was in some respects, had itself made one inroad on the democratic process at grassroots level, in providing that school boards should be thereafter appointed, not elected.[53]   It was evident that many Cubans, probably most of them, were in 1959 not interested in having a general election.   They supported Castro anyway.   There was not enough respect for law for it to be widely thought that legislation by decree was illegal or arbitrary.   After all, what had law been in the past?   A football for the President.   The roots of totalitarian democracy usually extend some way back.

No doubt in 1959 the 'liberal' men and women concerned were middle class, in the sense of having comfortable backgrounds, servants, and higher education.   Those few who were in the government or nearly at the top of the administration were essentially middle-aged members of the liberal professions, men who probably (being now about fifty years old) would have taken some part in the struggle against Machado in their youth.   Their own children would be less cautious supporters of Castro and might have re-enacted what their fathers had done twenty-five years before, in either the Civic Resistance or, more rarely, in the Sierra Maestra.[54]   Obviously, very young men might be expected to thrill at the thought of their contemporaries being in power.

But were they representative?   The professional middle classes were, in Cuba as everywhere else, less than half the total group who can be described as the bourgeoisie;[55] thus in 1953 there may have been about 20,000 school teachers,[56] together with maybe about 40,000 others who could conceivably have been regarded as of the professional classes.[57]   There were, however, nearly 100,000

1936 : honest elections, but victor only lasted a few months.
1940 : relatively honest elections, won by Batista with communist support.
1944 : relatively honest elections, won by Grau.
1948 : the same won by Prío.

[53] There were good reasons for this, since it was thought desirable that education should be outside politics.

[54] This point is pursued in depth by Lino Novás Calvo in 'La tragedía de la clase cubana', *Bohemia libre* (New York), 1 Jan. 1961.

[55] In the USA in 1950, professional, technical, and kindred workers numbered 5 million; managers, officials, and proprietors (excluding small farmers) numbered 5·2 million (*Historical Statistics*, p. 75).

[56] See above, pp. 253–4.

[57] Ranked thus:

Engineers, architects, surveyors	5,700
Professors & secondary schoolmasters	5,500
Chemists, &c.	5,100
Lawyers, judges, &c.	7,900

business men, merchants, bankers, other administrators, or directors of enterprises. This section of the community had committed itself to Batista. There was hardly a professional association which had not visited the national palace in 1957 to express their congratulations to Batista at his escape from assassination at the hands of a group which, if not now precisely in power, was nevertheless closely associated with it.[58] Even the most wild of the 1957 plotters, Ricardo Olmedo, a gangster who had held up the Royal Bank of Canada in the 1940s, found himself a hero's reward as police chief of a section of Havana. Hardly surprisingly, prominent business men fled. One or two were imprisoned and tried. Others changed their politics hastily and congratulated the revolutionary government, assuring them of their support, by means of embarrassingly fulsome advertisements in newspapers. But the whole business community was diminished in the public mind. Though it became known that some rich men had supported Castro and that others (along with the North American-owned Telephone Company) were going to pay their taxes in advance to assist the new government, this availed them little; for along with news of atrocities, described as a good round 20,000 killed—a guess almost certainly twice too high [59]—there also became known in January documentary evidence of all sorts of corrupt practices. Most striking perhaps, was the revelation of how the Telephone Company had managed to escape criticism when it raised prices in 1957:

there is a simple reason why the larger sections of the press is not complaining. They received their regular contribution, through the so-called barrage, in addition to the above-board advertising, thus getting paid more than double. Hence the only dissatisfaction came from *Bohemia*, the newspapers *Excelsior* and *País*, and José Parda Llada, the wireless commentator.[60]

Artists, writers, journalists, dancers, athletes ...	...	...	...	9,900
Priests & religious or social workers	...	...	...	2,200
Librarians, photographers ...	...	...	...	1,900

(Census of 1953)

[58] Several 26 July supporters joined in the attack on the palace. The leaders were the *Directorio* and the *Auténticos*, though apparently the latter had broken off relations with Prío before the attack.

[59] The exaggeration had the political effect of blackening the régime of Batista and its collaborators even further—which was its intention.

[60] A photocopy of this document was printed *in extenso* in *Revolución*, 18 Jan. 1959.

So there was little hope that the commercial middle classes of Cuba could do much to help preserve the liberals in Cuba. In a weak position, the liberals in power responded weakly. It is, of course, a characteristic of the Cuban middle class to show extraordinary heroism when in opposition, carrying out foolhardy acts without hesitation and showing themselves adept conspirators; when in power they are less deft. With most countries the contrary is true, as General Fellgiebel showed when he forgot to cut the telephone wire to Hitler's bunker in the plot of July 1944. There were no institutions for them to hold to, none to withstand, check, or even give pause to the revolutionary executive. Who had not been tarnished by collaboration, what bank had not held stolen cash? Both Miró (the Premier) and Urrutia (the President) wanted to resign in the early weeks—the former over the constitutional revisions,[61] the latter over the decision to keep the casinos after he, Urrutia, had wished them closed. On 15 February Miró finally resigned as Premier. He seemed in an unreal position. All real power lay with Castro, nominally only commander of the armed forces. Castro became prime minister.

Within three weeks came a decisive test of the régime. A court at Santiago found certain Batistiano pilots innocent of war crimes. Castro, furious, ordered a retrial presided over by the Minister of Defence, Augusto Martínez Sánchez, a lawyer who had been Raúl Castro's advocate-general in the Sierra. Castro himself intervened in the trial. The pilots were sentenced, this time to a long period of imprisonment.[62] But this arbitrary act could not be opposed by the judiciary, far too closely associated with the old régime to be able to protest in the new. One member of the cabinet (not the Minister of Justice) wanted to resign. Castro restrained his colleague: 'Ah, you do not understand. This revolution is an express train that knows where it is going. Your time to get off will be later.' The Minister remained on the train until Castro gave the word some months later.[63]

The liberals left the régime because of the movement of communism into the government, less because they objected to Castro's arbitrary use of power. Fear of communism became the dominant anxiety in Cuba by July 1959. Should the good men have left in

[61] Miró Cardona, in *Diario de la Marina* (Miami), 12 Nov. 1960.
[62] *Revolución,* Mar. 1959.
[63] Told to me by the minister in question. Knowing the person I have no doubt whatever that this evidence is truthful.

March? It is easy with hindsight to argue that this or that person should have done something other than he did, and to overlook the pressure that caused his inertia or his errors. In these circumstances, no doubt, the historian will overlook the continuing ebullience of the popular enthusiasm for Castro, who appeared so often on the television screen (how the State Department must have cursed the salesmen of those 400,000 sets) that he resembles less a de Gaulle or a Kennedy (who also used television to effect) than a kind of revolutionary link-man, a permanent confessor, a resident medicine man. And always, from the beginning, criticisms of the system bypassed Castro, falling on others. Had the liberals gone in March, they would have had a chance of moving into effective opposition. As it was, Castro was allowed to continue to think that he could act without criticism.

In May Castro made a somewhat feeble attempt, no doubt sincere, to launch a new ideology for the revolution, to be known as 'humanism'. His own temperament, his reluctance to organize a political movement, the weakness of the institutions of the country (thereby giving no democrat anything to lean on), and, maybe, to a lesser extent the stranglehold that the communists had already established in the army (and so in the real administration of the country) prevented this from reaching fruition.[64] It is hard to know how far Castro dictated events or surrendered to them. By the autumn, his still strong personal hold over the Cubans was being exercised in favour of the communists in both the army and the trade unions. The liberals did not make a fight of it. They went down without a shot fired. Immediately, they embarked on their real *métier*—conspiracy—with relish and courage. This was eventually based on Florida. The only leading commander in the army who disliked communism meantime asked to resign. He did not apparently organize resistance. He was sent to prison for twenty years for his pains.

The liberals left in waves: Miró in February; Urrutia, Agramonte, Elena Mederos, Sorí Marín in July; Ray, Pazos (not technically a cabinet member, though president of the bank), and even Faustino Pérez, the only *Granma* man in the original cabinet (apart from Castro), in October; López Fresquet not till March 1960.[65]

---

[64] I say 'maybe' since we are already in the land of mythology.
[65] All these except Pérez ultimately left Cuba as well as the government. Pérez stayed and later became chief of the hydraulics institution.

Others remained longer, remain perhaps even now, telling themselves that once out of power their influence would be nought, while if they hang on there is a chance of influencing policy: others, such as Dorticós, Boti, Buch, must have found the new system more appealing than they had earlier supposed.

Castro, of course, deceived the liberals; but people who place faith in a 'hero and guide' are usually deceived. Castro's alliance with these honest men was, after all, short—hardly more than the two years from July 1957 to July 1959. He owed them less than they supposed. They and international opinion deceived themselves almost as much as he deceived them. Castro never made such a pretence. The correspondent of the London *Times*, on 2 January 1959, described Castro as a devoted Catholic.[66] A year later, no doubt, readers of *The Times* were complaining that Castro's religiosity was a fraud. Whose fault was that? To conclude: Castro, if himself a man of education, always depended most on people who could not be described as middle class. He was never a social democrat, and the social democrats who attached themselves to him did so late (1957), after they had failed to unite round a leader of their own. He changed less than they said he did, for they credited him with their own opinions when, in fact, he was merely experimenting with some of his own. However well off Cuba might have been in the past on paper, it was not a just society. Its relative wealth, and the existence of United States consumer goods,[67] increased rather than diminished tension in society. The middle-class position in Cuba was historically unlike that of the middle class anywhere else in Latin America. Castro rode to power with a certain alliance with some middle-class parties, but his own programme was vague, if always vaguely millenarian too. Old Cuba destroyed her institutions, such as they were, and herself through collaboration with Batista, by her own hand; that is, not by the knife of revolution under Castro. The position of the coloured minority was not what the revolution later made it out to be, though the coloured people had other reasons for anxiety. In the past, Cuba has revealed her true character primarily in rebellion. The age of Castro has articulated this perfectly. The government is a rebel one, in permanent revolution against the United States; the

[66] This was the only time at that period that Cuba made the main news story in that Eurocentric organ.
[67] Or durables.

middle class, back in the United States as it was during the struggles against Spain, against Machado, and against Batista, is in permanent revolution against the Government of Cuba. Meantime the lesson for middle-class liberals caught up in a political maelstrom with a powerful popular leader is, of course, Lord Birkenhead's instruction on how to deal with Lloyd George: 'think clearly, think deeply and think ahead. Otherwise you will think too late.'

APPENDIX

Successful Military Coups, 1920–66

Argentina: September 1930; June 1943; February 1944; September 1955; November 1955; March 1962; June 1966.

Bolivia: June 1930; November 1934; May 1936; July 1937; December 1943; July 1946; May 1951; April 1952; November 1964.

Brazil: October 1930; October 1945; August 1954; August 1961; April 1964.

Chile: June 1932; September 1932.

Colombia: June 1953; May 1957.

Costa Rica: May 1948.

Cuba: August 1933; September 1933; March 1952; January 1959.

Dominican Republic: February 1930; January 1962; September 1963; April 1965.

Ecuador: August 1931; October 1931; August 1932; August 1935; October 1937; May 1944; August 1947; November 1961; July 1963.

El Salvador: May 1944; October 1944; December 1948; January 1949; October 1960; January 1961.

Guatemala: December 1930; July 1944; October 1944; June 1954; October 1957; March 1963.

Haiti: January 1946; May 1950; December 1956; May 1957; June 1957.

Honduras: October 1956; October 1963.

Nicaragua: June 1936.

Panama: October 1941; November 1949; May 1951.

Paraguay: February 1936; August 1937; June 1948; January 1949; February 1949; September 1949; May 1954.

Peru: August 1930; February/March 1931; October 1948; June 1962.

Venezuela: October 1945; November 1948; December 1952; January 1958.

NOTE ON CONTRIBUTORS

Richard N. Adams is Assistant Director of the Institute of Latin American Studies in the University of Texas. His publications include: *Cultural Surveys of Panama—Nicaragua—Guatemala— El Salvador—Honduras* (1957) and *A Community in the Andes* (1959).

François Chevalier, a former Director of the Institut Français de Mexico and Professor of Latin American Civilization at the University of Bordeaux, is now Director of the Casa de Velásquez at the University of Madrid. His principal published work is *La formation des grands domaines au Mexique* (1952), translated into English as *Land and Society in Colonial Mexico* (Berkeley, 1963). He is at present studying the contemporary history and agrarian problems of Latin America under the auspices of the Institut des Sciences Politiques of Paris.

Oscar Cornblit holds a research appointment at the Centro de Sociología Comparada of the Instituto Torcuato Di Tella at Buenos Aires. He is President of the Institute of Social and Economic Development (Argentina).

Emanuel de Kadt is Lecturer in Sociology at the London School of Economics. He is the author of *British Defence Policy and Nuclear War* (1964) and is at present engaged on a study of the Catholic Church and social reform in Brazil.

Alistair Hennessy is Reader in Spanish and Latin American History at the University of Warwick and Associate Fellow of St Antony's College, Oxford. He is the author of *The Federal Republic in Spain, 1868–1873* (1962) and numerous articles on Latin American affairs.

Eric J. Hobsbawm is Reader in the Department of History at Birkbeck College, University of London, and author of *The Age of Revolution, Europe 1789–1848* (1962) and *Labouring Men: Studies in the History of Labour* (1964).

José Nun, a graduate in Law and Social Sciences of the University of Buenos Aires, is director of a research project on social marginality in Latin America under the auspices of the ECLA Latin American Institute of Economic and Social Planning, Santiago, Chile.

Hugh Thomas is Professor of Modern History at the University of Reading. He is the author of *The Spanish Civil War* (1961), *The Suez Affair* (1967), and other books, and is at present engaged on a study of Cuba.

INDEX

Abdel Malek, 116
Acão Popular (Brazil), 146, 149, 150 n.,
211, 215
Acción Democrática (Venezuela),
65 n., 132, 146 ff., 152
Acción Popular (Peru), 61, 145 ff., 149,
152 n.
Acosta, Armando, 270
Adams, Dr R., 2, 4
Agramonte, Roberto, 269, 275
Agrarian question, 1, 48, 50 n., 53–56;
see also Landowners; Oligarchy;
Peasants; & *countries by name*
Agriculture: capitalist or cash-crop
economy, effect of, 29, 31, 45–46,
48, 55 f.; subsistence farming no
longer possible, 54; ' kulaks ', 55;
productivity, 97 n., 106; technicians,
lack of, 155; *see also* Mexico
Além, Leandro N., 236, 244
Alemán, Miguel, 170 f.
Alessandri, Arturo, 82–83, 85
Alianza Liberal (Chile), 82
*Alianza Popular Revolucionaria
Americana* (APRA) (Peru), 49 n.,
51–52, 53 n., 61 ff.; alliance with
conservatives, 124 n., 146; &
students, 125, 132 f., 141, 146–7,
152
Alliance for Progress, 10 ff.
Almeida (Cuban revolutionary), 259,
261–2
Almeijiras, Juan Manuel, 259 f.
Alsina, Adolfo, 236, 244
Alvear, Marcelo T. de, 94, 236
Amado, Isaias R., 240
Anarchism, anarchists, 50, 59, 61, 239
Andean regions: export economy,
46 n.; subsistence agriculture, 54;
agrarian unrest, 54, 144, 187
Anti-communism, 111 f., 146, 203 f.
Arango, Sánchez, 254
Arbenz, Jácobo, 269
Argentina, 12; trade unions in, 38,
63–64, 97, 239; urbanization, 45–46,
47, 58 ff., 68; *peronismo* in, 63, 95,
97 f., 152; urban proletariat, 88;
agrarian policy in, 95–97; Perón

Argentina—*cont.*
régime in, 95–97, 100; traditional
society, 236–7, 244; working class:
Partido Socialista &, 238–9; — &
Radicalism, 244; communists, 239
Armed forces: military coups, 66 ff.,
82, 94 f., 96, 98; officer corps:
middle-class origin of, 72; —
contacts with Radicals, 81–82; —
Union Cívica Radical &, 94;
political groups &, 103–4
Economy: before & after 1930,
45–46; industrial development,
67 f., 93, 94–95, 228–32; opening
up of interior, 221–2; development by immigrants, 223;
traditional-modern dichotomy,
230, 238; power of economic
groups, 230–1; protectionism,
230–1, 245–6; Radical economic
policies, 247
Elections: percentage participating
in, 100; suspension of, 113
European immigrants, 45; &
industrialization, 5–6; political
discrimination against, 6; as
supporters of *status quo*, 6–7;
& modernization, 93; nos. of
(1869–1930), 222; as technical
catalysts, 223; distribution in
urban/rural areas, 223–4;
regional distribution, 223–5, 238;
occupations, 225–8; participation
in industry, 231–2; & naturalization, 232–3, 241; political
apathy of, 232–4; supporters of
Yrigoyen, 236; political affilia-
tions, 238, 240–4; effects of
uprooting, 239–40; antagonism
to, 243–4; assimilation of
descendants, 244; industrial
groups: economic liberalism of,
245–6; — political parties &,
245–8
Middle class: alliance with landowners, 93; Yrigoyen &, 93 f.;
subordination of, 94; & 1930
coup, 94; under Perón, 95 f.;

281

288 *Index*

Mexico—*cont.*

Armed forces: military coups, 68, 71, 278; class origins of officer corps, 73; development of, 84–85; & revolution, 85; & bourgeois hegemony, 108–9; & political system, 109 n.; *see also below*, Middle class

Ejidatarios: no. of, 168, 176; present economic & social position, 175 ff., pride of ownership, 179, 183, 185 f.; attitude to revolution, 183, 186 f., 189–90; compared with smallholders, 183–4, 186; political role, 187–9

Ejido, the: defined, 159, 166, 175; communally farmed, 159, 173; statistical publications on, 159–60; as development of village community, 161–6; history of: (1912–34), 162–7; — (1934–40), 167–9; — since 1940, 169 ff., 189; area distributed to, 167–8, 170, 177, 189; collective *ejidos*, 168; local govt. of, 169, 187–8; no. of *ejidos*, 175; proportion of pop. depending on, 175–6; size of holdings, 178, 181; effect of mechanization, 182; *ejidal* peasant system, 182–3; fragmentation problem, 184, 186; population pressure, 186; & political stability, 190; future of, 190–1

Middle class: political aspirations of, 84; support of Carranza reforms, 84; army support of, 85, 104

Revolution, 11, 65 n., 84 f., 120; & agrarian problem, 84, 86, 108, 183, 186 f., 189–90; middle-class leanings of, 108; & capitalist system, 109; influence on universities, 130; role of cities & countryside, 158

Mexico City: population, 57; role in life of country, 158–9

Meyer, Jean, 168 n.

Middle class, 15–19, 33–34; as extension of traditional upper class, 4; & military régimes, 8; ' Lower Middle ', 18; ' Middle Middle ', 18, 24; proportion of

Middle class—*cont.*

population, 66; composition of, 79; & oligarchic system, 79–81, 100–1, 102; & economic development, 80; support by armed forces, 85, 103–4; adopts outlook of oligarchy, 85–86; effect of industrialization, 86–88; compared with British, 99; & populism, 100; institutional weakness of, 101; negative principles of, 111–12; & university reform, 129 f.; job mania, 141–2, 155; transformation into revolutionaries, 145 n.; *see also* Armed forces; Bourgeoisie; Students; & *countries by name*

Military coups, 66–71, 88, 278; *see also countries by name*

Mills, C. Wright, 73 n.

Miró, José, 269, 274 f.

Mitre, Bartolomé, 236

Molina, Pedro C., 234 f.

Molina, Víctor, 246

Mosca, Gaetano, 75

Mounier, Emmanuel, 205

Movimento de Educação de Base (MEB) (Brazil), 216–18

Movimiento de la Izquierda Revolucionaria (MIR): Venezuela, 145 f., 148 n.; Peru, 146

Movimiento Nacionalista Revolucionario (Bolivia), 152, 154 f.

Movimiento de Obreros, Estudiantes y Campesinos (MOEC) (Colombia), 144

Movimiento 15 de Mayo (Peru), 143 n.

Nasser, Nasserism, 8, 113–16; model of army as developmentalist force, 67, 114–15, 128

' Natal Movement ', 209

Nationalism: capitalists &, 30; & middle classes, 33; & university reform, 129–30

Negro slaves, 249; *see also* Cuba

Nelson, Lowry, 252, 254, 257

Nicaragua, 68

Nonconformist movement, 13

Nun, Sr José, 8

Obregón, Alvaro, 84, 164

Odría, Manuel, 61, 144